AIR STAFF HISTORICAL STUDY

HARNESSING THE GENIE:
SCIENCE AND TECHNOLOGY FORECASTING
FOR THE AIR FORCE, 1944-1986

Michael H. Gorn

OFFICE OF AIR FORCE HISTORY
UNITED STATES AIR FORCE
WASHINGTON, D.C., 1988

Library of Congress Cataloging-in-Publication Data

Gorn, Michael H.
    Harnessing the genie.

    (Air staff historical study)
    Bibliography: p.
    Includes index.
    1. Aeronautics, Military--Research--United States--
History. 2. Aeronautics, Military--United States--
Forecasting--History. 3. United States. Air Forces--
History. I. Title. II. Series.
UG643.G67 1988   358.4'0072'073   88-19554
ISBN 0-912799-52-8

For sale by the Superintendent of Documents,
U.S. Government Printing Office
Washington, D.C. 20402

**United States Air Force
Historical Advisory Committee**
(as of 31 December 1987)

Ms. Anne N. Foreman
The General Counsel, USAF

Dr. Norman A. Graebner
The University of Virginia

Dr. Dominick Graham
Canadian Royal Military College

Dr. Ira D. Gruber
Rice University

Lt. Gen. Charles R. Hamm,
USAF
Superintendent, U.S. Air Force Academy

Dr. Haskell M. Monroe, Jr. (Chairman)
The University of Missouri

Dr. John H. Morrow, Jr.
The University of Tennessee at Knoxville

Gen. Thomas M. Ryan, Jr.,
USAF, retired

Lt. Gen. C. Truman Spangrud,
USAF
Commander, Air University

Dr. Gerhard L. Weinberg
The University of North Carolina

iii

The Author

MICHAEL H. GORN is a historian with the Air Staff Branch, Office of Air Force History. He received a BA degree in 1972 and a MA degree in 1973 from California State University Northridge, and a PhD in U.S. colonial military history from the University of Southern California in 1978. Before joining the Office of Air Force History in 1985, he worked from 1978 to 1981 as chief archivist of the New England Historic Genealogical Society and from 1981 to 1985 as staff historian in the Headquarters Air Force Systems Command History Office. He has published a bibliographic essay entitled "Published Air Force History: Still on the Runway," as well as two historical monographs: The TFX: From Conceptual Phase to F-111B Termination, 1958-1968 (Air Force Systems Command History Office, 1986); and Vulcan's Forge: The Making of an Air Force Command for Weapons Acquisition, 1950-1986 (Air Force Systems Command History Office, 1986).

Foreword

Air power has always been closely linked to science and technology. The very reality of flight depended upon a technical innovation. Unlike the other services, where machines merely support the mission, technology is for the Air Force at the very heart of its existence as an institution. As a consequence, the USAF and its predecessor organizations have always recognized the singular importance of science to their survival.

This lesson was driven home with new urgency on December 7, 1941. No longer were American borders secure against aerial bombardment. The Japanese proved at Pearl Harbor that U.S. territory was not immune from attack; waves of bombers might strike without warning and with devastating effects. Commanding General of the Army Air Forces Henry H. Arnold countered the threat, at least in part, with brainpower from the universities. Three years later, with victory close at hand, Arnold began to consider the safety of the country once the war was over. The danger of sudden and devastating raids had greatly increased since Pearl Harbor. He turned, as he had during the war, to academia and enlisted the help of Dr. Theodore von Karman, asking him to assemble a group of top scientists to review aeronautical research and make recommendations about the future of air power in light of probable scientific opportunities in the decades to come.

The result is felt in the Air Force yet today, for Toward New Horizons, written by von Karman's USAF Scientific Advisory Group, has endured as the model for Air Force science and technology forecasts. Renamed the USAF Scientific Advisory Board, the institution von Karman created has also endured. Harnessing the Genie tells us that while both the report and the board continue to be regarded with the utmost respect, their roles have been imperceptibly transformed over time. Toward New Horizons was followed in 1957 and 1958 by the Woods Hole Summer Studies, in 1964 by Project Forecast, in 1975 by New Horizons II, and in 1986 by Project Forecast II. The pattern suggests that every ten years or so the USAF revisits the concept behind Toward New Horizons and attempts to look into the future of aerospace technology.

But with each report, the likeness to von Karman's model has become more remote. The extent of reliance on independent advice has steadily lessened and greater emphasis placed on internal USAF sources for forecasting the future. As a consequence, the Scientific Advisory Board is no longer involved in long-range, broadly based forecasting envisioned by von Karman, but devotes itself to giving advice on technical subjects. Moreover, no institution has arisen to claim control over the process of forecasting and directing the pace and direction of technological change. Instead, the direction of technological forecasting of long-range research and development has wandered from the National Academy of Sciences to the Air Force Systems Command to the Air Staff, and back again to Systems Command. The reports themselves have changed accordingly. Toward New Horizons, rooted in the basic sciences, stressed the abstract principles of nature and how they related to air-power advancements. As their participants have gradually become more closely associated with the Air Force, the subsequent studies have become more technological than scientific, reflecting a declining representation of independent scientists on the succeeding panels.

Thus, Harnessing the Genie describes and analyzes the methodologies and conclusions of the five main science and technology forecasts undertaken by the Air Force since before its birth as an independent service. Hopefully, this work will provide useful background as the Air Force grapples with the technological demands of national security in the 21st century.

RICHARD H. KOHN
Chief, Office of Air Force History

Acknowledgments

I am indebted to a number of people who made important contributions to Harnessing the Genie. Without good sources there is no history, and for invaluable help in locating often obscure documents I wish to thank the following people: Ms. Janice Goldblum, archivist at the National Academy of Sciences; Master Sergeant Roger Jernigan, (USAF ret.), former reference librarian at the Office of Air Force History; the late Mrs. Helen Manthos, senior secretary and archivist of the USAF Scientific Advisory Board; Mr. William Mattson, formerly information specialist at the Air Staff Studies and Analysis Office; Mrs. Thelma Smith, archivist at the Headquarters Air Force Systems Command History Office; Mr. Larry Wilson, reference librarian for the National Air and Space Museum; and Lt. Col. Chuck Williams, formerly Project Forecast II Administrative Director, who guided me through piles of office files relevant to this study. To augment the written record, I interviewed several figures involved in science and technology forecasting through the years. They were all generous with their time and insights. Dr. H. Guyford Stever, former Chairman of the USAF Scientific Advisory Board and Chief Scientist of the Air Force, spoke about Toward New Horizons and the Woods Hole Summer Studies of 1957/1958. Former Secretary of the Air Force Eugene M. Zuckert and former Assistant Secretary of the Air Force for Research and Development, Dr. Alexander Flax, shed light on Project Forecast. Major General (then Brigadier General) Eric Nelson, co-director of Project Forecast II, told me about its overall objectives, while Major David Glasgow, the Forecast II Deputy Program Manager, filled in the specifics.

Members of the Office of Air Force History provided invaluable comment and criticism of this study. Mr. Jacob Neufeld, Air Staff Branch Chief, did more than anyone to improve the manuscript, untangling contorted phrases and straightening twisted lines of logic. Dr. Richard H. Kohn, Chief of the Office of Air Force History, provided keen insight on its general focus and purpose. Several other readers offered very useful suggestions: Col. John F. Shiner, Mr. Herman Wolk, Dr. Fred Beck, Dr. Frank Cooling, Dr. Daniel Mortensen, Dr. Rebecca Welch, and Lt.

Col. Donald Baucom. My two branch colleagues, Drs. Richard Davis and Richard Wolf, offered helpful informal comments and acted as thoughtful listeners on many occasions. Dr. Wolf also did a superb job formatting the entire text. In addition, several readers outside the Office of Air Force History were asked to review Harnessing the Genie. Dr. Stever provided invaluable reflections on the national context of science and technology advising. Lieutenant Colonels Al Barbier (USAF, ret.) and William Reynolds, Executive Secretaries of the Scientific Advisory Board, both offered fine suggestions. Major Glasgow added much needed corrections on the last chapter. The general style and presentation of the text was enriched by the editorial comments of Prof. John A. Schutz of the University of Southern California.

Finally, Ms. Laura Dahljelm of the Editorial Branch of the Office of Air Force History deserves credit for top quality copy editing and layout. Thanks are also due to the 1100th Resources Management Group Graphics Office which did an excellent job reproducing the diagrams and photographs. Most important of all, I wish to thank my wife Annette for listening to my ideas with patience, and for stifling countless yawns to spare the feelings of her enthusiastic husband.

Contents

                                                          Page

The Author   iv
Foreword   v
Acknowledgments   vii
Diagrams and Photographs   x
Source Abbreviations   xi

Introduction   1

  I. A Mandate for Civilian Science, 1944-1950   11
       Notes   51

 II. The Decline of Civilian Science, 1950-1958   59
       Notes   81

III. Conforming Science to Military Necessity,
       1956-1966   87
       Notes 125

 IV. Scientists in Uniform, 1966-1986   131
       Notes 173

Conclusion   183

Bibliographic Note   189

Glossary   191
Index   195

Diagrams and Photographs

Diagrams   Page

1. Project Forecast Organization Chart 100
2. Project Forecast Flow Chart. 101
3. New Horizons II Organization Chart. 137
4. Project Forecast II Organization Chart. 146
5. Project Forecast II Matrix 152

Photographs

Cover
 1. Dr. Theodore von Karman at the Chalkboard

Following Chapter 2
 2. Commanding General of the Army Air Forces
     Henry H. Arnold
 3. Dr. Theodore von Karman
 4. Gen. James H. Doolittle
 5. Gen. Thomas S. Power
 6. Dr. H. Guyford Stever
 7. Lt. Gen. Donald L. Putt

Following Chapter 4
 8. Hon. Eugene M. Zuckert
 9. Gen. Bernard A. Schriever
10. Gen. David C. Jones
11. Maj. Gen. Foster Lee Smith
12. Dr. Michael I. Yarymovych
13. Gen. Lawrence A. Skantze
14. Brig. Gen. Eric B. Nelson
15. Brig. Gen. Charles F. Stebbins

Source Abbreviations

A. AFHRC= Air Force Historical Research Center
B. AFSC= USAF Systems Command History Office Archives
C. FII=   Project Forecast II Papers
D. NAS=   National Academy of Sciences Archives

   File Folder Designations:
   1. Finance and Accounting: Contracts: Air Force
      Special Study: AF 18(600)1661, 1957-1960
   2. Division NRC: Physical Sciences: NAS-ARDC
      Study on Long Range Scientific and Technical
      Trends: General: 1957-58
   3. Division NRC: Physical Sciences: General: 1960
   4. Government: Agencies and Departments: Air
      Force: 1959
   5. Division NRC: Physical Sciences: NAS-ARDC
      Study on Long Range Scientific and Technical
      Trends: Participants: 1957-1958
   6. Divisions of the NRC: Physical Sciences:
      General: 1959
   7. Division NRC: Physical Sciences: Air Force
      Summer Study: Participants: 1957
   8. Division NRC: Physical Sciences: Air Force
      Summer Study: 1958
   9. Division NRC: Physical Sciences: Air Force
      Summer Study: General: 1957
   10. (Air Force Studies Board Deposit) from file
       entitled "von Karman Study Info, 1957-1958"
   11. (Air Force Studies Board Deposit) NAS-ARDC
       Summer Study, 1957-1960
   12. Divisions of NRC: Physical Sciences: General:
       1962-1963

E. SAB=   Papers of the USAF SAB

   File Folder Designations:
   1. SAB Historical Report, 1944-1959

2. USAF SAB Organization, 1944-1966
3. USAF SAB 20 Year History
4. Organization-Background of SAB
5. USAF SAB Membership, 1946-1966
6. Air Force Review of Final Report—USAF SAB Tactical Air Capabilities Task Force
7. USAF SAB Operations
8. SAB Operating Procedures
9. Distribution of Sturm's History—1969
10. USAF SAB Organization, 1967-1971
11. Improving the Operation of the SAB—Col Manci
12. Final Report—SAB Tac Task Force
13. USAF SAB Report of the Tactical Air Capabilities Task Force
14. SAB Staff Review Group Meetings, 1967-1968
15. SAB Regulations
16. SAB General Files
17. Report of the Ad Hoc Committee on Aircraft Technology (1971 Summer Study)-- November 1971
18. SAB Panel Structure Review—1972-1973
19. Report of the SAB Ad Hoc Committee on the Air Force and Space—December 1972
20. Special Report of the USAF Scientific Advisory Board Executive Committee on Basic Research--October 1977
21. SAB Reorganization, 1978
22. Memorandum of Understanding Concerning USAF SAB/AFSC Division Advisory Groups
23. USAF SAB USAF in Space Report, July 1980
24. SAB/DAG Relationships; SAB By-Laws

F. SP= Schriever Papers at the Office of Air Force History
G. TVK=Theodore von Karman Collection at the California Institute of Technology

I listened with fascination. I had always admired [Commanding General of the Army Air Forces Henry H.] Arnold's great vision, but I think then that I was more impressed than ever. This was September 1944. The war was not over; in fact, the Germans were to launch the Battle of the Bulge in December. Yet Arnold was already casting his sights far beyond the war, and realizing, as he always had, that the technical genius which could help find answers for him was not cooped up in military or civilian bureaucracy but was to be found in universities and in the people at large.

-Theodore von Karman,
The Wind and Beyond,
p. 268

INTRODUCTION

This monograph on the forecasting of long-range Air Force science began as an attempt to describe the five major scientific studies undertaken by the U.S. Army Air Forces (USAAF)/U.S. Air Force (USAF) since the end of World War II. These reports included Toward New Horizons (1945), the Woods Hole Summer Studies (1957-1958), Project Forecast (1964), New Horizons II (1975), and Project Forecast II (1986). They seemed at first to represent nothing more than isolated efforts to predict the technological future. But shortly after initiating research on the subject, it became clear that several themes linked the five reports. Rather than a collection of unrelated analyses, common threads were seen to run through them.

The realization of this pattern was surprising. Taken at face value, the reports appeared to be entirely different. They were not produced in any one place; they were not directed by people with similar backgrounds or educations. Both in number and type of participants, they differed widely. Methodologies were not at all uniform. Their conclusions varied significantly. In fact, they did not even have the same purposes. Toward New Horizons was initiated to summarize the most advanced air power technologies of World War II and project them into the future. The Woods Hole Summer Studies organized hundreds of academic scientists to predict the short and long-term military uses of space.[*] Project Forecast had the mandate of revitalizing Air Force thinking by linking national policy issues to scientific vistas and new weapon systems. New Horizons II endeavored to point the way toward technological improvements in a period of expected scarcity. Finally, Project Forecast II sought to infuse the Air Force laboratories with new avenues of basic science research. Thus, for a variety of internal and external reasons, at roughly ten year intervals since the Second

---

[*]The 1958 study in particular struggled with the space question.

1

World War, the Air Force launched major science and technology forecasts.

Despite their unique aims, the five did have several factors in common. From first to last, they reflected a steady decline in the role of civilian science for long-range forecasts. Moreover, as the importance of independent scientists gradually diminished, the USAF's locus of in-house science -- the Scientific Advisory Board (SAB) -- lost its influence over the process of predicting the future of technology.[*] Paralleling and hastening this trend, military scientists and engineers trained in R&D came gradually to dominate science forecasting. Finally, cut loose from the SAB in the 1950s, the practice of doing periodic reports on the future of science and technology found itself an institutional orphan, unattached to any particular Air Force organization, and redefined according to the imperatives of each new study director. The course

---

[*]This study touches only on scientific forecasting for the Air Force. Since the Second World War, the U.S. defense establishment as a whole has had at its disposal a growing number of institutions able to provide expert science advice: the Defense Science Board, the White House Science Office, think tanks, and many other organizations. The Army and Navy also developed their own corps of technology experts. But the USAF SAB served as the model, indeed the grandfather of all the later boards. As such, it eventually found itself competing for talent with the others. Studies it alone was capable of undertaking in the 1950s were being done all over the defense landscape during the 1960s, 1970s, and 1980s. Indeed, during the 1980s one-half of every R&D dollar expended by the U.S. government was devoted to the armed forces. Thus, the role of the USAF SAB not only narrowed due to internal dynamics; its position outside the USAF also eroded as long-range science advising for the Defense Department became better funded and more diffuse. For reasons internal and external to the Air Force, over time the SAB found itself doing fewer and fewer studies of broad scope, becoming an institution devoted to short-term advice on relatively narrow subjects.

of these events did not occur suddenly. They progressed slowly and unobtrusively, almost absent-mindedly, with so little notice that neither military nor civilian scientists and engineers fully appreciated their occurrence, or their significance.

The long-range Air Force science forecasts also had in common a few basic objectives. They were all embarked on to predict trends in scientific knowledge one to three decades in the future, and to isolate those advances likely to yield significant advances for air power. Second, they sought to relate scientific and technological principles to specific weapons requirements, the presumed foreign threat, questions of cost, and ease of manufacture. Third, they suggested a number of likely weapon systems to be derived from the new frontiers of science.

But some common aspects could not conceal fundamental differences. The four reports which followed Toward New Horizons diverged increasingly from the pattern established by its director, Dr. Theodore von Karman. He did not deliberately set out to provide the USAF with a model for doing science forecasts. He only sought to draft an analysis as comprehensive, far-seeing, and practical as possible. But its warm reception at USAF Headquarters, its wide influence throughout the Air Force, and von Karman's powerful reputation contributed to its permanence and emulation. His unintentional model stressed four factors: to ensure fresh, disinterested views, advice should be given by people outside the confines of the Air Force; senior academic scientists, equipped by temperament and long experience to be informed generalists, should populate the panels; the reports should be comprehensive, the product of sufficient time to allow serious reflection; and the findings should place scientific or technological possibilities in the contexts of usefulness to national defense, air power requirements, and technical practicality.

Von Karman, perhaps the leading aeronautics expert of his generation, selected for Toward New Horizons 33 academic colleagues, chosen mainly from the California Institute of Technology (Cal Tech) and the Massachusetts

Institute of Technology (MIT). The project originated with a request to von Karman from the Commanding General of the Army Air Forces, H.H. Arnold, to search the world for the most advanced aeronautical ideas generated by wartime research and project them into the future. After a year of wide-ranging study in the U.S., Europe, and the Orient, the von Karman team — known as the USAAF Scientific Advisory Group (SAG)[*] — issued a fourteen-volume precis of the scientific lessons of World War II, and the technical implications likely to result from these breakthroughs. The product principally of physicists and mathematicians, it related advanced theoretical concepts to practical military objectives, evident in such titles as "High Speed Aerodynamics," "High Temperature Materials," and "Terminal Ballistics." Von Karman delivered his study with two chief recommendations: scientific inquiry must be pursued constantly and applied quickly to support air power; and a separate, distinct AAF agency should be devoted exclusively to aeronautical R&D.

Von Karman and the report proved highly persuasive. The Air Force took both of his suggestions. It established the USAF SAB in 1947 and the Air Research and Development Command (ARDC) three years later. But the need remained for comprehensive, long-term scientific advice for the Air Force, and on the urging of ARDC Commander General Thomas S. Power, a sequel to Toward New Horizons was begun in 1957. Held in Woods Hole, Massachusetts, during the summers of 1957 and 1958, the sessions were again directed by Dr. von Karman, but this time the facilities of the National Academy of Sciences (NAS) were contracted to attract the nation's finest scientific talent from academia and industry.

It had a basic kinship with Toward New Horizons. Academic scientists dominated the proceedings, led the panels, and decided for themselves the subjects for discussion. But in its mechanics it differed sharply. An army of scientists almost ten times the size of that enlisted for Toward New Horizons assembled on Cape Cod. Over 300 people--198 participants and 105 consultants--

---

*Foreunner of the USAF SAB.

passed in and out of the study site. Too many for long-term residence or coherent group discussion, the contributors to the Woods Hole Summer Study stayed at the Massachusetts location for only a few days at a time, disbanded, and left von Karman's personal assistants to weave the committee findings into 13 coherent volumes. Unlike Toward New Horizons, Woods Hole organized itself into weapon system/subsystem panels, rather than the basic science committees of its predecessor. As a result, a wide-ranging but conservative report was published. The USAF leadership responded with little enthusiasm. They did not find Woods Hole wrong or invalid; rather, it was irrelevant to a question of profound national importance: how to meet the defense crisis implicit in the October 1957 launch and orbit of the Soviet satellite Sputnik. Consequently, the influence of Woods Hole proved to be nil.

At an hour when Air Force officials were almost desperate to find measures to overcome the Soviet lead, this omission in the Woods Hole studies, based on a belief that long-range reports must provide balanced coverage of new technologies, had serious ramifications for the forecasts which followed. Uniformed USAF leaders concluded from the experience that civilian scientists required military oversight to ensure that their work furthered U.S. air power interests. These reforms, begun at the USAF SAB, subjected civilian scientists to greater military control than previously known.

No one did more to harness academic science to military objectives than Gen. Bernard A. Schriever, Commander of ARDC and its successor, Air Force Systems Command (AFSC). A distinguished Air Force R&D leader who brought the American ICBM force to fruition and almost single-handedly established a USAF command for weapons acquisition, he also erected a chain of AFSC mini-SABs (known as Division Advisory Groups, or DAGs) to serve his Product Division commanders. Then, directed in March 1963 by Secretary of the Air Force Eugene M. Zuckert, he undertook a major review of technologies applicable to USAF needs through the mid-1970s.

Called Project Forecast, it enlisted almost 500 people. The report balanced military R&D experts who understood the requirements of war with the nation's top civilian scientists and engineers from academia, industry, think tanks, and government. Schriever drew participants from the USAF, 63 other federal agencies, 26 institutions of higher learning, 70 corporations, and 10 non-profit organizations. Both Schriever and his project manager, Major General Charles H. Terhune, not only understood the scientific world, but represented a growing number of scientists and engineers in uniform able to grasp both the technical and military aspects of weapons development.

Schriever and Terhune structured Forecast so that all ideas produced by the technology panels were "filtered" through the mediums of cost and military requirements. Considerations of threat and national foreign policy objectives further winnowed the choices. Finally, the concepts which survived this screening were then translated into weapon systems by the capability panels. Far more hierarchical than the Toward New Horizons model, it nonetheless depended on independent academic scientists to make the basic judgments about the appropriate avenues of science and technology to pursue. Also, like Toward New Horizons, it was a comprehensive study, producing a massive 25-volume document which related its findings to the world in which the Air Force found itself. Each volume dealt with an aspect of aeronautical or military science. Its major conclusions presumed the status quo in strategic nuclear relations between the superpowers. Under the existing nuclear umbrella, Forecast recommended the development of weapons to fight small-scale nuclear wars, as well as protracted conventional conflicts. Schriever and the Forecast staff pressed for low-yield tactical nuclear devices, huge intercontinental transports, light composites for aircraft and engine designs, and vertical take-off and landing aircraft for light transport and strike reconnaissance.

Project Forecast enjoyed widespread influence throughout the USAF, and much of it was finally implemented. Could Schriever's success be duplicated in the next long-range forecast? This awaited an answer, but in the interim, the SAB produced a study called the

"Tactical Air Capabilities Task Force Report," in which it tried unsuccessfully to echo the work of Schriever and recapture some of the von Karman luster. Following its publication, the board experienced still greater USAF oversight.

Almost ten years after Forecast, the Air Force undertook a follow-on to Schriever's milestone work. Known ambitiously as New Horizons II, it was begun in August 1974 at the direction of the Air Force Chief of Staff, Gen. David C. Jones. Its executive director, Maj. Gen. Foster Lee Smith, the Headquarters USAF Assistant Deputy Chief of Staff for Plans and Operations, led an all Air Staff steering group of two-star generals. Completely divergent from the pattern established in Toward New Horizons, civilian scientific advice had little weight in the deliberations. Indeed, outside civilian scientists and members of the SAB functioned only as expert consultants, not as recognized participants in the study process, as they had in Forecast. All of the 49 study members but one---the Chief Scientist of the Air Force--were military men, and almost half worked in the offices of the Deputy Chief of Staff for Plans and Operations.

The methodology of New Horizons II lacked the comprehensiveness of Toward New Horizons, or, for that matter, of Forecast. Its five technology panels were mission, rather than scientifically, oriented, and the crucial Forecast feature of "filtering" the technologies through cost, capability, and threat factors were all but absent. Its conclusions, presented to General Jones in seven short volumes, generally involved subsystem improvements in the force structure. These included advances in data processing relative to command and control; survivable military satellites; laser weapons in the atmosphere and in space; and aircraft upgrades for night and all-weather flying. They did propose one new weapon system: a heavy lift, global range transport airplane of far greater capability than the C-5 aircraft.

Lacking General Schriever's prestige and close connections to the R&D and scientific communities, New Horizons II had only limited influence on weapon system planners. It did, however, foster the idea that independent civilian input in long-range science should be sharply limited. After minor attempts by two AFSC commanders to bring the process under control, AFSC Commander General Lawrence A. Skantze initiated the most recent long-range report. It continued—and in some ways added to—the tradition of military leadership in forecasting. Project Forecast II, begun in August 1985, was comprehensive in the style of Forecast I. It utilized a similar "filtering", or matrix process, considering threat and cost in its analysis panels; scientific possibilities in its ten technology panels; and military requirements in the mission panels. Some 200 people contributed to Forecast II. But there the similarities ended. Distinctly different from Forecast I were the occupational affiliations of the 200; all were Air Force employees. Although a majority of the 107 panelists were civilians, most of them worked for the AFSC laboratory commanders. Indeed, part of Forecast II's raison d'etre was to infuse the Systems Command lab structure with new ideas. Independent civilian advice was widely solicited, but not much used. The SAB was not even consulted until the report was completed. Altogether, about 2,000 technical ideas flowed from the Forecast II process: 900 originated in the Forecast II offices and 1,100 came from outside sources (academia, industry, and think tanks). While all of the 900 were considered in the project's screening process, 90 percent of the 1,100 were rejected without recourse to the formal review procedures. Long-range forecasting, controlled by military scientists, had reached a new plateau. The principal features of the von Karman model—applying independent, academic brainpower to long-term advising—had all but disappeared. Gone too was the Toward New Horizons practice of relating the technological future to the institutional life of the Air Force, and the nation's defense needs as a whole.

Eventually, 70 candidate systems and technologies emerged from the rigorous Forecast II review system. Unlike its namesake, Forecast II did not relate them to national security policy or overall military objectives, but simply presented them as the technological "best bets" of the future. They included such highly advanced concepts as knowledge-based computer systems, ultrastructured materials, anti-proton technology, the transatmospheric vehicle, widely distributed phased array radar in space, and the super cockpit. Implementation of the massive 1,700-page final report began almost immediately with significant AFSC laboratory funding devoted specifically to further exploration of the Forecast II technologies. But unlike Toward New Horizons and Forecast, which originated at Headquarters USAF, Forecast II was totally a product of AFSC. It remained, therefore, to be seen whether Forecast II would become ingrained in Air Force thinking like its two famous predecessors.

The story of how the USAF went about guiding aerospace science toward long-term air power requirements encompassed many institutions and personalities. Basically, it reflected a history of increasing military control over the process, and a decline in outside scientific advice (in particular, the USAF SAB). Air Force science forecasting became increasingly preoccupied with aerospace technologies as ends in themselves, rather than viewing them in organizational and national contexts. Much had changed between the time General Arnold asked Dr. von Karman to "make me a report" and the present, when a major Air Force command, out of its own resources, compiled a gargantuan study of the USAF's future in science. This monograph traces the evolution of the change.

CHAPTER ONE

A MANDATE FOR CIVILIAN SCIENCE, 1944-1950

At the end of the Second World War the U.S. air power establishment, especially the Commanding General of the Army Air Forces (AAF), Henry H. Arnold, faced a dilemma: how to introduce top quality scientific ideas into peacetime long-range planning. During the war many of the best brains from industry and academia rallied to the nation's defense, working for the government directly or undertaking research in university laboratories. Their discoveries had proven invaluable to U.S. air power, adding to the speed, range, payload, and accuracy of strategic bombing, and multiplying the destructiveness of armament. The air war was transformed by advances in propulsion, materials, fuels, radar, and explosives.

After Allied victory appeared certain, however, Arnold realized these gifted scientists would soon return to civilian life. At the same time, he knew the absence of overt warfare in no way guaranteed that the new weapons of sudden and mass destruction would not be aimed by hostile powers at U.S. targets. The only way to prevent surprise attack, he reasoned, was to maintain technological superiority in the skies. To do so, some method had to be found to tap at least part of the enormous reservoir of civilian talent, persuading them to continue to do AAF work. The answer came piecemeal. Before the war ended and the scientists returned to civilian pursuits, Arnold decided to assemble some of the finest minds to initiate a comprehensive review of future technologies useful to the Army Air Forces. He selected to lead the review Dr. Theodore von Karman, a distinguished scholar who dominated the field of aeronautics, and whose very presence on the panel assured a noteworthy result. Von Karman succeeded so well at the task that the very concepts of independent civilian technical advice and scientific forecasting became ingrained practices of the AAF, and later, the USAF. Thanks to these achievements, von Karman presided for more than a decade over a period in which civilian scientists guided U.S. air power toward the technological future.

*   *   *

The process of predicting scientific and technical developments for the Air Force began on a cloudless, breezy day early in September 1944, when two men sat alone in an automobile parked at the end of a runway at La Guardia Field, New York. The older man was in his 60s, small in stature and pale from a recent illness. The younger, by just a few years, was stocky and broad shouldered, but tired-looking. They conferred for some time, discussing the course of the war, the role of air power in it, and the future of the Army Air Forces in the postwar world. As aircraft roared overhead and cool winds rocked the car, they chatted about a preoccupation of the younger man: harnessing science to assure U.S. technological superiority in the skies in the decades to come. When the talk finally ended, an informal understanding had been reached which would exert a profound influence on American military aviation.

The men who met on that late summer day were Dr. von Karman, the founder of modern American aerodynamics, and General Arnold, Commanding General of the AAF. The general arranged the meeting to coincide with a scheduled change of planes during a flight from Washington, D.C., to Canada, where he would attend the second Quebec Conference of World War II. Out of friendship and patriotism, von Karman left a hospital bed, where he had been recovering from cancer surgery, to see Arnold. They had known each other since 1936 when the general, commanding March Field, California, visited von Karman "very many times" to discuss lighter-than-air technologies. In 1938, when Arnold was Chief of the Army Air Corps, he invited von Karman to Washington, D.C., to review problems related to pilot visibility and military rocketry. During World War II, Dr. von Karman accepted a part-time appointment as scientific adviser both to Arnold and to the commanding general of the research laboratories at Wright Field, Ohio. General Arnold asked him to develop test facilities to accelerate the growth of aviation knowledge. Both agreed that the construction of a 40,000-horsepower, 20-foot wind tunnel at Wright Field would do most to spur aeronautical innovation. The scientist supervised its study and design phases. Later in the war, he undertook analyses on the Bell XS-1, responding to Arnold's request to contribute to the development of a supersonic aircraft. As one official who had worked closely with both men observed, they made a superb team and worked together very well. The general was not really a technical man. But he had a gift for anticipating the future and recognized the importance of science and technology in achieving his objectives. Dr. von Karman, on the other hand, understood only the rudiments of military affairs, yet he grasped clearly which aspects of science would be of most use to the AAF.[1]

The friendship and trust they had developed over a decade stood them in good stead at the meeting at La Guardia. In fact, the outcome of their talk had been at least partly determined well before their impromptu conference. General Arnold had already spoken to another scientist with whom he had a long friendship, Dr. Robert A. Millikan, von Karman's superior at the California Institute of Technology (Cal Tech). Asked whom he would select to head a committee of eminent scientists to advise the Air Force on long-range science, Millikan picked von Karman. Based on his own experience and Millikan's recommendation, Arnold told von Karman to forget the present war, which he considered won. Arnold could not be sure whether sheer force of numbers or superior equipment made victory possible; in a sense, he considered it irrelevant. "What I am interested in," he said, "is what will be the shape of the air war, of air power, in five years, or ten, or sixty-five." Arnold asked von Karman to assemble a group of scientists in the Pentagon, study such things as jet propulsion, atomic energy, and electronics, and "make me a report."[2]

Von Karman raised some objections. A gentle, warm-hearted man, he had no desire to give, or take, orders in a military environment. He did not want to work in the Pentagon. But Arnold assured him that he would be von Karman's only boss, and that he would give all the

necessary orders. Moreover, the general set no time limit
for completing the report. Von Karman would undertake
the study at his own pace, using his own methods. He
would not consider merely the next generation of air
power, or the one after that; but project years into the
future. He and his associates were free to travel
anywhere they chose--including Germany, Russia, and
Japan--to learn from their colleagues abroad. More than
this, Arnold wanted the scientists assembled at the
Pentagon to "forget the past; regard the equipment now
available only as the basis for [the] boldest predictions."
They would study supersonic aircraft, crewless airplanes,
advances in bomb lethality, defenses against future
aircraft, air-to-air and air-to-ground communications,
television, weather, medical research, atomic energy, and
all other likely and appropriate avenues of research.
Forced for four years to think in incremental terms,
General Arnold now sought the best people in the
scientific community to spur air power technology far
beyond present limitations. The chance to share Arnold's
dream of aviation progress, rather than promises of
institutional autonomy, inspired von Karman. It also
persuaded him to accept the general's offer to act as the
link between civilian science and the Air Force. Von
Karman later admitted that as Arnold made these proposals
on a wind-swept landing strip at La Guardia, he sat
fascinated, absorbed by the remarkable insights into the
future. The end of the war was not yet in sight, but the
general realized that the AAF would not maintain its
dominant position in the postwar world by relying on
government technologists; the genius of civilian science, he
said, must be enlisted to assure U.S. air power superiority
in the years to come.[3]

Whom had Arnold entrusted with integrating the
wonders of science into the Army Air Forces? Theodore
von Karman was born in Budapest, Hungary on May 11,
1881, the son of Maurice von Karman, a distinguished
professor of education at the University of Budapest. By
contrast, past generations of his family had simple Jewish
roots; his paternal grandfather was a tailor for Hungarian
noblemen. Maurice von Karman received his title of
nobility for the sweeping reforms he had instituted in the

secondary education system of his country, and for overseeing the curriculum of the Archduke Albrecht. Although Theodore showed a genius for mathematics at a very early age, his father insisted he receive a liberal education before narrowing his sights on the sciences. The elder von Karman wanted no child prodigies. After several years of home tutoring and matriculation at an elite gymnasium, he studied at the Budapest Royal Polytechnic Institute, and in 1902 took a degree with honors in mechanical engineering. Von Karman pursued the study of aerodynamics under one of the discipline's founding geniuses, Professor Ludwig Pradtl of Gottingen University, Germany, and received the doctor of philosophy degree there in 1908. His research at Gottingen on aerodynamic drag had profound implications for aircraft, ship, and bridge design. With a reputation second only to his mentor's, he accepted a chair at the Polytechnic Institute at Aachen and taught there until World War I, when he served as an aircraft designer for the Austrian Air Service. Between the end of the war and 1929, he was Director of the Aachen Aeronautics Institute and pursued research in fluid mechanics. By the end of the decade he had at least equalled Pradtl's stature as a research aerodynamicist.[4]

Von Karman's fame spread to America, where aeronautical research had not yet reached the degree of sophistication it had in Europe. To remedy the situation, the Guggenheim Foundation provided funds to establish the Guggenheim Aeronautical Laboratory at the California Institute of Technology (GALCIT). Von Karman's name topped the list of world renowned candidates for director. In 1926 Professor Robert A. Millikan had invited von Karman to lecture at Cal Tech. The trip persuaded Millikan that von Karman should be the Guggenheim director. Millikan and Harry Guggenheim were deeply impressed by von Karman's intellectual capacity, practical insight, and organizational finesse. His charm and warmth also won converts. After three years of negotiation, in October 1929, von Karman accepted the Cal Tech offer. His reasons were compelling. Nazism had begun to manifest itself on the Aachen campus, and the facilities and salary offered by Guggenheim were too generous to refuse.[5]

HARNESSING THE GENIE

During the 1930s, von Karman exerted a significant influence over aeronautical research and development (R&D) in the U.S. Due largely to his efforts, Cal Tech came to rival Aachen as a center of advanced aviation studies. Indeed, Southern California became the hub of the nation's aircraft industry in large part thanks to the brainpower assembled by von Karman in Pasadena. But as war loomed over Europe, General Arnold invited the scientist to sit on a special committee of the National Academy of Sciences (NAS) which reviewed scientific projects of interest to the Army Air Corps. Professor Millikan, who had introduced the two men in 1936, urged von Karman to go. His acceptance initiated almost twenty years of continuous association with the air power establishment. He and his students undertook an Air Corps-sponsored research project to develop small rocket engines propelled by liquid and solid fuels. Their solid rocket motors proved so successful that in 1942 von Karman and his group formed the Aerojet Engineering Corporation (forerunner of the Aerojet General Corporation) to fabricate these engines. Two years later, Cal Tech received a contract from the Army Ordnance Department to develop tactical ballistic missiles, resulting in the restructuring of the GALCIT as the Jet Propulsion Laboratory (JPL).[6]

Undoubtedly, von Karman's crowning service to the nation began in fall 1944, just after he agreed to act as General Arnold's scientific adviser. Appointed on October 23, 1944, he proceeded immediately to Eglin Field, Florida, where he and a few colleagues spent a month laying the groundwork for the long-range study requested by Arnold. On his return to Washington, von Karman quickly began to select personnel to serve on functional area panels. Luckily for the project, many of the top scientists employed by the government in wartime research were just completing their work and had not yet undertaken new duties. He contacted three dozen "first-class" scientists and engineers including Dr. Hugh L. Dryden, a leading aerodynamicist with the National Bureau of Standards; Drs. Lee A. DuBridge, Frank C. Wattendorf, and Hsue-shen Tsien from Cal Tech; George E. Valley, Ivan Getting, E.M. Purcell, and Vladymir K. Zworykin from the Massachusetts

Institute of Technology (MIT) Radiation Laboratories; and Norman Ramsey of Harvard University, a pioneer in nuclear research. Despite resistance from some Air Forces officials, Arnold permitted von Karman to also select able men from industry, including George Schairer of Boeing. Von Karman did not care what walk of life his panelists came from; only that they be men of the highest ability.

Von Karman threw himself into his new responsibilities. His appearances in Pasadena became less frequent, and despite the pleas of his students to return, he persisted in his tasks in the Pentagon. General Arnold had brought in an able administrative staff headed by Col. Frederic E. Glantzberg to assist the men of learning being assembled by von Karman, and the scientist relished the recognition which came with his position. Suddenly, he found his knowledge much in demand among senior USAAF leaders. Maj. Gen. Oliver Echols, the Air Staff Deputy for Materiel, sought out his counsel on R&D questions. Brig. Gen. Frank Carroll, commander of the Air Materiel Command (AMC) research facilities at Wright Field, Ohio, asked him to visit his center. But, for the time-being at least, General Arnold insisted Karman stay in the Pentagon and concentrate on providing him first-hand scientific advice. Indeed, Arnold deserves a large share of the credit for von Karman's early successes. During the late 1930s the general had sat on the National Advisory Committee for Aeronautics (NACA) where he learned much about scientists and how they did their work. Arnold also had a gift of interesting people in his projects and channeling their energies toward his goals. The more he pressed NACA for a 500 mph aircraft, the more enthusiasm he generated for the idea. When Arnold spoke to von Karman and his colleagues in December 1944 he brought to bear this knowledge and dynamism. As they were about to embark on the long-range report, he asked them to consider a pilotless Air Force. Why, he asked them, should men in fighter planes shoot down bombers? Why should bombers, each of which required thousands of man hours to contruct, be the sole means of long-range aerial offense when a V-2 rocket could be fabricated in a fraction of the time? "For twenty years the Air Force was built around pilots, pilots, and more pilots," said Arnold.

"The next twenty years is going to be built around scientists."[7]

Arnold urged them to search every corner of every scientific field to unearth discoveries for U.S. air power. Taking their cue from him, by the beginning of 1945 several weeks of group meetings had resulted in progress on high-speed aerodynamics, power, and communications.[8]

Although General Arnold and Dr. von Karman had set the overall tone and direction for the scientists, there remained in fall and winter 1944 mountains of work for von Karman to do to prepare for the long-range study and establish his organization on the Air Staff. It would have taxed a man half his age. First, he had to complete several commitments to GALCIT, from which he had chosen to take a leave of absence rather than resign. He also was compelled to disassociate himself from several private enterprises: Northrop Aircraft and General Electric, where he acted as a paid consultant; and Aerojet General, where he served as a major shareholder and chairman of the board of directors. At the Pentagon, most of his time was devoted to a whirlwind of conferences with Air Staff leaders, as well as other scientific agencies in which he described the objectives of the new organization.[9]

Fortunately for von Karman, official recognition and structuring of his office came quickly. On November 10, 1944, Lt. Gen. Barney M. Giles, Deputy Commander of the AAF, announced to the Air Staff that von Karman would direct the AAF Long Range Development Program. As "Expert Consultant to General Arnold," he would receive "full cooperation and expeditious action" in carrying out Arnold's mandate. Almost two weeks later the new office was designated the "AAF Consulting Board for Future Research" and given official status at HQ USAAF. Its members would study for the AAF Commander long-range R&D, preparing on demand special reports pertaining to "scientific thought, technical research, and air power." Subjects of particular interest included propeller-and jet-powered aircraft, guided missiles, fuels, and explosives.

Assigned a four-room office in the Pentagon, the board included a director, an executive officer, full-time scientific advisers, and on-call consultants. The permanent staff of scientists included Morton Alperin, technical assistant; Dr. Frank Wattendorf, gas, turbo, and jet propulsion; George Schairer, aircraft; Dr. Louis Alvarez, radar; Dr. S. J. Zand, controls; Dr. Hsue-shen Tsien, rocket motors; and Dr. Vladymir Zworykin, television. Finally, effective the first day of December 1944, HQ USAAF Office Instruction 20-76 renamed the Board for Future Research the AAF Scientific Advisory Group (SAG), and designated it as "an office attached to the Commanding General, AAF." Dr. Dryden was listed as von Karman's scientific deputy, while Colonel Frederic E. Glantzberg was named military deputy.* [10]

Once the SAG office had been organized and established on the Air Staff, one task became paramount: researching and writing for General Arnold the report on long-range science for the USAAF. The commanding general had been most explicit in setting forth the guidelines for the study. He based them on his understanding of the experiences of World Wars I and II. During both conflicts, aggressor nations sought to maintain American neutrality, only to find U.S. power arrayed decisively against them. The lesson for the next war, Arnold wrote, "is too plain for the next aggressor to miss: the United States will be the first target." Consequently, American air power would have no grace time to mobilize, and must be the leading force in the skies from the very first engagement. He concluded that research was the principal ingredient for an Air Force capable of defending the country. The imagination and genius of the whole nation—in industry, academia, and the armed forces—"must have free play, incentive, and every encouragement." Rapid advances in aerodynamics, physics, chemistry, electronics, rocket-related sciences, jet propulsion, and radar demanded comprehensive and continuing programs of research both inside and outside the AAF.[11]

On the basis of these presumptions, he presented the SAG with a set of axioms to guide their research. As one of the world's predominant powers, the U.S. would continue

---

*Those who advised on an irregular basis — the SAG consultants — included Drs. Charles W. Bray (Princeton), Lee A. DuBridge (Cal Tech), Pol Duwez

to encounter adversaries who threatened the nation. While most wars would still be fought between the 30th and 60th parallels, General Arnold asked the scientists to consider technologies appropriate for global conflict north of the European and North American centers of population. He also observed that pre-war aeronautical research in the U.S. had "often been inferior to our enemies'," and suggested von Karman concentrate on offensive weaponry, rather than countermeasures. Arnold felt the American people would not support large standing armies, nor wars of human attrition. Hence, machines must be enlisted to make the work of the air forces safer and more efficient by overcoming problems of long distance, darkness, and weather. This would leave human intelligence—assisted by television and radar—free to determine weapons delivery. The general also urged the SAG to explore radically new means of aerial warfare: more potent explosives; faster aircraft with more flexibility and control; greater offensive efficiency in mass operations; and terror weapons such as "buzz" bombs, napalm, gas, and bacteriological warfare. The scientists must at the same time keep costs in mind. In peacetime, the AAF's large portion of the War Department budget would be reduced, and Congress might cut R&D funding based on a mistaken faith in the masses of stockpiled, but obsolete, weapons.

Finally, General Arnold asked Dr. von Karman to rely on the current war only as a "baseline" for understanding existing aeronautical science, but in all other respects to

---

(Cal Tech), George A. Gamow (Johns Hopkins), Ivan A. Getting (MIT), Louis P. Hammett (Explosives Research Laboratory), Walter S. Hunter (Brown), Irving P. Krick (Cal Tech), Duncan P. MacDougall (Naval Ordnance Lab), George A. Morton (Sarnoff Research Center), Nathan M. Newmark (Illinois), William H. Pickering (Cal Tech), Edward M. Purcell (Harvard), Galen B. Schubauer (National Bureau of Standards), William R. Sears (Cornell), Arthur J. Stosick (Cal Tech), William J. Sweeney (Standard Oil), George E. Valley, Jr. (MIT), Fritz Zwicky (Cal Tech), Mr. Irving L. Ashkenas (Northrop Aircraft), and W. Randolph Lovelace II, M.D. (the Lovelace Foundation).

"divorce yourselves from the present war." As well as highlighting potential development programs in their final report, he also wanted the scientists to pose organizational questions. To what extent should government underwrite peacetime scientific research in universities and industry? Should scientists be asked by the government to donate a small portion of their time to do research in the interests of national security? How should the AAF go about acquiring modern testing and support equipment? How much of the AAF budget should be invested in R&D? [12]

Despite the general's reassuring pledge to place at the disposal of the SAG whatever services his staff could render, von Karman now knew how formidable a task lay ahead. He and Arnold agreed that the report would achieve true comprehensiveness only if a SAG team of scientists traveled to the European war zone and interviewed colleagues both in the allied and enemy nations. Early in December 1944 Dr. Wattendorf, one of von Karman's closest aides in the Pentagon, drafted a highly ambitious list of eleven countries. Perhaps most promising were facilities in the United Kingdom: the national laboratories at Teddington and Farnborough, as well as leading industrial plants. They were targeted for review in the fields of jet propelled aircraft, guided missiles, radar, television equipment, fuels, materials, and explosives. In France and Belgium plans were made to show the American delegation the National Aeronautical Laboratories and coastal launch sites of robot bombs, respectively. The tour of Holland would center on the Phillips Corporation, actively engaged in advanced radar research. Germany (Aachen, Metz, Strasbourg), Switzerland (the Zurich Institute), Sweden, Finland, Poland, and Italy all offered the fruits of German science, either in German laboratories or in facilities directed by Germans abroad. Dr. Wattendorf considered it "very important" to see Russian developments at Moscow's Central Aero-Hydrodynamic Institute, hoping for reciprocation by Soviet visits to U.S. research installations.

Once preliminary work had been undertaken, General Arnold's staff formally asked the Chief of Staff of the U.S. Army, Gen. George C. Marshall, to direct Gen.

Dwight D. Eisenhower, Commander of the European Theater of Operations (ETO), to clear the SAG to enter these countries. Dr. von Karman and eight colleagues—Col. Frederic E. Glantzberg and Lt. Col. Godfrey T. McHugh, military members of the SAG; Dr. Hugh L. Dryden; Dr. Lee A. DuBridge; Dr. Vladimir K. Zworykin; Dr. Hsue-shen Tsien; Dr. Frank Wattendorf; and George Schairer—asked to embark in February 1945 on a 60-day trip. But the progress of the war delayed the process. General Marshall had already suspended all ETO travel by War Department civilians and had recently directed General Eisenhower to limit his concerns to the immediate problems of prosecuting the war. Moreover, State Department officials warned of persistent Soviet resistance to granting visas for travel in the U.S.S.R., adding that the von Karman party had already been pre-empted by the mission of Brig. Gen. John R. Deane to obtain first-hand technical information from Soviet scientists. Hence, a decision on the SAG trip was put off until February 1945.[13]

When the request for travel was submitted that month, the itinerary and agenda had been refined greatly. General Marshall was asked once again to expedite a tour to Europe by von Karman and the SAG personnel. Upon arrival in the ETO, they requested permission to contact allied scientists and industrialists; interrogate German scientists and inspect German laboratory facilities under allied and Russian jurisdiction; gather data on German R&D activities in neutral countries (Sweden and Switzerland); and confer with military and technical officers in the Headquarters ETO and MTO.* Lt. Gen. Barney M. Giles, Deputy Commander of the AAF, suggested Drs. von Karman, Dryden, Zworykin, and DuBridge, who had been given informal assurances by the Soviet ambassador of Russian willingness to receive them, be permitted to visit the U.S.S.R. Giles further suggested an April 15 departure date.[14]

The Army Chief of Staff received General Giles' requests favorably, and the following day (February 17,

---

*Mediterranean Theater of Operations.

22

1945) the bureaucratic machinery began to turn at full speed. Plans were made to obtain clearances via cable to General Eisenhower, and passports and re-entry visas were issued quickly. The Russian visit would be expedited by the Deane Mission and Ambassador Averill Harriman in Moscow. A preliminary itinerary proposed a tightly scheduled trip of 44 days, beginning in London and progressing through Stockholm, Leningrad, Rome, Bern, the Western Front, and Paris. To expedite the movement of personnel and ensure suitable accommodations, arrangements were made to provide temporary ranks of colonel and (for von Karman) general, as well as AAF uniforms, to the traveling scientists. They were also assured transportation on a specially designated transport aircraft. A letter from General Giles introducing von Karman asked that those assisting him "take any steps necessary to see that the... mission is facilitated and that he is shown every courtesy."

Just before their departure, General Giles also wrote to Gen. Carl Spaatz, Commanding General, United States Strategic Air Forces in Europe, informing him of the SAG's high priority objectives and requirements during their stay. While the group would be available for consultation with Spaatz and his staff, its main goal of gathering information for General Arnold must be furthered. Giles suggested that the data assembled by the von Karman team must be obtained only by direct means: through face-to-face discussions with Allied (as well as neutral nation) scientists and industrialists; inspection of German R&D facilities in the occupied zones; and conferences with military and technical leaders in both the Mediterranean and European Theaters of Operation. Giles added that von Karman and his associates would remain in Europe for six to eight weeks. During that period, Spaatz was asked to provide them an aircraft to facilitate full freedom of movement, make appropriate contacts for them, and in general give the group his personal attention.[15]

The work of the von Karman party in Europe proved to be more successful than anyone could have guessed. Once the arrangements were in hand, "Major General" von Karman and his associates stepped aboard a C-54 transport bound for London. They arrived on April 28, 1945, and met a recently arrived group of twenty-nine senior American engineers from private industry known as the Alsos mission. While interested in basic aeronautical science, the Alsos delegation was more concerned with the practical aspects of German air power innovation.* The two parties shared the unusual code name Operation Lusty, which Dr. von Karman called "unlikely but pleasant." After a few days of rest in the British capital, von Karman's contingent journeyed on to Paris. Since the war continued to rage in its last stages in Germany, their plans had to be adapted to battlefield circumstances. While awaiting orders in Paris, von Karman received an urgent message describing the existence of a clandestine, top secret scientific institute, located by U.S. soldiers in a forest near Braunschweig, northern Germany. The group arrived at Headquarters United States Strategic Air Forces in Europe (HQ USSTAF) on May 4 and traveled immediately to the hitherto unknown site. They found the laboratories in shambles from the American troops, but even the ruins deeply impressed von Karman. Built by his former assistant, Adolph Baumker, the facility's fifty-six buildings were disguised as farmhouses and camouflaged by trees. Advanced work was done there in ballistics, aerodynamics, and jet propulsion.

Von Karman set about collecting documentary and microfilm data scattered about the premises, and interviewed German scientists "who had not the time or the inclination to flee." Between the various sources he was able to uncover most of the projects undertaken at the clandestine site. He came to an ominous conclusion. Had the Germans further developed their discoveries and better organized their scientific research, they might have prolonged or even won the war. While the scientists enjoyed all the funding necessary to pursue whatever inquiries they chose, they lacked close ties to the military establishment, which regarded them as unrealistic intellectuals who should be isolated from military activities.[16]

Excitedly, von Karman cabled General Arnold and described the enormous cache of materials quite literally

---

*To avoid duplication of effort, on May 16 and 17, the von Karman group met with members of the Alsos

unearthed at Braunschweig. About 3,000,000 documents weighing 1,500 tons had been amassed, were microfilmed in Europe, and returned to the U.S. to form the backbone of the War Department Documentation Center.* Information on swept-wing aircraft, ejection seats, and the effects of high speed on human physiology topped the list of crucial research subjects gleaned from the Braunschweig laboratories.

Once he had finished there, von Karman visited the devastated city of Aachen, the seat of the aeronautical institute he had once directed, and Gottingen University, where his mentor, Dr. Ludwig Prandtl, still presided over long-range aeronautical research. While von Karman interviewed Prandtl about his wartime experiments in nuclear power, Drs. Wattendorf and Dryden traveled south to Munich, a relatively new center for air power studies. Here they met over 400 engineers and technicians who had been evacuated from the Peenemunde rocket facility. Chief among them were Dr. Wernher von Braun and Gen. Walter Dornberger. From these two men Dryden and Wattendorf learned much about the V-1 buzz bomb and the V-2 long-range rocket. Once the interviews at Gottingen and Aachen had been completed, on May 27 von Karman boarded an aircraft bound for Paris. He continued on to London where Royal Air Force (RAF) officials briefed him on progress in jet propulsion and missiles. Von Karman and his party then departed for additional fact-finding in Switzerland, and by June 8 were back in Paris.[17]

While several more weeks of exhausting travel lay ahead for the buoyant von Karman, his younger colleagues had begun to wrap up their work. Drs. Tsien, Wattendorf, and Dryden prepared to return to America around mid-June, but not before arrangements had been made to

---

mission. The aims of the two parties were found to be compatible, and as only one man on the Alsos team specialized in aeronautical research, it was agreed that members of the groups should be exchanged to work in cooperation on each other's projects.
*Today known as the Defense Technical Information Center (DTIC).

ship to the U.S. a great prize: a complete, uncrated Swiss-made wind tunnel, destined originally for Germany. Despite the high priority given at the time to personnel aboard cargo aircraft, Dryden insisted upon "immediate action" to transship this invaluable equipment from its hangar at Orly Field to Wright Field, and late in the month a B-17 was made available for the purpose. The Swiss wind tunnel, as well as the interviews with the European scientists, the boxes of documents and laboratory equipment, and the regular technical intelligence reports assembled by the von Karman group, all added luster to the SAG's reputation.[18]

The next leg of the von Karman odyssey took him to the U.S.S.R. He was invited to attend the 220th anniversary of the founding of the Soviet Academy of Sciences, and General Arnold urged him to "look around and let us know what you see." Preparations for the departure were complete by June 14 thanks to the efforts of Ambassador Harriman, who had secured the necessary clearances for von Karman. He flew to Moscow aboard a lend-lease DC-3 dispatched by the Soviets to pick him up. He found the Russian capital alive with victory. To his delight, he was asked to share the reviewing stand at Red Square with Premier Josef Stalin. There he saw a massive military parade, followed later by a sumptuous Kremlin banquet hosted by the Soviet Marshal himself. In spite of the elation of the moment, the trip revealed more about the manner in which the Russians organized science than about Russian science itself. Unlike wartime conditions in Germany, Soviet scientists received both high salaries and top military awards for their service in the war. Indeed, von Karman remarked with approval that several of the leading Soviet professors wore general's uniforms and enjoyed direct access to the highest levels of military authority. Von Karman was also impressed by the extent of the Soviet laboratory system. "The supreme scientific organization," it ranged from the Ural Mountains to the eastern Ukraine. He saw laboratories in Moscow and Leningrad which specialized in chemistry, power, semiconductors, and nucleonics, and visited a cyclotron. However, he observed no equipment or installations related directly to military research and was told by his hosts that they had no control over these facilities. "This struck me as surprising," he would later recall, "since they were all in general's uniforms." Worse still, he found it difficult to meet scholars or students informally to discuss their work, most contacts having been arranged in advance.[19]

Tired by a whirlwind of parties and meetings, Dr. von Karman happily journeyed back to Paris early in July. As General Arnold had arrived in nearby St. Germaine (en route with President Truman to the Potsdam Conference for meetings with Stalin and Churchill) von Karman visited him and described the bonanza of knowledge yielded by his travels. Arnold was delighted by what he heard. He also praised the scientist for his work in persuading many German scientists to emigrate to the U.S., and for retrieving their documents and equipment for AAF use. The general asked him to prepare an interim report which summarized his European experiences.*

Accordingly, von Karman returned to the Pentagon and, with the aid of his staff, feverishly wrote down his impressions. Six weeks later—on August 22, 1945—he submitted the product of his labors to Arnold in a seminal volume entitled Where We Stand. As its name implies, Where We Stand was a summary of the existing state of aeronautical knowledge as related to air power. But in listing eight "fundamental realities" characterizing postwar aerial combat, von Karman reached several astonishing conclusions:

> Aircraft, manned or pilotless, will move with speeds far beyond the velocity of sound.
> Due to improvements in aerodynamics, propulsion, and electronic control, unmanned devices will transport means of destruction to targets at distances up to several thousands of miles.
> Small amounts of explosive materials will

_____

*The two men understood this to be an interim report, not the long-range study requested by Arnold in December 1944.

cause destruction over areas of several square miles.

Defense against present-day aircraft will be perfected by target-seeking missiles.

Only aircraft or missiles moving at extreme speeds will be able to penetrate enemy territory protected by such defenses.

A perfect communication system between fighter command and each individual aircraft will be established.

Location and observation of targets, take-off, navigation and landing of aircraft, and communication will be independent of visibility and weather.

Fully equipped airborne task forces will be able to strike at far distant points and will be supplied by air.[20]

What secrets had the scientists unearthed in Europe on which to base such expansive predictions? First, the Germans had made significant advances in supersonic flight through experiments in jet propulsion, aerodynamics, and rocketry. Almost unlimited government funding provided them with the finest, most expensive equipment, including highly sophisticated wind tunnels. Wind tunnel tests taught the Germans that maintaining stability at transonic speeds required rapid acceleration; and that wing forms—especially the swept-back arrowhead shape—with sufficient lift over drag ratios for supersonic flight could indeed be designed. To achieve the feat of transonic aircraft, von Karman recommended building supersonic wind tunnels of sufficient size to test whole model airplanes, as well as major sub-structures and components. In order to obtain performance and flow mechanics data, he proposed flight tests at the speed of sound in rocket-launched research aircraft. Only a heavily funded program of government research could solve the still formidable problems of supersonic flight. Von Karman could not predict the best methods of employing these high velocity aircraft for tactical warfare; he did know, however, that "we cannot hope to secure air superiority in any future conflict without entering the supersonic speed range."[21]

Pilotless aircraft and guided missiles rated a close second in importance. The Peenemunde group under the leadership of Dr. Wernher von Braun had carried out a number of important experiments. Perhaps their greatest achievement was to show that winged missiles like the second generation V-2 were superior to their finned counterparts. Indeed, calculations had been completed for a transoceanic missile, a vehicle whose practicality had been borne out to von Karman's satisfaction by wind tunnel tests, ballistic computations, and the V-2 experiences. A closely knit group in one location under one leader, the Peenemunde community comprised within itself a total missile development program, with experts in aerodynamics, structural design, electronics, servomechanisms, gyros, control devices, and propulsion. This fact was the central lesson of the Peenemunde group for the U.S. military. Von Karman suggested the establishment of a center expressly for missile research which would enjoy the support of top ranking civilian and military leaders and be funded adequately. As he wisely foresaw, once German rocketry was linked to American atomic bomb expertise, "future methods of aerial warfare (will) call for a reconsideration of all present plans."[22]

Jet propulsion was next on Von Karman's list. He recalled that many patents had been granted for jet designs well before World War II. They became practical during the war because military aircraft suddenly required the speed of non-propeller powered systems, and the poor fuel economy normally associated with jets no longer mattered (provided the new engines weighed less and were simpler to manufacture than reciprocating engines). Due to hastened research between 1938 and 1945, knowledge of combustion in high speed air flow improved greatly and metallurgists discovered new materials resistent to high temperatures. Finally, imaginative designers built turbine and compressor prototypes which far surpassed those of conventional engineering. Additional research, wrote von Karman, would soon enhance both jet economy and reciprocating engine performance.

Rocket propulsion, unlike jet power, propelled objects without using atmospheric oxygen, instead burning solid or liquid propellant and oxygen mixtures at slow rates of combustion. Rocket motors suggested several uses to von Karman: for trans-atmospheric missiles which must operate without oxygen; guided anti-aircraft missiles; and launch of supersonic, long-range aircraft. German tests during World War II demonstrated that various combinations of rocket fuels had little bearing on overall effectiveness. Nonetheless, von Karman urged the AAF to develop rocketry as a main auxiliary form of aircraft power by establishing centers for the testing of rocket propulsion and by attracting the best minds in the field to government service.[23]

Von Karman also had great faith in atomic power as a method of aerospace propulsion. In the decades ahead, once the problems of producing it continuously and at a constant rate had been solved, atomic energy would be the perfect source of power. At 1.5 million times the volatility of gasoline, nuclear power promised an extremely lightweight propulsive force, capable of fueling rockets or aircraft for years rather than hours. He suggested the AAF bring to bear the best engineering minds on the problems of atomic propulsion: conversion of the energy released by nuclear reactions into heat usable in rockets or aircraft; heat transfer; and resistance of materials to heat and corrosion. Should atomic propulsion become feasible, the AAF would command the air with no range limitations whatever.[24]

Finally, Where We Stand urged advanced study in two fields of research still very much on the minds of aeronautical engineers in the 1980s: tailless (flying wing) aircraft and radar detection. The first flying prototypes of tailless aircraft were made by German scientists during the 1930s, and Northrop's XP-56 followed suit. But lack of flight control dogged the experiments. Should the problems of stability and maneuveribility be mastered, von Karman felt that the aerodynamics of these aircraft promised significantly longer ranges than conventional airplanes of his day. Moreover, "the recent recognition of the advantages of swept-back wings for very high speeds makes the tailless airplane particularly attractive for transonic airplanes." After completion of extensive wind tunnel testing to improve control at high speeds, the SAG suggested the AAF seriously consider development of the tailless aircraft.

Radar had been used extensively in aerial combat in World War II. A fantastic aid to human vision, it allowed "sight" in darkness, fog, and rain; instant calculation of distance from objects; recognition at up to 200 miles; and reckoning of bearing, elevation, and range in seconds. Pilots would have at their command powerful systems to relieve some of the stresses of combat, including surer control from the ground or air of large operations. Pilotless aircraft likewise would be subject to greater control. In words which still ring with prophesy today, von Karman urged the AAF to avoid complacency and apply engineering talent for "clever adaptation" and refinement of existing radar techniques. It was not, he said, "a facility or attachment which will occasionally be used under bad conditions." Rather, von Karman predicted for radar the primary role of controlling the skies, opening darkness and inclement weather to operational use. Bombing, gunfire, navigation, landing, and control would all fall under the guiding hand of radar. Indeed, the scientist ranked its significance with the development of jet-propelled aircraft, and called for changes in operational planning, training, and organization to account for its tremendous influence.[25]

Despite the enormous contributions of Where We Stand toward illuminating the realities of postwar air power, von Karman felt his investigations of some scientific subjects were not complete. In particular, he sought more information on the German transoceanic rocket—that is, the intercontinental ballistic missile—in order to give General Arnold the fullest possible picture of future aerial warfare. Questions about supersonic flight also awaited further study. He decided another trip to Europe was needed to satisfy these and other loose ends.

Before he embarked, the framework for Arnold's long-range study had to be erected. In an August 1945 SAG meeting, von Karman exhorted his staff and assembled consultants to research and write the study with all possible speed. Pressures to complete it had begun to mount. The Japanese surrender in August and War Department plans to centralize under civilian control all long-range defense research persuaded him to streamline the SAG's approach. Hoping to bring out a first-rate study in time to blunt the movement for scientific centralization,* he persuaded his colleagues to abandon the idea of producing a textbook style report which categorized their conclusions by academic discipline (e.g., physics, chemistry, engineering, etc.). Instead, they each agreed to write a brief monograph related to their scientific specialty on subjects of specific interest to the AAF—missiles, propulsion, radar, and so on.[26] They set a year-end deadline for themselves. As von Karman prepared for his second European sojourn, the SAG members and consultants, led by Deputy Director Dryden, gathered their thoughts and began a hard three months of setting their conclusions on paper.

As von Karman's departure date of September 23, 1945, neared, a list of his traveling companions was drawn up, and included Wattendorf, Tsien, Colonel Glantzberg, Colonel McHugh, and Lt. Col. Frank W. Williams of Wright Field. The civilians would again enjoy the privileges of temporary military rank. Their passports would take them first to the U.K., France, Holland, Switzerland, Sweden, and Italy. Once they completed their business in the ETO, in mid-October they would fly to the Pacific Theater, stopping in Australia, India, and China. In a verbal directive of August 25, General Arnold also asked the group to visit Japan, for which von Karman scheduled two weeks at the end of the trip. The journey did involve some risk. The chaotic situation in Japan might "entail delicate involvements," but General Arnold nonetheless felt the opportunity to "observe, correlate, and draw deductions" from Japanese science had to be seized. These aims would be furthered by von Karman's friendship with several Japanese scientists, dating back to his pre-war lectures at the Imperial University of Japan. Placing General Arnold's own C-54 transport at the group's disposal for the duration of the trip, Lt. Gen. Ira C.

---

*Centralization did not occur and each of the services retained its own weapons development establishments. The National Science Foundation provided scientific

Eaker, Deputy Commander, AAF, asked Gen. George C. Kenney, Commanding General of the Far East Air Forces, to provide the "fullest cooperation" to the von Karman party. Rather than mere intelligence gathering, these men would require first-hand inspections of research centers in order to exercise "imagination and scientific acuity in recognizing important scientific trends."[27]

The European portion of the journey enjoyed mixed success. Late in September von Karman held useful discussions with Professor Jacob Ackeret of Zurich on laminar flow control, a method of reducing aerodynamic drag and maximizing aircraft speed by pumping air through small crevices on the bottom and top surfaces of wings, thus "bleeding out" turbulence across the wings. Back in Germany, von Karman attended to a number of problems. He conferred with British representatives to avoid unseemly competition in luring German scientists to emigrate to one or another allied country. He discussed with Colonel Glantzberg and Colonel McHugh the format of the long-range study summary volume, which he himself would write for General Arnold. But the sessions did not satisfy von Karman, who agonized over the appropriate action to take. How far should the report go? Should it suggest a total restructuring of the AAF, or emphasize just one or two aspects of Army Air Forces R&D? Nothing seemed to jell in his mind.

Misfortune suggested the course he ought to take. In mid-October General Arnold suffered a serious heart attack. From his sickbed in Washington, D.C., he called von Karman, urging him to hasten the drafting of his report. When von Karman suggested a completion date of January 1, 1946, Arnold said he would "greatly appreciate" an earlier time frame. The general wanted to devote his remaining energies to reading and publicizing the von Karman report, and knew his time was limited. A December 15 deadline was agreed upon. The new due date, as well as past months of traveling, interviewing, and report writing compelled von Karman to rearrange his

———————————

support as required.

schedule. By now, he was worn out. He cabled Arnold on October 29 saying he was "much worried" about completing his work on time, especially in light of the upcoming trip to Japan. He suggested sending his group to the Orient immediately,* while he remained in Paris "about twenty days...using the time for writing up my ideas conceived in recent months. I feel this is the best way to accomplish the job," he told the general, and "am very anxious not to disappoint you." Working undisturbed, he hoped for mental concentration and physical rest.[28]

During November 1945, von Karman concentrated exclusively on this crucial project. Comfortably installed at the Prince of Wales Hotel in Paris with excellent secretarial help and a fine scientific library, he wrote the general outline of volume one, expecting to fill in details and polish the language between his return to Washington on November 28 and the mid-December deadline. Meanwhile, he transacted SAG business through his deputy, Hugh Dryden. As von Karman finished portions of the report, he sent it piecemeal to Dryden for review. Between guiding the work of the monograph writers, commenting on von Karman's copy, sending his chief a number of collateral studies, and writing sections on locating and hitting targets, Dryden had an even busier November than von Karman. To speed up the process, substantive research and writing occurred simultaneously with layout and graphics work. Nonetheless, von Karman insisted that the present undertaking should be on the "same level" as Where We Stand, which was "very well received." Toward that end, the two men carried on a dialogue over transatlantic teletype, relaying portions of chapter one and the monographs back and forth as needed. By the third week in November von Karman's chapter was well in hand and the others were taking form. Von Karman decided to use a decimal system of paragraph marking, making the style of the report "more decisive." He also added a discussion on the AAF and the atomic bomb. Finally, he determined from Paris which volumes needed to be filled in or improved upon, and which scientists ought to write which sections. For these

---

*The night he learned of Arnold's heart attack, von Karman asked Glantzberg, McHugh, Tsien, and Wattendorf to leave for Japan. Hastily added to their number

judgments he relied heavily on Dryden, DuBridge, and, in the final analysis, Wattendorf. Von Karman's return to Washington on November 28 was scheduled to coincide with the arrival of the Tokyo group, whose findings would be added to the report in the final two weeks.[29]

Just days before the deadline a draft was at last on the table. What should it be called? Teddy Walkowicz suggested Toward New Horizons. Some on the SAG disliked the title, arguing it implied the present scientific horizons were muddled. But the weary von Karman, in no mood for debate, insisted that they had, in fact, looked "at the basic scientific potential which could change the future. The name remained." Von Karman's first volume, entitled Science, the Key to Air Supremacy, arrived on General Arnold's desk as promised, on December 15. The remaining twelve volumes (which included Where We Stand) were distributed on a limited basis to the Air Staff and bore a Restricted security classification. A truly comprehensive work, its twenty-five authors--most of whom had been drawn from or were returning to academia from government service--produced thirty-two separate monographs which directly linked the latest scientific knowledge to the future of air power. All but von Karman, Dryden, Glantzberg, and McHugh were board members hired on a consulting basis.* The thirty-two studies were grouped by subject matter in these volumes: Technical Intelligence, Aerodynamics and Aircraft Design, Future Airborne Armies, Aircraft Power Plants, Aircraft Fuels and Propellants, Guided Missiles and Pilotless Aircraft, Guidance and Homing of Missiles and Pilotless Aircraft, Explosives and Terminal Ballistics, Radar Communications, Weather, and Aviation Medicine and Psychology.[30]

---

were Professors Fritz Zwicky of Cal Tech and William Pickering of the Jet Propulsion Lab; Col. W. Randolph Lovelace, M.D., of the Wright Field Aeromedical Lab; Maj. Teddy Walkowicz, military member of the SAG, and Lt. Col. Frank Williams, also of the SAG.
*See page 19-20 for a full list of SAG members and their institutional affiliations.

HARNESSING THE GENIE

When he presented <u>Science, the Key to Air Supremacy</u> to General Arnold, von Karman attached a memorandum in which he summarized the most essential findings of the entire study. He emphasized in particular a question posed by Arnold in his November 7, 1944, letter empowering the study: "what proportion of available money should be allocated to research and development?" Von Karman consulted American industry for a model. U.S. corporations invested roughly five percent of annual profits in research. Gearing this figure to AAF needs, he proposed a yearly outlay for R&D of five percent of total annual <u>wartime</u> expenditures. If an average AAF peacetime budget totalled fifteen or twenty percent of the costs for one wartime year, then von Karman's formula actually yielded an annual R&D fund of one-quarter to one-third of the total AAF fiscal pie.

A share of such size exceeded the wildest expectations of all but a few R&D advocates. How could von Karman justify it? He argued that in an age of atomic weaponry, the security of the nation demanded a powerful Air Force for offensive and defensive purposes. If applied to air power, discoveries in aerodynamics, propulsion, electronics, and nuclear physics would result in an Air Force suited for nuclear warfare. Von Karman proposed a large proportion of the new R&D funding be invested in a ten-year program of scientific exploration leading to supersonic flight, pilotless aircraft, all-weather flying, perfected navigation and communication, remote controlled/automatic fighter and bomber forces, and airborne transportation of whole armies. All research, he warned, must be directed toward these goals, and not become mired in an attitude of abstract inquiry for its own sake. Interdisciplinary development centers, rather than laboratories, would help scientists focus on the practical solutions. To complement the sharp upswing in R&D expenditures, Army Air Forces personnel, training, and organizational practices had to undergo significant change to accommodate the surge in scientific thought. Von Karman suggested the AAF develop a global strategy for applying the new technologies—such as a wing of experimental pilotless aircraft—to the battlefield, and institute a three-tiered typology of weaponry: human directed, electronically assisted, and purely automatic. Finally, von Karman asked the AAF leadership to always keep an open mind toward potential scientific breakthroughs. "Problems never have final or universal solutions," he wrote, "and only a constant inquisitive attitude toward science and a ceaseless and swift adaptation to new developments can maintain the security of this nation...."[31]

Von Karman based these conclusions partly on the experiences of the two world wars, and partly on the global review he had just completed of science and aerial warfare. He drew several lessons from World Wars I and II. The twentieth century transformed war from a drama of human endurance to a technological contest for control of the air. Aided as never before by scientists in the last war, military men must learn that the future hinged on cultivating the closest cooperation with the nation's laboratories and researchers. His observations of fascism and Nazism taught von Karman that the worst acts of international terror could never again be ruled out. Atomic explosives only heightened the danger of foreign aggression and underscored the crucial role of air power in modern warfare. Surprise attacks using nuclear weapons were not unthinkable, and science could offer no sure umbrella against this eventuality. If only one missile carrying one bomb penetrated a nation's air defenses, immense destruction would ensue. The answer, argued von Karman, lay in a powerful offense which deterred aggression. Offensive aerial systems must give U.S. air forces the capability of reaching remote targets quickly and striking them with maximum impact; attaining air superiority over any region of the world; and landing, in short order, large contingents of men and equipment at any trouble spot. Over her own territory, America must establish total air superiority, and erect a network of highly sophisticated warning and homing devices to detect incoming enemy forces. To achieve these objectives, "only an Air Force which fully exploits all the knowledge ...science has available now and...in the future, will have a chance of accomplishing these tasks."[32]

The science of aircraft design and construction had progressed immeasurably during the war, and pointed toward continued improvements in the decades ahead. Since 1939 a string of breakthroughs in aerodynamics brought the velocity of aircraft nearer and nearer the speed of sound. Flying wing shapes and laminar flow devices on wings greatly reduced drag, leaving engineers on the threshold of aircraft designs capable of breaking the sonic barrier. New propulsion systems, particularly jets, had the potential for very high speed because of their light weight and their tendency to become more efficient with greater velocity. Improvements in reciprocating engine design and aerodynamic form also resulted in spectacular increases in the economy, range, and cargo capacity of transport aircraft. Von Karman believed non-stop distances could be further enhanced using nuclear power, which would eliminate the problems associated with the more combustible fuels required for longer range.

Great progress had also taken place in navigation and instrument flying. Radio transmissions, as well as pulse and echo radars, had begun to penetrate the main inhibitors of aviation—weather, clouds, and darkness. In the years ahead, developments in communications and electronics would result in highly accurate blind bombing and landing, location of remote and invisible objects, pinpoint ground control of tactical aircraft, and the conquest of night and inclement weather. Likewise, von Karman predicted great strides in gyroscopic and servo-motor devices, whose main impact would be on automatic piloting and remote control mechanisms for pilotless aircraft and guided missiles. Electromagnetic radiation techniques—especially in infrared, radio, and radar—would make "possible and effective" automatic bomb target seeking and fire control. By combining automatic and remote control systems with homing apparatuses, drone aircraft would be developed with "tremendous speed, extraordinary range, and ability to hit targets accurately." As such, they would augment manned forces in appropriate missions.[33]

A major conclusion in Science, the Key to Air Supremacy involved organizational changes to ensure the preeminence of science in the AAF of the future. Von Karman insisted upon an institutional alignment in which science permeated the entire Army Air Forces structure. "Scientific results," he observed, "cannot be used efficiently by soldiers who have no understanding of them, and scientists cannot produce results useful for warfare without an understanding of the operations." How did he suggest bringing this revolution to bear on the AAF? First, person to person cooperation between scientists and the air forces' leadership needed to be strengthened. Measures to encourage this atmosphere included direct issuance of research contracts by the AAF to scientific institutions, exchanges of personnel among military officers and civilian laboratories, employment of scientific consultants, and establishment at major universities of laboratories dedicated to research facilities in fields related to air power. Secondly, industry and the AAF required greater unity of effort. This von Karman would undertake by separating the management of R&D from procurement, establishing large applied research centers at which industries would work on a contract basis on large projects, and underwriting pilot programs at aerospace plants with an option to expand to full production should the products prove useful.

Von Karman's third point suggested that the AAF reorient its R&D structure to combine complementary technologies in unified research centers. The centers should be devoted to supersonic and pilotless aircraft development, operational aircraft development, nuclear aircraft development, as well as a conventional armament center at Eglin Field and a separate site at which aerodynamics, propulsion, control, and electronics were studied on an integrated basis. The fourth organizational problem facing the AAF was how to infuse scientific ideas and methods into command and staff work. Von Karman recognized a number of promising methods, chief among which were permanent establishment of the SAG on the Air Staff; creation of liaison offices in the HQ AAF R&D hierarchy to coordinate AAF science with that of other government agencies; inclusion of scientific personnel in intelligence services; and continuation into peacetime of the employment of scientists for operational analyses and target studies. In addition, officers commanding laboratories must enjoy long tenure without penalties in promotion, and hold rank commensurate with the importance of their research, not the size of their organizations. To obtain for government service the finest scientists available, their compensation and conditions of work should be removed from civil service regulations.

Finally, the vital question of providing scientific and technical education for AAF personnel required action. Von Karman recommended special training at scientific institutes for some young officers and broad scientific schooling toward the masters degree for technical officers recruited through the ROTC. About twenty percent of officers with scientific training should undertake doctoral degrees in their chosen disciplines. Von Karman felt the AAF Engineering School should confine itself to teaching scientific fundamentals related to the air forces, leaving more advanced training to the civilian institutions. Refresher courses every five years, retention of R&D officers, and flight training for uniformed scientists ought to be pursued vigorously by AAF personnel experts.[34]

The Air Staff's reaction to Science, the Key to Air Supremacy and Toward New Horizons could not have been more positive. In part, this resulted from months of discussion among von Karman and top AAF leaders about the same questions treated by the report. As early as November 1944--months before his first European trip—von Karman and his colleagues had drafted an outline of the final report very much like the ultimate form of Toward New Horizons. During Spring 1945 von Karman suggested to Arnold that to flourish, air power science must have its own facilities, staff, and funding. Hence, he proposed continued AAF support for the research laboratories established during the war. Staffed by civilian scientists, these labs represented the germ of the research center idea found in Toward New Horizons. Indeed, almost as soon as German experimental facilities had been examined, SAG members reported back that the foreign labs were "more ambitious and forward looking than our own," and asked AAF leaders to consider construction of a development center featuring a cluster of large wind tunnels for aeronautical research. Informal discussion and circulation of many of the concepts in Toward New

Horizons prior to its publication helped the SAG understand the general Air Staff perspective on R&D and also readied internal opinion for the conclusions of the report. Its findings met with widespread praise and acceptance.[35]

No one praised the report more vigorously than General Arnold, calling it "the first of its kind ever produced" and a boon to research and development planning in the years ahead. Lt. Gen. Nathan F. Twining, Commander of the Air Materiel Command, endorsed its recommendations and said the implementation of the first volume alone would provide a sound foundation for the future of the AAF. Years later, Gen. Jimmy Doolittle—Chairman of the SAG's successor, the Scientific Advisory Board (SAB)--described Toward New Horizons as "the most important thing" ever accomplished by the SAG or SAB. Von Karman felt the report did make a significant contribution to U.S. air power. Together, Toward New Horizons and Science, the Key to Air Supremacy represented the first exhaustive review of future science as it related to the military services. They made plain the preeminence of the AAF in protecting the nation, but also asserted that its success rested in large part on technological progress. The reports also fostered an atmosphere favorable to basic research. Finally, von Karman pointed out that both studies cautioned against Air Force long-range science becoming the captive of civilian or military control. It must, he argued, be "dispersed among all the people and their institutions."[36]

Despite the hindrance of Secret and Restricted security markings and initial dissemination limited to the Air Staff and top levels of the Air Materiel Command,[*] Toward New Horizons quickly found its way into the institutional fabric of the AAF. At least partly as a result of Toward New Horizons, AAF planners rejected the widely publicized views of the eminent physicist, Dr. Vannevar Bush, who regarded as futuristic the possibility of perfecting intercontinental missiles. Instead, they embraced von Karman's predictions on the feasibility of ballistic missiles and inserted a missile development

---

[*]The entire report was declassified in 1960.

program in the five-year R&D projections. As a result, during 1946 Consolidated-Vultee Aircraft Company received a study contract for Project MX-774 which funded the exploration of ICBM guidance, control, and lightweight structures technology. Meanwhile, North American Aviation won a contract to review rocket propulsion for pilotless aircraft (cruise missiles). While these programs went forward, both the AMC and HQ USAAF staffs drafted detailed plans to implement the von Karman recommendations. Most of their work was scuttled when Congress slashed 1947 R&D funds from a requested $186 million to $111 million, and persisted with similar austerity for the rest of the decade. Nonetheless, for many years to come the reputation of von Karman and his report would exert a powerful influence over the American air power establishment. Always mindful of the impermanence of technological leads in an age of breakneck discovery, von Karman elevated science to a matter of national survival. In the process, he fixed the agenda of research and development for decades to come. Moreover, Toward New Horizons, highly persuasive to the air power establishment on its own merits, set the precedent of establishing periodic, special panels to study the latest technology as applied to future air power needs. As the first such report, it influenced profoundly each of the four succeeding studies on long-range science and aerial warfare.[37]

* * *

Though fatigued from the rigors of the past year, von Karman cast about for a way to perpetuate the lessons of Toward New Horizons. He reasoned that the survival and implementation of the ideas in the report hinged, for the most part, on the institutional standing of the SAG, the office which originated the study. Hence, he took the opportunity of its publication and acclaim to ask for its permanent establishment on the Air Staff. Taking his cue from one of the recommendations in Science, the Key to Air Supremacy, on December 20, 1945, von Karman told General Arnold that the Air Forces had a continuing—not just an intermittent—need for the finest scientific advice available. The scientist predicted that the passage of time would only increase the necessity for AAF leaders to have on hand sound technical guidance. To render these judgments, von Karman asked Arnold to establish a body of "scientific consultants of high standing, who are familiar with the AAF, but whose main activities are outside the AAF." Called together by the Commanding General as needed, they would not concern themselves with the current research projects of the Air Staff Director of R&D;[*] rather, they would give him suggestions on "future trends and long range possibilities."[38]

Von Karman envisioned a board attached directly to the AAF Commander's office, consisting of a military director (preferably of brigadier rank), a full-time military or civilian scientist, and clerical support. Finally, ten to fifteen consultants "of a very high scientific standing" would prepare recommendations and reports for General Arnold and his successors. The quality of Toward New Horizons sold Arnold on the idea. He sent copies of von Karman's request to Lt. Gen. Ira C. Eaker and the Director of Air Staff Research and Development, Maj. Gen. Curtis E. LeMay. Arnold also asked General Spaatz to review Toward New Horizons and to consider von Karman's request for a permanent SAG as he read it.

Several days after Christmas 1945, Arnold received further evidence supporting von Karman's suggestion. A letter from Lt. Gen. John K. Cannon, Commanding General of the USAAF in Europe, implored Arnold to send to the Continent men experienced in questioning German scientists, many of whom were fast repatriating themselves to other countries in search of work. The top man Cannon asked for was Colonel Frank W. Williams, a SAG veteran who had accompanied von Karman on his European travels. The need for an organization able to "speak the language" of scientists had become clear. After discussions among Dr. von Karman and Generals Arnold, Spaatz, Fairchild, Norstad, Eaker, LeMay, and Vandenberg, the concept of a permanent group of scientific advisers was agreed upon. Only LeMay argued that the SAG should be subsumed under the rubric of his own directorate. The

---

*A Deputy Chief of Staff for Air Staff Development was established in January 1950. Until then, the Director of R&D reported to the Deputy Chief of Staff for

final statement of the SAG mission drafted by von Karman and LeMay for Arnold, clarified who the scientists would work for and what they would do. It provided that the group inform the Commanding General of new developments in science; prepare special studies for him on the relationship between scientific thought, technical research, and air power; assemble and evaluate facts on long-range plans for scientific research and development; advise on problems of scientific organization both inside and outside the Air Forces; make additional studies of scientific problems as required by the Commanding General; report and make its recommendations directly to the Commanding General and receive its directives from him.

LeMay and von Karman also agreed that Arnold and his successors should appoint the members, and that the SAG should meet as a body semi-annually. Its make-up would include a chairman, the Director of R&D (ex-officio), and thirty members organized in five scientific panels: aircraft and propulsion; guidance of missiles and pilotless aircraft; fuels, explosives, and nuclear energy; radar, communications, and weather; and aeromedicine/psychology. A vice chairman would head each panel. Meeting at least four times per year as an executive committee would be the chairman, the five vice-chairs, and the Director of R&D. Together they would nominate members, draft policy, and appoint ad hoc panels from outside the SAG roster to study special subjects. The Director of Research and Development would act as liaison officer with the Air Staff and furnish clerical and other administrative assistance, such as preparation of reports. One of his civilian scientists would act as SAG Secretary, whose chief responsibility was to keep the members of the executive committee informed of all requests from the Commanding General.[39]

The charter of the SAG—issued expressly to facilitate Toward New Horizons--expired on February 6, 1946. As a result, Dr. von Karman temporarily resigned the chairmanship. No concrete action had been taken to establish a permanent group in its place. The reason

_____

Materiel.

involved people, not policy. Though Arnold supported the idea in the strongest terms, ill-health* forced him to announce his retirement, and he decided to allow his successor, General Spaatz, to take this important step. Less than a week after Arnold's departure date (February 9, 1946) the machinery of government began to draw together the elements of the new scientific advisory office, now designated the Army Air Forces Scientific Advisory Board (SAB). However, to the great surprise of von Karman, the movement of people and offices did not result in independence for the SAB. General LeMay directed that the remnant SAG positions be moved to the Directorate of R&D. Done ostensibly to provide the fledgling board with a fixed institutional home and a secretariat, the scientists would now report to LeMay, not Spaatz. They would advise the director on advanced research trends, suggest levels of funding for scientific endeavors, and survey laboratory and technical facilities. On March 14 General Spaatz invited several dozen leading American scientists to join the first SAB term (July 1, 1946 to June 30, 1947) as paid consultants. Although the new organization was officially called the Scientific Advisory Board to the Commanding General of the Army Air Forces, only General LeMay's name—not von Karman's—appeared in the text of the invitation.[40]

What could be done to preserve General Arnold's original concept of a body of civilian scientists to advise the Commanding General of the AAF? Was there some way to prevent Toward New Horizons being thought of as a freak of wartime necessity, rather than the initial step in a permanent process? Fortunately, the Army hierarchy concurred with Arnold's position on civilian science. Chief of Staff of the Army General Dwight D. Eisenhower† expressed the same enlightened views von Karman heard from Arnold. Eisenhower admitted that victory in World War II depended heavily on the natural and social sciences.

---

*General Arnold never fully recovered from the heart attack he had suffered in mid-October 1945 and died in January 1950.

†Eisenhower succeeded George C. Marshall as Army Chief of Staff in November 1945.

HARNESSING THE GENIE

"The armed forces could not have won the war alone," he maintained. "Scientists...contributed techniques and weapons which enabled us to outwit and overwhelm the enemy." He added that in peacetime, this pattern of integrating civilian and military knowledge must continue, not simply in a way which familiarized the armed forces with recent scientific developments, but by drawing into the planning process itself "all the civilian resources which can contribute to the defense of the country." [41]

After convening the SAB on June 17, 1946, von Karman's first task was to persuade the AAF to provide the board direct access to General Spaatz. Despite making successful appointments to the panels and providing expert advice on the establishment of one of the world's foremost wind tunnel facilities,[*] the main problem persisted. Aside from the wind tunnel project, none of <u>Toward New Horizons</u> had been implemented. Indeed, von Karman complained he spent "a good deal of...time...arguing the merits of maintaining the Scientific Advisory Board as a meaningful and active group within the Air Force structure, and not as a showpiece or letterhead of elder statesmen."[42]

The situation worsened until October 1947 when the leadership of the newly established United States Air Force (USAF)[†] considered abolishing the SAB entirely. In fact, the board disappeared from the organization charts, and while von Karman vacationed in Paris, his secretary had to keep the guided missile division (of the R&D directorate) from taking over his office and her desk! Resentment emerged as some officers at Wright Field wondered why a group of civilian scientists was so highly placed in the Air

---

[*]Later established as the Arnold Engineering Development Center (AEDC), Tullahoma, Tennessee. Air Force Secretary Stuart Symington supported the building of AEDC with great energy, finally persuading an economy-minded Congress to appropriate $100 million for the undertaking. As a center for aerodynamics, propulsion, and missile testing, it would have a profound influence on Air Force weapons development.

[†]Effective September 18, 1947, the Congress and the President established the National Military Establishment whose provisions provided for the USAF

Force structure. Several SAB members, including Dr. Ivan Getting, Vice President of Raytheon and later President of the Aerospace Corporation, resigned from the board in disgust with its inactivity. Maj. Teddy Walkowicz, one of von Karman's principal aides and one of his closest friends, pleaded with the aging scientist to fight for civilian science in the USAF. "If you let them shove the SAB down into an unimportant position," he said, "the whole future becomes very glum." Walkowicz asked von Karman to be tolerant of the Air Force tendency to side-track or ignore SAB advice; at least the top leadership was for the first time receiving "good, reliable ideas or opinions" on technical matters. Should the board disappear from the Air Staff organization charts, the future of USAF research and science would fade with it. "If the pilots reign supreme in peace time as they do in war time," Walkowicz warned, "the whole cause will be lost...and the...tragic course of any future war will be decided long before the first shot is fired." In his view, many young engineers in uniform looked hopefully to von Karman and his associates for a needed jolt of scientific and institutional innovation, and depended on him to bring vigor to Air Force technological thinking.[43]

When von Karman returned to America, he discussed the issue with the new Director of R&D, Maj. Gen. Laurence C. Craigie, and the SAB members. On April 6, 1948, he wrote to General Spaatz suggesting that the board be directly responsible to the Air Force Chief of Staff and that General Craigie be named as SAB Military Director. Nine days later, at a meeting between Spaatz, Vandenberg, Craigie, and von Karman, the military director position was adopted and the SAB was attached organizationally to the Chief of Staff's office. Subsequently, an Air Force regulation was published clarifying the board's relationship to the Air Staff and the major commands. The Deputy Chief of Staff for Materiel was informed of the SAB's new status and told also that the board's members would be appointed by the Chief of Staff, that they would report their recommendations directly to him, and that the SAB secretariat would be

---

as a military service co-equal to the Army and Navy.

manned from the Chief's own personnel pool. Moreover, Maj. Gen. William F. McKee, the Assistant Vice Chief of Staff, advised all offices to "cooperate with and aid the Board in their mission of advising and keeping the Chief of Staff informed on all scientific matters." Finally, Air Force Regulation 20-30, dated May 14, 1948, restored to the SAB those functions agreed upon by von Karman and LeMay in January 1946.[44]

These actions improved immeasurably the institutional position of the board. But even more important to reviving the SAB was the appointment in September 1948 of Brig. Gen. Donald L. Putt to the R&D Directorate. Putt's whole career had been devoted to research and development. He earned a B.S. degree in electrical engineering, and a masters degree in aeronautical engineering from Cal Tech. His mentor and good friend was Theodore von Karman. During the war Putt served as Chief of the Experimental Bombardment Aircraft Branch at Wright Field, where he was instrumental in fitting B-29 aircraft for the first operational atomic weapons. Here, and as Deputy Chief of the Air Materiel Command's Engineering Division, he assembled a cadre of scientifically trained young officers he called his "Junior Indians," chief among whom was Colonel Bernard A. Schriever.* [45]

Before Putt could begin his duties as R&D Director, he underwent a period of recovery from a torn knee cartilage. Confined to bed at Walter Reed Hospital, he received many visits from his Junior Indians. Together, they hatched a plan to revitalize both the SAB in particular and Air Force R&D in general. They would ask Dr. von Karman to call a general meeting of the board in April 1949 and invite the new Air Force Chief of Staff, General Vandenberg, to speak. Von Karman agreed, Vandenberg accepted, and Teddy Walkowicz wrote the speech. Vandenberg was forced to cancel his appearance and Vice Chief Muir S. Fairchild† delivered it instead.

---

*Later, as commander of Air Research and Development Command (ARDC) and Air Force Systems Command (AFSC), General Schriever became a major force in shaping Air Force long range science.

†Named Vice Chief of Staff of the Air Force in May 1948, Fairchild served successively in World War II as

The conclusion of the talk called upon the SAB to study the entire Air Force R&D organization and issue a report on its reform.

Accordingly, Von Karman and Putt selected Dean Louis N. Ridenour of the University of Illinois to chair a SAB working group and persuaded Lt. Gen. Jimmy Doolittle to serve as well.* Both men were already sympathetic to reform, as von Karman and Putt well knew. Fortunately, the board had already prepared a report for General Vandenberg in November 1948 which recommended Air Force R&D changes, so ground had been laid for the Ridenour findings. After two months of preparation, in September 1949, the Ridenour Report was completed. It advocated a sweeping reform of Air Force science: a separate command for R&D; a Deputy Chief of Staff for Development on the Air Staff; and unitary budgeting for USAF development outlays. These suggestions were not popular on the Air Staff. Every dollar added to research and development activities would reduce operations, personnel, or plans—indeed, all budgets—by an equal amount. Despite nearly unanimous rejection of the proposals at a January 2, 1950, staff meeting of top HQ USAF leaders, the following day General Fairchild announced implementation of the Ridenour reforms.† [46]

* * *

Donald Putt's crucial assistance in making the SAB the instrument of a massive R&D restructuring brought the board a degree of prestige and standing absent since the

---

Secretary of the Air Staff and as HQ AAF Director of Military Requirements. After the war he served for two years as Commandant of the Air University.

*The Ridenour panel also included Dr. George P. Baker, Harvard Business School; Dr. James B. Fisk, Bell Telephone; Dr. Carl Overhage, Eastman Kodak; Dean Ralph Sawyer, University of Michigan; Professor John M. Wild, Cornell University; Professor Raymond Woodrow, Princeton University; and Dr. Frank Wattendorf, AMC's principal aeronautical engineer.

†The Research and Development Command (RDC)—later the Air Research and Development Command (ARDC)—was established on January 23, 1950. Maj. Gen. David M.

publication of Toward New Horizons, breathing into it a new life and vitality. Never had the board been at a higher point. Nor had Putt.[*] He and his Junior Indians represented the new Air Force, in whose ranks the technical man in uniform would one day lead USAF science. Indeed, Putt likened the R&D officer to his operational counterpart. Just as the SAC or USAFE man dedicated his life to winning air battles, "the technical man devotes his career to the task of putting in the hands of the operational man the best weapons which American science and technology can produce." Putt hoped—perhaps with undue optimism—that the establishment of an Air Force R&D organization would lead eventually to a close and equal partnership among scientists, strategists, and pilots. Instead, it resulted in a vast pool of technically trained officers who gradually assumed the role of science forecasting once performed by civilian scientists.[47]

Schlatter served as its first commander. Lt. Gen. Gordon P. Saville was named as the first Air Staff Deputy Chief of Staff for R&D.

*Putt removed yet another hurdle for von Karman. He reduced the ill feelings between the SAB and AMC's R&D establishment at Wright Field. He scheduled the first two days of the November 1948 SAB meeting at Wright Field in order to improve relations by face-to-face contact. He asked the AMC Commander to appoint a liaison office for SAB affairs. This group would expedite action on board recommendations respecting AMC, distribute board reports throughout the command, seek out suitable technical problems for SAB review, and familiarize itself with the board, its workings, and its members.

NOTES

1. von Karman, Theodore and Lee Edson, The Wind and Beyond: Theodore von Karman, Pioneer in Aviation and Pathfinder in Science. Boston and Toronto: Little, Brown, 1967, pp. 225-227, 233, 267-268; Interview, Dr. Theodore von Karman with Donald Shaughnessy, 27 January 1960, AFHRC K1214, pp. 1-2, 8-9; New York Times, p. 1 of 8, 9, 10, and 11 September 1944 issues; Interview, Lt Gen James A.   Doolittle with unknown interviewer (NASA interview), n.d., p. 9; Sturm, Thomas, The USAF Scientific Advisory Board: Its First Twenty Years, 1944-1964, Washington, D.C.: Government Printing Office, 1967, p. 3.

2. Arnold, Gen Henry H., Global Mission, New York: Harper Bros., 1949, p. 532; Interview, von Karman, p. 8.

3. Interview, von Karman, pp. 8-9; Karman, Wind and Beyond, p. 268; Arnold, Global Mission, pp. 532-533.

4. Hanle, Robert A., Bringing Aerodynamics to America, Cambridge, Massachusetts and London, England: M.I.T. Press, 1982, pp. 53-92; Karman, Wind and Beyond, pp. 3-20; Neufeld, Jacob, "Theodore von Karman" (unpublished article), n.d., p. 1.

5. Interview, Harry Guggenheim with Donald Shaughnessy, 6 April 1960, AFHRC K1214, pp. 1, 26-29; Hanle, Aerodynamics, pp. 93-97, 123-139.

6. Neufeld, "Theodore von Karman," p. 2; Karman, Wind and Beyond, p. 226.

7. Perkins, Dr. Courtland D., "Recollections" (unpublished memoirs), vol. 3, chapter 9, "Mini Bio-Theodore von Karman," p. 34; Interview, Lt Gen James A. Doolittle with Mr. Leish, April 1960, AFHRC K1214, p 22; Interview, Dr. Hugh L. Dryden with Donald Shaughnessy, 23 February 1960, AFHRC K1214, pp. 22-23, 35; Karman, Wind and Beyond, pp. 268-271; Sturm, SAB, p. 4.

8. Karman, Wind and Beyond, p. 271.

9. Ltr, Dr. Theodore von Karman to Dr. Clark B. Millikan, subj: Cal Tech vs SAG duties of von Karman, 4 November

1944, TVK 73.6; Ltr, Drs. H.S. Tsien, C.C. Lin, W.Z. Chien, and Y.H. Kuo to Dr. Theodore von Karman, subj: von Karman and Cal Tech in SAG period, 7 November 1944, TVK 30.37; Ltr, Dr. Theodore von Karman to Gen H.H. Arnold, subj: von Karman's divestiture, 20 November 1944, TVK 90.1.

10. Memo, Lt Gen Barney M. Giles, Deputy Commander, Army Air Forces and Chief of Staff to the Air Staff, subj: AAF long-range development program—Dr. von Karman, 10 November 1944, SAB 4; Memo to AC/AS (mgmt control) and AC/AS (operations, commitments, and requirements), subj: AAF development program, 22 November 1944, SAB 2; HQ Office Instruction No. 20-76, "Organization, The AAF Scientific Advisory Group," 1 December 1944, SAB 4; von Karman, Theodore, Science, the Key to Air Supremacy, 1944, p. xvii; Sturm, SAB, pp. 136-143.

11. The War Reports of General of the Army George C. Marshall, General of the Army H.H. Arnold, and Fleet Admiral Ernest J. King. Philadelphia: J.B. Lippincott, 1947, p. 415.

12. Memo, General H.H. Arnold to Dr. Theodore von Karman, subj: AAF long-range development program, 7 November 1944, SAB 4.

13. Ibid.; Memo, Dr. Frank L. Wattendorf to Col Frederic Glantzberg, subj: proposed itinerary for overseas mission, 6 December 1944, TVK 90.1; Memo, Brig Gen Frederic H. Smith, Jr., Deputy Chief of the Air Staff to the Assistant Chief of Staff, Operations, subj: proposed mission—AAF SAG, 16 December 1944, TVK 90.1; Memo, Lt I.W, Mitchnick to Lt Col Carr, subj: proposed ETO trip, SAG, 14 December 1944, TVK 90.1; Memo, Maj Gen J.E. Hull, Assistant Chief of Staff, Operations to the commanding general of the AAF, subj: proposed mission, AAF SAG, 24 December 1944, TVK 90.1.

14. Memo, Lt Gen Barney M. Giles, Deputy Commander AAF, and Chief of Staff to the Army Chief of Staff (Gen Marshall), subj: proposed mission—AAF SAG, 13 February 1945, TVK 90.2.

15. Memo for file, subj: clearance for foreign visits of SAG, 17 February 1945, w/attch: itinerary, TVK 90.2; Memo, Maj O.W. Hammonds, Air Corps to Col Glantzberg, subj: processing of Dr von Karman for overseas mission, 19 February 1945, TVK 90.2, ; Memo, Lt Gen Barney M. Giles, Deputy Commander, AAF to AC/AS, Intelligence Collection Division, subj: mission of the SAG, 3 April 1945, TVK 90.2; Memo, Lt Gen Barney M. Giles, Deputy Commander AAF to whom it may concern, subj: von Karman mission, 11 April 1945, TVK 90.2; Ltr, Col Frederic Glantzberg, Deputy AAF SAG to Commissioner of Immigration and Naturalization, subj: Dr. Tsien's re-entry visa, 17 April 1945, TVK 90.2; Ltr, Lt Gen Barney M. Giles, Deputy Commander AAF to Gen Carl Spaatz, Commanding General, U.S. Strategic Air Forces in Europe, subj: von Karman party, TVK 90.2.

16. Brig Gen George C. McDonald, Director of Army Intelligence to unknown correspondent, subj: exploitation of air intelligence objectives, 22 April 1945, w/attch: draft of recommended teletype, list of SAG travellers, memo requesting billeting arrangements, memo detailing Operation Lusty, AFHRC C5098, pp. 668-670, 675-676; Von Karman, Wind and Beyond, pp. 272-275; Weekly Activity Report from the office of the Director of Intelligence, HQ USSTAF, 4 May 1945, AFHRC A5720, p. 1887; Weekly Activity Report, Office of the Chief of Staff, Exploitation Division, HQ USSTAF, 19 May 1945, ARHRC A5720, pp. 1860-1861; Sturm, SAB, p. 6.

17. Von Karman, Wind and Beyond, pp. 277-283; Daily Report, Executive Sub-Section, Exploitation Division, HQ USSTAF, 30 May 1945, AFHRC A5720, p. 19; Sturm, SAB, p. 6; Daily Report, Executive Sub-section, Exploitation Division, HQ USSTAF, 31 May 1945, AFHRC A5720, p. 5; Weekly Activity Report, Office of Assistant Chief of Staff, Exploitation Division, Personnel and Reception Section, HQ USSTAF, 31 May 1945, AFHRC A5720, p. 1814; Weekly Report, Executive Sub-Section, Exploitation Division, HQ USSTAF, 31 May 1945, AFHRC A5720, p. 1798; Weekly Activity Report Ending 31 May 1945, HQ USSTAF, AFHRC A5720, p. 1799.

18. Daily Activity Report, Office of the Assistant Chief of Staff, Exploitation Division, HQ USSTAF, 18 June 1945, AFHRC A5720, p. 490; Daily Activity Report, Assistant Chief of Staff, Exploitation Division, HQ USSTAF, 19 June 1945, AFHRC A5720, p. 509; Weekly Activity Report, HQ USSTAF, 22 June 1945, AFHRC A5720, p. 1580; Daily Activity Report, USSTAF Main Supply Section, 25 June 1945, AFHRC A5720, p. 404; Routing and Record Sheet, Lt Gen Ira C. Eaker, Deputy Commander, AAF to Theodore von Karman, SAG, subj: appreciation of work of SAG, 18 July 1945, w/attch: Ltr, G.W. Lewis, NACA Director of Aeronautical Research to CG AAF (Gen Arnold), subj: usefulness of technical intelligence reports, 30 June 1945, TVK 90.2.

19. Weekly Activity Report, Office of the Assistant Chief of Staff, Exploitation Division, HQ USSTAF, 14 June 1945, AFHRC A5720, p. 775; von Karman, Wind and Beyond, pp. 283-289.

20. Daily Activity Report, Office of the Director of Intelligence, Exploitation Division, HQ USSTAF, 13 June 1945, AFHRC A5720, p. 614; von Karman, Wind and Beyond, p. 289; Sturm, SAB, pp. 7-8; von Karman, Theodore, Where We Stand, August 1944, p. iv.

21. von Karman, Where We Stand, pp. 1-7.

22. Ibid., 9-17.

23. Ibid., 18-35.

24. Ibid., 36-37.

25. Ibid., 41, 48-54.

26. Sturm, SAB, p. 8; von Karman, Wind and Beyond, pp. 289-290.

27. Memo, Lt Col Godfrey T. McHugh, SAG Exec to members of SAG going overseas, subj: overseas mission, 29 August 1945, TVK 90.3; Memo, Lt Col Godfrey T. McHugh, SAG Exec to CG, Army Services Forces, subj: passports

for SAG, 31 August 1945, TVK 90.3; Request for Orders for Civilian Personnel, AAF SAG, Lt Col Godfrey T. McHugh, SAG Exec, 31 August 1945, TVK 90.3; Ltr, Dr. Fritz Zwicky, Astrophysical Lab, Cal Tech to Dr. von Karman, subj: visit to Japan, 4 September 1945, TVK 90.3; Ltr, Theodore von Karman to Fritz Zwicky, subj: visit to Japan, 20 September 1945, TVK 90.3; Memo for CG, Air Transport Command, subj: assignment of C-54 to von Karman mission, 17 September 1945, TVK 90.3; Ltr, Lt Gen Ira C. Eaker to Lt Gen Geo. C. Kenney, CG of Far Eastern Air Forces, subj: von Karman visit to Japan, 6 September 1945, TVK 90.3; Memo, Gen H.H. Arnold to whom it may concern, subj: SAG visit to European, Mediterranean, and Pacific Theaters, 21 September 1945, TVK 90.3.

28. von Karman, Wind and Beyond, pp. 290-291; Memo, von Karman to unknown correspondent, subj: disposal of German scientists, 10 October 1945, TVK 90.3; Request for Orders for Mr. Henry Nagamatsu, Dr. Fritz Zwicky, and Col W. Randolph Lovelace, 16 October 1945, TVK 90.3; Ltr, ? to Col Fritz Glantzberg, subj: date of completion of report to Arnold, 23 October 1945, TVK 90.3; Cable, von Karman to Gen Arnold, subj: completion of report to Arnold, 29 October 1945, TVK 90.3.

29. Ltr, von Karman to Dr. Hugh L. Dryden, subj: preparing vol one of report to Arnold, 7 November 1945, TVK 90.3; Ltr, von Karman to Dryden, subj: preparing vol one of report to Arnold, 9 November 1945, TVK 90.3; Ltr, von Karman to Dryden, subj: preparing vol one of report to Arnold, 22 November 1945, TVK 90.3.

30. von Karman, Wind and Beyond, pp. 291-294; von Karman, Theodore, Science, the Key to Air Supremacy (volume one of Toward New Horizons) 15 December 1944, pp. xix-xxiii.

31. Ltr, von Karman to Gen Arnold, subj: transmittal of Toward New Horizons, 15 December 1945, SAB 2.

32. von Karman, Science, the Key to Air Supremacy, pp. 1-4.

33. Ibid., 4-6

34. Ibid., 81-82, 85, 87, 91, 92, 95, 97, 101, 104, 107, 108-109.

35. Memo, "Outline of a Report on Future Trends of Development of Military Aircraft," 16 November 1944, TVK 30.37; Memo, von Karman to Gen Arnold, subj: establishment of AAF research labs, 30 April 1945, TVK 90.2; Ltr, Dr. Frank L. Wattendorf to Gen F.O. Carroll, subj: proposal for a new air forces development center, 19 June 1945, TVK 87.1.

36. Von Karman, Wind and Beyond, p. 296; Interview, Lt Gen James H. Doolittle with unknown interviewer, 23 June 1965, AFHRC oral interview #623, p. 29; Sturm, SAB, pp. 10-11; Ltr, Brig Gen Laurence C. Craigie to Gen Carl Spaatz, subj: classification of von Karman report, 1 March 1946, TVK 90.4; Ltr, Col Donald L. Putt to Gen Carl Spaatz, subj: classification and arrangement...of von Karman report, 13 March 1946, TVK 90.4; Ltr. von Karman to CG, Air Technical Services Command, subj: arrangement of Toward New Horizons, 15 March 1946, TVK 90.4; Ltr, Maj Ted Walkowicz to Mrs. Marie Roddenberry, subj: publication of Science the Key to Air Supremacy, 11 July 1946, TVK 31.38.

37. Futrell, Robert Frank, Ideas, Concepts, and Doctrine: A History of Basic Thinking in the USAF, 1907-1964, Maxwell AFB, AL: Air University Publications, 1971, pp. 111-112; Sturm, SAB, pp. 11-12; Interview, Dr. Ivan Getting, SAB member, with Michael Gorn, 12 March 1986; von Karman, Wind and Beyond, p. 291.

38. von Karman, Wind and Beyond, p. 294; Ltr, von Karman to Gen Arnold, subj: establishment of a permanent SAG, 20 December 1944, SAB 4.

39. Memo, von Karman to Gen Arnold, subj: organization of AAF SAG, 9 January 1946, SAB 2; Memo, Gen Arnold to Gen Spaatz, subj: establishment of a permanent SAG, 21 December 1945, SAB 4; Ltr, Lt Gen John K. Cannon, CG UAS to Gen Arnold, subj: supervision of German

experimental research, 27 December 1945, TVK 90.3; Ltr, Gen Arnold to Maj Gen Edward H. Powers, subj: distribution of Toward New Horizons, 3 January 1946, SAB 2; Memo, Maj Gen Curtis LeMay to Gen Spaatz, subj: establishment of a permanent SAG, 3 January 1946, SAB 4; Sturm, SAB, pp. 13-14.

40. Sturm, SAB, pp. 13-15; Routing and Record Sheet, DCS/R&D (Maj Gen LeMay), to Deputy Commander, AAF, subj: transfer of responsibilities and job vacancies of SAG to DCS/R&D, 13 February 1946, SAB 4; HQ Office Instruction 20-76, "Organization—AAF SAG," 4 March 1946, SAB 2; Memo, Dr. Edward L. Bowles to Gen Eaker, subj: potential SAG/SAB members, 5 March 1946, w/attch: letters by Gen Spaatz inviting membership in SAG/SAB, SAB 5; Plan for SAB Operation (by Brig Gen Alden R. Crawford, Chief, Engineering Division, DCS/R&D), 18 April 1946, SAB 2.

41. Memo, Chief of Staff of the U.S. Army Gen Dwight D. Eisenhower to directors and chiefs of the War Department general and special staff divisions, subj: scientific and technical resources as military assets, 30 April 1946, AFHRC 35252, pp. 61-64.

42. Sturm, SAB, pp. 15-16; von Karman, Wind and Beyond, pp. 298-299; Ltr, Maj Gen LeMay to von Karman, subj: new Air Engineering Development Center, 12 March 1946, TVK 87.1; Ltr, von Karman to Gen Spaatz, subj: the Air Development Center, 9 July 1946, TVK 87.1; HQ Office Instruction 20-76, "Organization—the USAF SAB," effective 10 October 1947, SAB 2.

43. Interview, Dr. Getting with M. Gorn, p. 1; Ltr, Maj Ted Walkowicz to von Karman, subj: status of SAB, 14 October 1947, TVK 31.38.

44. Ltr, Maj Walkowicz to von Karman, subj: status of SAB, TVK 31.38; Ltr, von Karman to Gen Spaatz, subj: SAB access to AF Chief of Staff, 6 April 1948, SAB 2; Memo for Record, subj: SAB role, 15 April 1946, SAB 4; Memo, Maj Gen William F. McKee, Assistant Vice Chief of Staff to DCS/Material, subj: relationship of SAB to Chief

of Staff, 26 April 1948, SAB 2; Air Force Regulation 20-30, "Organization—SAB to the Chief of Staff, USAF," 14 May 1948, SAB 2.

45. Interview, Lt Gen Donald L. Putt with Dr. James C. Hasdorff, 1-3 April 1974, USAF Oral History Program Interview #K239.0512-724, pp. 77-80; Memo, Maj J.C. De Hart to Brig Gen Putt, subj: SAB, 29 September 1948, SAB 4; von Karman, Wind and Beyond, pp. 303-304; Sturm, SAB p. 31; HQ ARDC Annual History, 23 January 1950-30 June 1951, pp. 28-49.

46. Sturm, SAB, pp. 32-34; Interview, Putt, pp. 80-87; HQ ARDC Annual History, 23 January 1950-30 June 1951, pp. 28-49.

47. Sturm, SAB, pp. 34-35; Memo, Brig Gen Putt to CG, Air Materiel Command, subj: SAB Liaison Office, 21 October 1948, SAB 2; Putt, Donald L. "USAF R&D," lecture by Maj Gen Donald L. Putt at the Air War College, 17 November 1949, AFHRC K239.716249-74.

CHAPTER TWO

THE DECLINE OF CIVILIAN SCIENCE, 1950-1958

The SAB had done great things in its first five years. It had produced two models of science forecasting, <u>Where We Stand</u> and <u>Toward New Horizons</u>, exhaustive treatises on the present and future of aeronautical science. It followed these seminal works with the <u>Ridenour Report</u>, a study which determined the profound influence R&D would one day have in Air Force counsels. The board enjoyed a sophisticated organizational structure in which 48 distinguished members served on eight technology panels: aircraft, guided missiles and pilotless aircraft, explosives and armament, aerospace medicine, fuels and propulsion, electronics and communications, geophysical research, and social sciences. Its place on the Air Staff as direct advisor to the Chief of Staff--not to any intermediary authority-- was secure. Finally, the SAB still had Theodore von Karman as its chairman, which alone assured it a measure of respect and visibility. The board, in short, had reached its stride.

But none of these factors could prevent a subtle decline in the board's status, and a consequent fall in the prestige of civilian science for periodic forecasting. During 1950 von Karman turned 69 years of age, and he began to look for challenges suited to his seniority. The forging of the western alliance known as the North Atlantic Treaty Organization (NATO) fired his imagination. Why not a scientific advisory board for NATO? With the approval of General Vandenberg, in the summer of 1950 von Karman traveled to Europe to study the state of aeronautics in a number of western countries. When he returned to the Pentagon, he solicited the Chief of Staff's support for a permanent, international committee of scientists to harness European and North American science for the common defense. The following February, twelve nations were invited to send representatives to Washington, D.C., to discuss the idea. Eight countries sent scientists, who quickly drafted a proposal for a NATO Advisory Group for Aeronautical Research and Development (AGARD). They recommended that AGARD act as a clearinghouse for

European technical information relating to aeronautics and advise the NATO governments as to the ways in which European science should be employed in the interests of the Atlantic Alliance.[1]

Before AGARD could begin operation, it had to be approved not only by the NATO General Staff, but by the military leadership of each participating country, as well as the governments of all NATO signatories. The group was established officially in February 1952, and von Karman accepted General Vandenberg's invitation to serve as its first chairman. During Spring of that year, von Karman asked Dr. Frank Wattendorf to go to Paris and set up the preliminary organization. The first General Assembly of AGARD was met with great enthusiasm by the scientists of the twelve NATO nations, and von Karman spent a very busy summer in Paris erecting a panel structure much like the one he had invented for the SAB.[2]

As he became more and more preoccupied with his AGARD responsibilities, the duties of the SAB fell increasingly to von Karman's vice chairman, General Jimmy Doolittle. While von Karman did chair the fall 1952 and spring 1953 general SAB meetings, the attendees remarked that the dual workload had taken a heavy toll on him. Recognizing the inevitable strain on his health, he wrote in September 1954 to Gen. Nathan F. Twining, the new Air Force Chief of Staff, tendering his resignation effective January 1955. His appraisal of his association with the Air Force was generous, especially of the man who first convinced him to serve. Looking back over ten years as SAG/SAB chairman, he "cherished the memory of many episodes of working for General Arnold," was grateful for the support of the succeeding Chiefs of Staff, and deemed it a privilege to have served the Air Force.[3] Thanks probably to Donald Putt, with whom von Karman had dinner during his Christmas-time return to Washington, he was informed in January 1955 that he would not only receive a "very nice letter" from Twining accepting his resignation, but be named chairman emeritus of the SAB.[4]

During the next two years, von Karman concentrated on AGARD and Cal Tech affairs, while the SAB was chaired by Dr. Mervin J. Kelly (January to November 1955) and Jimmy Doolittle (November 1955 to December 1958). Early in 1957, however, a project was begun in Washington, D.C., which attracted von Karman's attention, and for which he was again asked to serve the Air Force. It involved a long-range study equal in scope to Toward New Horizons. Von Karman had had an opportunity in 1953 to recreate his earlier success when Putt, a lieutenant general and ARDC Commander, urged him to update the 1945 report. But he declined, arguing that scientific knowledge had expanded to such an extent that the board could no longer adequately encompass the subject. During the final months of World War II there were unique chances to interview the world's foremost aeronautical experts, who had been mobilized to serve their governments in the conflict. He wondered whether equally fruitful discussions were possible in the Cold War atmosphere of suspicion and propaganda. In all likelihood, his absorption with AGARD contributed to his disinclination to do Toward New Horizons over again. Rather than one sweeping survey, he suggested the Air Force undertake "a continuing series of studies on a modest scale."[5]

But the terms of the offer made to him at the start of 1957 were different, and by now AGARD was on its feet. Perhaps most appealing to von Karman about the proposed long-range study was the open intention of its organizers to parallel Toward New Horizons in breadth of subject matter and quality of participants. The idea originated with Lt. Gen. Thomas S. Power, Commander of ARDC. When Power assumed command in April 1954, he asked his staff whether long-range plans had been made for new, elaborate test facilities, on the order of the Tullahoma, Tennessee, wind tunnels. Dissatisfied with the answers, Power directed his senior staff to produce a series of R&D forecast reports, much like those proposed by von Karman when he declined to draft a second Toward New Horizons. During 1955 Power appointed six panels and six panel chairs: Propulsion (Maj. Gen. Troup Miller); Missiles (Maj. Gen. D. N. Yates); Aircraft (Brig. Gen. Ralph Wassell); Electronics (Maj. Gen. Thomas L. Bryan); Materials (Brig. Gen. Marvin C. Demler); and Aerosciences (Maj. Gen. Edward P. Meckling). Panel members were selected from ARDC and the Office of Scientific Research (OSR). Power did not impose a deadline on the committees and intentionally left unstated what he intended to do with the reports. He simply directed the chairmen to forecast the future and take whatever time needed to present their findings.

Powers' chairmen reported back within a year, but the panels' conclusions differed widely and more discussions were held to integrate the subject matter. During one session, Maj. Gen. Bernard A. Schriever, Commander of ARDC's Western Development Division (WDD) and a former member of Putt's inner circle, told Power that only an outside body of scientists could reconcile these differences and provide a coherent vision of what lay ahead. Schriever suggested von Karman be enlisted to lead a second major long-range report. Power agreed, and asked the elder scientist to direct a sequel to Toward New Horizons. This time he accepted. To meet von Karman's well-known objections to conducting large-scale studies within the confines of the SAB, ARDC would negotiate a contract with the National Academy of Sciences (NAS) to undertake a major report on the future of USAF science.[6]

The proposition was made to the NAS during fall 1956. In November its council recommended consideration of the project, and the following month General Power and SAB chairman Doolittle met with the NAS President, Dr. Detlev V. Bronk, to discuss its terms. The two Air Force representatives asked Bronk for "an independent, unbiased appraisal of the scientific program and problems," which would result in a "systematic evaluation of the scientific and technological possibilities and requirements of the Air Force covering the next 10 to 25 years." Hoping the NAS would initiate the study in summer 1957, Power turned over portions of the six ARDC committee reports to Dr. Bronk to hasten a decision and promised full ARDC cooperation should the NAS accept the proposal. After careful consideration and several more meetings with Power, Doolittle, Putt, and Air Force Vice Chief of Staff Gen. Thomas D. White, Dr. Bronk announced in January 1957 that his Governing Board had agreed to launch a full-scale report for the Air Force.

The Air Research and Development Command at first wanted a two-phase contract which included initial planning, followed by a six-month preparation period lasting from April 1 to September 30. By April 1957 a clearer and more expansive picture had emerged. A large team of the nation's finest scientists would gather at Woods Hole, Massachusetts, during 1957 and 1958. They would take as points of departure the six committee reports produced for General Power at ARDC. During phase one of the study (summer 1957) they would gain familiarity with Air Force scientific problems and provide an interim report of immediate use to ARDC. In phase two (summer 1958) they were asked to produce a comprehensive plan for Air Force long-range scientific purposes. The overall objective of the NAS project was to mobilize the "experience, wisdom, and breadth of viewpoint of outstanding scientists and engineers not regularly available for this concerted purpose." The NAS would recruit these researchers from the universities, government, and industry, seeking "cooperation and assistance" from the National Advisory Committee for Aeronautics (NACA) and the SAB. Indeed, the board did more than offer advice. The study director (Dr. von Karman) and two of his chief assistants (Drs. Dryden and H. Guyford Stever) had close SAB connections, which they would use freely in these deliberations.[7]

Initially, in May 1957 eighty-four distinguished men of academia, government, and corporate science were contacted to participate in phases one and two of what was officially called the "NAS/ARDC Study Group Relating to Long-Range Scientific and Technical Trends of Interest to the United States Air Force." In Air Force parlance it had the more digestible name of The Woods Hole Summer Study, 1957/1958. Organized in the manner of Academy studies, panels were established and a nationwide search undertaken for the leading scientists to chair and staff each committee. The Scientific Advisory Board had a marked effect on the selection process. Since the Woods Hole report involved Air Force science, von Karman asked Doolittle to choose several senior SAB members—including Drs. Charles Draper, Ivan Getting,[*] Joseph Kaplan, Clark

---

[*]Getting returned to the board in 1952 after resigning in 1948.

B. Millikan, and Edward Teller—to serve on the Academy panels, and to submit the names of others who might serve. Ultimately, of the thirty-six original members of the SAG, ten would act as participants and seven as consultants on the Woods Hole study.

Despite the strong SAB representation, the sheer number of participants in the Woods Hole process far exceeded previous gatherings of scientists to forecast technical trends of military interest. Also, while the SAB enjoyed close ties to Cal Tech, MIT, and Princeton, the NAS reached out to almost every academic institution in the country. Over the course of 2 summers, more than 300 people contributed: 198 attended the sessions at Woods Hole as participants, and 105 served as consultants. To make the planning process manageable and facilitate solving problems of coverage and organization, von Karman assembled a small advisory council, composed mostly of his former SAG/SAB colleagues. Wattendorf and Dryden, in Paris with von Karman on AGARD business, flew home to join the council, which also included Stever, Getting, Walkowicz, and Drs. Francis H. Clauser and George Kistiakowsky. During their deliberations, these men clearly conceived of the upcoming report as a second Toward New Horizons, a chance to guide Air Force science as they had 12 years earlier.[8]

Meanwhile, preparations went forward for the opening meetings at Woods Hole, scheduled for late June 1957, at which von Karman and the council would hear Air Force briefings and assign scientists to the various panels. During July participants would start to arrive, and by August the full complement would be in residence. The advisory council would oversee and guide the discussions of the panels, review their work, integrate their results and objectives, and formulate plans for the more in-depth studies due in 1958.

A Woods Hole contract worth $300,000 laid out the minimum study requirements. The Academy would organize and supply all needed personnel and services for an intensive review of "scientific and technical trends and possibilities...pertinent to the development of air power in the United States." During the first phase of the study—running through the end of 1957—the NAS agreed to explore the feasibility of and plan for an in-depth report on the future of Air Force R&D, and produce a preliminary forecast on aerospace materials for the period 1967 to 1977. Phase two, ending February 1, 1958,[*] included the preparation of one report by each panel, as well as a final, integrated volume "which will prescribe those scientific and technical avenues of approach which show the most promise of assuring that the U.S. Air Force maintain scientific and technical superiority in the atmosphere and exosphere." The participants were allowed to examine Top Secret material, but the panel and summary reports would have no higher classification than Secret. To protect proprietary information which might be revealed during discussions or briefings, each member of the Woods Hole Study would sign a pledge to refrain from disclosure or use of technical ideas to which contractors claimed ownership.[9]

When the advisory council first convened at Woods Hole from June 24 to 26, it found a casual and relaxed atmosphere, with von Karman dressed in shirt sleeves and a sailor's cap. Despite the friendly spirit of the gathering, he and the study's executive director, Guyford Stever, were impressed by the Academy's efforts to make this a serious and productive undertaking. More than 100 scientists representing 26 universities, 20 industrial firms, and 8 government research agencies had agreed to serve in the 1957 sessions. In short order the council sketched a panel structure, following the outline of General Power's[†] 1955/1956 ARDC reports:

---

[*]Later extended to February 1, 1959.
[†]On 30 June 1957 Power became Commander in Chief, Strategic Air Command, succeeding Gen. Curtis E. LeMay, who was appointed Air Force Vice Chief of Staff. On 1 August 1957 Power was succeeded at ARDC by Gen. Samuel E. Anderson.

HARNESSING THE GENIE

1. Guided Missiles and Space Vehicles
2. Propulsion
3. Electronics
4. Materials
5. Aircraft
6. Aero-sciences
    a. Nuclear Air Ordnance
    b. Non-Nuclear Air Ordnance
    c. Guidance and Control
    d. Geophysics
    e. Aero-Medicine and Bio-Sciences
    f. Psychological and Social Sciences

Before the official proceedings began, Air Force Chief of Staff General Thomas D. White[*] expressed firm support for the project. White felt the USAF had reached "a critical stage in which our broad planning, as exemplified in ...'Toward New Horizons'...must be projected into the future as far as possible if we are to maintain a qualitatively superior Air Force." Since the Air Force lacked the capability to carry out long-range scientific forecasts by itself, an external agency had to be relied on to gather a national pool of scientific talent.[10]

The council heard a number of distinguished speakers during its late June meetings. Mr. James H. Douglas, Secretary of the Air Force, recapitulated those themes in Toward New Horizons germane to the NAS/ARDC collaboration: that professional scientists held the security of the nation in their hands; that much research remained to be done on air power problems such as distance, darkness, and weather; and that through scientific endeavors supersonic speed and nuclear weapons had become realities. Douglas challenged his audience to rise to the standards of Toward New Horizons and to recall the words of von Karman during their discussions: "men in charge of the future Air Forces should always remember that problems never have final or universal solutions, and only a constant inquisitive attitude toward science and a ceaseless and swift adaptation to new developments can

---

*White became Chief of Staff of the Air Force on 1 July 1957.

maintain the security of the nation through world air supremacy."[11]

General Donald Putt seconded Douglas's call to follow the path blazed by Toward New Horizons. Lingering questions about what direction the USAF should take in propulsion systems, electronics and radar, and manned aircraft versus unmanned missiles, perplexed Air Force planners in 1957, as in 1945. The military uses of space, said Putt, might constitute the next technological horizon.

Maj. Gen. Howell M. Estes, ARDC's Deputy Chief of Staff for Development, concluded the sessions with a briefing on the major Air Force weapon systems scheduled for completion in the next few years. Estes made plain that ever more demanding military requirements since World War II had lead to increasingly complex weapon systems. Because the necessary technologies had to be hurried along and were often pressed into service before they were fully mature, technical deficiencies arose which could not be predicted prior to development. Solving the problems once the programs were underway was often costly, and frequently resulted in systems with permanent design flaws and reduced performance.[12]

Enlightened by these talks, as well as several informal briefings on overall defense planning, von Karman and friends got down to work. The critical meetings were set for July 29-30 and August 22-23, and the Advisory Council made the final selections for the six panels and six sub-panels. An on-the-spot library of 134 technical volumes was carted in by the Academy for basic reference. During the week before the July meeting, intensive critique and review of the ARDC reports took place. During August, the full assemblage checked in and heard briefings on the ICBM by General Schriever, as well as discussions by other Air Force officials on anti-ballistic missiles, materials, aircraft, guided missiles, and propulsion. The committees then met to hammer out positions and put their findings on paper. General Samuel Anderson was briefed on the conclusions on November 22, 1957. He listened with interest to tentative recommendations for ARDC and plans for the second, far more comprehensive, study next summer.[13]

HARNESSING THE GENIE

Anderson had a compelling reason to continue the study in 1958. On October 4, 1957, just as the first Woods Hole Report was being completed, the U.S.S.R. launched into orbit Sputnik, the first artifical earth satellite. Several scientists, including von Karman, had wanted to explore the satellite question during the 1957 sessions, only to be discouraged by military officials who felt Congress would seize on it as another example of extravagance in the development requests of the Air Force. Until October 4, the top priority business of the USAF had been ICBM development, and Air Force leaders did not want satellites or any other projects diverting resources from ballistic missiles. Indeed, when some of the scientists tried to discuss openly the general subject of the military uses of space, the idea was "ridiculed by most and ruled off the agenda."[14] The American public demanded to know how the U.S. scientific and defense establishments could let this dangerous situation occur. The Air Force responded by scrapping the 1957 NAS report and asking the Academy to produce a new one which reflected the realities of the space age.

Despite a feeling of disappointment at ARDC and the NAS over the outcome of the first Woods Hole Summer Study, staff work and informal discussions continued during winter 1957 and spring 1958. Luckily, the administrative procedures relating to salary, travel expenses, and housing all remained intact from the 1957 report. By December 1957, participants in the forthcoming study began to consider the course it should take. Propulsion had suddenly become one of the great issues. How should America lift advanced missile systems? How should satellites, space platforms, and space flight vehicles be placed into orbit? Early discussions focused on six possible technologies: chemical rockets, nuclear power, radioactive isotopes, particle and plasma jets, solar energy, and magnetohydrodynamics.[15]

These and other ideas were suggested during meetings held on February 14 and 15, 1958, at HQ ARDC. General Anderson and his staff reviewed with von Karman and a number of his former SAB associates* the overall agenda

---

*Drs. Dryden, Stever, Wattendorf, William Sears, Courtland Perkins, Pol Duwez, W. Randolph Lovelace,

of Woods Hole II. The committee chairmen[*] agreed to submit possible topics by April 1, and meet as a group late that month in Denver, Colorado, to finalize their choices. The project would open officially on June 23, and, after a week of registration, orientation, and briefings, carry through July and August. Between sixty and seventy scientists, most of whom had served the previous year, would convene on the pleasant grounds of the Whitney Estate at Little Harbor Farm, Woods Hole, a private, nine-acre waterfront property, and stay until they completed the report. While the 1957 panel categories would be reestablished, the military uses of space would occupy center stage.[16]

A supplemental contract for $400,000 with the NAS reflected the change in emphasis. The agreement covered the costs of holding technical symposia; determining future R&D facilities requirements; amassing scientific and technical information relative to long-range capabilities in offensive, defensive, and limited warfare; reviewing methods of collecting, interpreting, and disseminating physical intelligence data; completing by December 31, 1958 an integrated final report which treated the period 1958-1978; and briefing the ARDC Commander on its conclusions and recommendations.[17]

Prior to the opening session, von Karman sent invitations to fifty-one academic and seventy non-academic scientists. But, when full and part-timers were finally averaged, von Karman could count on only fifty pairs of hands for the project. On the positive side, to the list of attendees were added eight young officers with scientific or engineering backgrounds, each of whom was assigned to one committee to provide military insight and to learn first hand from the scientists. The committee chairmen suggested, and von Karman accepted, the establishment of eight new "joint" panels to complement the eight technical committees. They would assess problems which cut across

---

John R. Markham, Joseph V. Charyk, Clark Millikan, William Shockley, William Pickering, Clifford T. Morgan, Allen Puckett, and John H. Hollomon.

[*]Drs. Joseph V. Charyk (Aircraft, Guided Missiles, and Space); Frank L. Wattendorf (Propulsion); John H. Hollomon (Materials); Pol Duwez (Materials); Louis

scientific disciplines, including the military implications of space vehicles, subsidiary power, limited warfare, human physiology in advanced weapon systems, approaches to R&D planning, miniaturization and research, reliability and maintenance, and facilities.[18]

On the eve of the second Woods Hole conference, a disturbing difference of opinion emerged between von Karman and the ARDC leadership. The scientist looked upon the 1958 study as a more comprehensive version of Toward New Horizons, designed to expand the scientific potentialities of the Air Force on a very broad front. At the same time, responding to public pressure to counter the Russian presence in space, ARDC officials issued statements to the media pledging to emphasize space research in their R&D programs. "They have apparently decided to become a Space Force," warned William Sears in a letter to von Karman. To this he responded with uncharacteristic vehemence. An "exaggerated emphasis" on rocketry and new types of rocket propulsion, he wrote, must not be allowed to overshadow all of the many aeronautical research problems. "I believe less emphasis should be given" in the upcoming report, "to examine any one weapon system or any particular mission." Despite clear signs that the Air Force desired a space-oriented study, von Karman argued eloquently for balanced weapons development and a balanced forecast of the future. While space flight for military and civil purposes was at hand, he cautioned that "it will still be a long time before the foot soldier, the boat, and the airplane vanish completely from the 'surface' of the earth." Von Karman reminded his Air Force friends that the 1957 Woods Hole Study had already probed the use of satellites for reconnaissance and communications and that the subject would be again discussed fully in the 1958 sessions. He suggested that "forward-looking considerations" of conventional air power should also receive a complete hearing.[19]

An unstated compromise was worked out between the two points of view. Although the study went forward

---

T.E. Thompson (Weapons); and Clifford T. Morgan (Life Sciences).

under von Karman's broad rubric, it did come to stress to a significant degree the Air Force role in space. Unfortunately, its ambivalent character—neither a true space study nor a second Toward New Horizons—would eventually cast doubt on its entire validity, at least in the eyes of top Air Force and ARDC leaders.

The working proceedings of the 1958 Woods Hole II Study group began on June 26 after addresses by Dr. Bronk, Air Force Vice Chief General Curtis LeMay, Dr. von Karman, Assistant Secretary of Defense for Research and Engineering Paul D. Foote, and Assistant Secretary of the Air Force for Research and Development Richard E. Horner. Briefings by ARDC officials on the twenty-seventh of June were followed by the convening of panels to review agendas prepared in advance by von Karman's Advisory Council. The committees then split up into mission area groups, within the framework of which they would analyze individual weapon systems. For instance, those panel members who sat on the aircraft committee were also assigned to the strategic warfare mission area where they deliberated on likely types of weapon systems for atmospheric and trans-atmospheric flight. Mindful of the pressures imposed by Sputnik to produce a report quickly, von Karman scheduled rigid due dates for each committee: chapter outlines completed late in July, rough drafts in by mid-August, chapters out for peer review two weeks later and completed in September, and the final draft sent to the printer by November 15. Once the chapter outlines were briefed to Mr. Horner, Maj. Gen. Leighton I. Davis (HQ ARDC Deputy Director for Research), and other Air Staff and ARDC officials, von Karman and his council reviewed all subsequent committee work at each stage of production. They looked, in particular, for cogent introductory essays which presented clearly the choices open to the Air Force, preferred solutions, research areas pertinent to the solutions, technical development issues, and facility requirements.[20]

Working frantically to comply with the terms of the contract with ARDC,* the scientists spent exhausting days debating points, reaching consensus, and rendering

*Two more supplements were appended to the Woods Hole contract before it was terminated. On September 22, $45,000 was added to widen the facilities studies; on

their findings in report form. Much of the discussion centered on advanced rocketry and strategic weapons as they pertained to orbiting satellites. No concept, no matter how remote, failed to receive at least a hearing. The idea of overflight of U.S. territory by foreign satellites, which was regarded as a grave menace at the beginning of the space age, engendered long talks on possible anti-satellite weaponry. As one participant later recalled, everyone present would have been shocked to know that in a few years time, satellite-based reconnaissance, communications, weather, and navigation would be considered peaceful uses of space! Speculation about manned vehicular exploration of space ran almost to the fantastic, and von Karman felt the groups "went wild" in this respect. Talk ranged from the applicability of low space laboratories to space platforms for launches into deep space, leaving von Karman wondering about the usefulness and productivity of scientific teamwork at all.[21]

Despite the misgivings of the study director, the work was rushed to completion. A day-long series of briefings was set for December 15, 1958, for General Anderson and his senior staff, with identical presentations for working-level ARDC personnel the following day. The attendees assembled in the conference room of the Academy Building on Constitution Avenue in Washington, D.C., to hear the conclusions contained in volume one of the final report, which embraced each committee's summary findings. Dr. von Karman introduced the briefings by suggesting once again that the Woods Hole II Summer Study represented an updating of Toward New Horizons. Yet, he did acknowledge differences. The 1945 report appeared at a time of Allied victory, in a relatively uncomplicated international climate. Since then, the scientist told his audience, nuclear weapons had re-shaped global politics and made it necessary to hedge technological projections with considerations of limited war, deterring war, and winning

---

November 19 an additional $80,000 was agreed upon to cover the publication costs of 1,000 summary volumes and 500 copies of the committee reports. Total outlays for the NAS study amounted to $825,000.

war. Secondly, the Woods Hole participants did not feel it necessary to touch on organizational questions; Toward New Horizons had already succeeded in establishing the Air Staff Deputy Chief of Staff for Research and Development, the SAB, and ARDC. Finally, substantial discussions of space flight, satellites, and rocketry differentiated this report from its predecessor. However, to the chagrin of many listeners, von Karman warned that "in high places, the pendulum of support has swung from indifference...of the word 'space' to all out enthusiasm and 'crash' programs." He called for orderly growth in all of the important branches of air power technology, adding that "in our enthusiasm for new horizons we [must] not overlook those [weapons] that still remain in the more classical domains of flight within the atmosphere, communications, reconnaissance at low altitudes, and so on. In thus giving adequate thought to all aspects of military necessity, the Air Force will do its share...."[22]

Summations of the findings of the twelve committees were then presented to the ARDC leadership. From the viewpoint of the Air Force, the committee responsible for panels on aircraft, guided missiles, and space vehicles produced the most significant recommendations. They suggested that Minuteman be developed with twice the payload of existing designs, and include decoy and cluster features. To improve deterrence, their silos should be hardened and widely dispersed. To further deter nuclear attack, the committee proposed adding an additional stage to Titan or Atlas missiles so they could lift 8,000-pound payloads, sufficient to penetrate hardened Soviet sites. The scientists supported development of the B-70 bomber as an effective weapon against Soviet strategic targets whose precise location could not be ascertained. Military uses of space could be furthered by the Dyna-Soar, a boost-glide aircraft-like vehicle in which men could be sent into earth orbit and returned after periods of experimentation. Improvements in the accuracy of ballistic missiles required a concentrated research effort.* Tactical aviation needed two new weapons: subsonic vertical take-off and landing (VTOL) strike aircraft and supersonic VTOL aircraft,

_____

*The Military Uses of Space Flight Panel divided space exploration into categories of short, medium, and long-term programs. The short-term included recon-

featuring day/night all-weather capability and anti-missile defenses. A better air defense required augmentation of the Ballistic Missile Early Warning System (BMEWS) with orbiting satellites and high-altitude airborne radar-infrared coverage. The committee recommended that transport aircraft should be developed along the lines of increased size, higher speed, and VTOL capabilities. Finally, it was felt that reconnaissance of the future demanded orbiting satellites for global surveillance, mapping, warning, and weather forecasting, as well as improved manned high flight aircraft.[23]

The propulsion committee presented its findings according to the main types of engines and rockets. Among air-breathing engines, turbojets were already a mature technology, but development remained to be done on light turbojets for short take-off and landing (STOL) and VTOL aircraft. Hypersonic ramjets held out great promise for reconnaissance aircraft. Nuclear air-breathing engines also showed potential for very long range and endurance, but radiation shielding for the crew and reduction of heat transferred from the reactor to the working fluid had yet to be solved. Chemical rockets, in liquid and solid forms, had high military importance, although their characteristics differed. Liquid rockets provided greater thrust; solid offered greater reliability. Good as both rockets had been, nuclear rockets were worth close study as they offered far higher energy release. The heat transfer nuclear rocket, which could boost heavy payloads into space with only one stage, as well as the gaseous fission rocket, both required intensive exploration. Electric propulsion based upon lightweight generation of electrical power and conversion of electricity

---

naissance, communications, and "investigation" satellites, as well as counters to Soviet reconnaissance orbiters; the medium-term held the promise of orbital weaponry (bombardment and air defense), Dyna-Soar for logistics support and space station construction, and more sophisticated satellites. The long-term prospects (the 1970s and beyond) included manned lunar flight, which suggested the possibility of a lunar base for military operations.

to kinetic energy held out the hope of even greater thrust than nuclear rockets. Facilities for experimentation with atomic and electrical rocketry would be large and costly, but were believed worth the investment.[24]

The committee on electronics posited Air Force applications in space and in general research. In the field of navigation, electronics held the key to improved accuracy for missiles and satellites. Guiding ICBMs to within 1500 feet of their targets was considered possible. Communications would also be revolutionized using highly reliable and low noise systems. Radar would remain the main tool for detecting enemy movements, but electronics advances would add great sophistication to existing processes. Electronic countermeasures would likewise remain the main defenses of bomber and attack aircraft, but would also be applied to tactical aircraft, satellites, and missiles.[25]

Questions about future materials were reported by the materials panel. In contrast to the past, when Air Force material requirements were much like those of civilian industry, the next generation of USAF systems would demand types of metals and plastics unknown in 1958. Implicit was the necessity for high strength-to-weight ratios. The strongest steels and titanium alloys would eventually be replaced by lighter, more ductile materials. The blending of the best characteristics of several substances using composite technology held great promise. Most importantly, the committee members agreed the Air Force should begin exploration of new materials-making techniques using thermal protection, refractory materials for high temperatures, compound semi-conductors, and graphite compounds. The panel implored the USAF to broaden its materials research, warning that unless it followed this course of action vigorously, a time would come when the Air Force would be unable to acquire needed materials from U.S. suppliers. Demands for ever more exotic substances for new weapon systems would diverge increasingly from the private sector's interest in commonplace materials for commercial purposes. Hence, the government must fund universities, non-profit organizations, industries, and the Air Force laboratories to initiate exploratory projects, both to exploit new ideas and to accumulate data for future applications.[26]

The weapons panel cautioned the USAF that nonnuclear weapons development was "being dissipated" by an overemphasis on nuclear weaponry. Despite the official U.S. defense policy of massive nuclear retaliation in the face of aggression, the committee recommended greater emphasis on conventional force programs. They suggested research on such weapons as nonnuclear ordnance for fighter and bomber aircraft, airborne anti-tank weapons, and new guidance control using sensory devices to detect ground targets. Chemical and biological weapons research should be pursued to determine the most useful agents, and a wide range of companion delivery systems and field testing must be undertaken. The panel did concede the necessity of developing tactical nuclear weapons, but recommended they carry very small yield values (one to a few hundred tons), and be considered for use only under conditions of excellent intelligence and highly precise delivery. Radiation weapons also had potential. Concentrated electromagnetic radiation beams might have anti-satellite and anti-ballistic missile applications, and, if mounted on airborne platforms, be targeted against aircraft, conventional missiles, and ground sites. Particle beam weapons based in space had several advantages: excellent focus, target heating, and secondary radiation effects. Finally, the panel proposed feasibility studies for a new generation of ballistic missiles with payloads of 2,000 to 10,000 pounds, delivery accuracies of 2,500 feet, and hidden or mobile basing.[27]

* * *

Toward New Horizons and the Woods Hole Summer Studies present a paradox. Directed by the same man and undertaken by many of the same scientists, the 1945 report became embedded in Air Force consciousness while the influence of its successor was minimal. Perhaps the normal postwar feelings of relief and euphoria contributed to the effectiveness of Toward New Horizons, reflecting the hope and expansiveness of its authors. Woods Hole, a product of the Cold War and the nuclear age, looked upon further scientific advances with less optimism. But the differences could also be laid to more concrete factors. The sponsors of the two reports had a significant effect on their outcomes. General Arnold was a man of international reputation and his enthusiastic support of air power science was well known. His views on the importance of R&D had been demonstrated for years, as had his reliance on the judgment of Theodore von Karman. On the other hand, General Power, who launched the Woods Hole Study, was reassigned before it began. Power was a fine commander, but even had he stayed on to direct the study he could not have imparted Woods Hole with the luster Arnold gave Toward New Horizons. Secondly, Toward New Horizons advanced a number of truly revolutionary ideas. Woods Hole, by contrast, was comparatively conservative and failed to phrase the important points with the aphoristic panache of thirteen years before. Moreover, though von Karman directed Woods Hole in name, in fact he spent little time in Massachusetts during the summers of 1957 and 1958. Still immersed in AGARD and NATO matters, his preoccupations had shifted to Europe. Just like General Arnold's, his leadership was sorely missed. Finally, von Karman was now in his mid-70s and somewhat unprepared for the rigors of molding the loose impressions of a dozen committees into a solid, worthwhile volume of practical advice.

Several other factors explain why the Woods Hole report did not have greater impact. The leaders of ARDC, pressed by outcries from Congress and the public to close the space gap posed by Sputnik, asked that satellite technology take center stage in the 1958 final report. Space was given much consideration, but at von Karman's insistence, was only one subject among many. He fought hard to produce a study which followed the pattern of Toward New Horizons, treating the wide horizon of air power science. This approach displeased the ARDC leadership who demanded the focus be on space. Worse still, many top Air Force generals were men of long SAC experience who had reservations about the Woods Hole conclusions. They disliked the treatment of space as a mission, which they regarded as a potential infringement of SAC's strategic role. They also objected to the limited war* aspects of the report, claiming that nuclear deterrence must remain paramount. Consequently, Woods Hole lacked a strong constituency within the Air Force. It seemed to teach the lesson that without proper military controls, scientists would produce reports useful to their academic specialties, but of little utility to the Air Force.

Hence, the Woods Hole Summer Studies never achieved the fame of Toward New Horizons. The work of "outsiders" who were unaware of the perspectives and agenda of various groups within the organization, Woods Hole foundered on institutional politics. Nonetheless, von Karman acted courageously in insisting upon a broad treatment and avoiding what he called "fads" in research. Despite the urgency to enter the space race, he continued to press for balance in long-range scientific studies. But von Karman himself had misgivings about the Woods Hole reports. Though the nation's foremost scientists had gathered under ideal conditions to draft a blueprint for Air Force R&D, he knew it did not turn out as well as his report for General Arnold. He began to wonder whether the more intimate environment of the SAB—where he and a few colleagues conceived of and wrote Toward New Horizons—might not have been the better of the two approaches after all. Do "continous communal sessions" like Woods Hole really produce useful ideas? Von Karman had serious doubts. Imaginative impulses were submerged in committees, and specialists tended to dominate the proceedings. To the extent this occurred, the scientific generalist, who could perceive patterns among seemingly isolated phenomena, was stifled. "In the long run," wrote von Karman, "I still think that the finest creative thoughts come not out of organized teams but out of the quiet of one's own world."[28]

---

*The Limited War panel reasoned that nuclear fallout and ineffectiveness against widely dispersed targets made it dangerous to rely on nuclear weapons in limited war operations. They recommended joint service cooperation in collecting and analyzing intelligence data; development of STOL and VTOL aircraft with non-nuclear armament; development of air-to-surface armament better able to hit small ground targets; a guerilla force featuring joint service cooperation; development of large, inter-theater transports; and

---

integration of weapon requirements by the four services to improve interoperability.

1. von Karman, Wind and Beyond, pp. 325-329; Sturm, SAB, pp. 49-50; AFR 20-30A, "Organization—General, the Scientific Advisory Board to the Chief of Staff, USAF," 25 July 1951, SAB 2; Membership Lists, SAB, 7 July 1949 1 March 1950, SAB 2.

2. von Karman, Wind and Beyond, pp. 325-329; Sturm, SAB, pp. 49-50.

3. Sturm, SAB, p. 50; Ltr, Gen Hoyt S. Vandenberg, AF Chief of Staff to Lt Gen James H. Doolittle, subj: Doolittle's leadership of SAB, 18 December 1952, SAB 5; Ltr, Gen Vandenberg to von Karman, Subj: SAB vs. AGARD activities, 18 December 1952, SAB 5; Ltr, von Karman to Gen Nathan F. Twining, AF Chief of Staff, subj: resignation from SAB, 17 September 1954, SAB 2.

4. Ltr, Putt to von Karman, subj: von Karman retirement from SAB, 6 January 1955, TVK 24.10.

5. von Karman, Wind and Beyond, p. 305; Sturm, SAB, pp. 56-65.

6. Article, Anon., "Woods Hole Conference Maps Long Range Air Force Plans," Astronautics, v.2, September 1957, p. 4; Paper, Harris, Dr. W.J., Jr., "A Personal View of the Origins of the 1957-1958 von Karman Studies," February 1983, NAS 10.

7. Ltr, Dr. Detlev V. Bronk, NAS President, to Professor Wallace C. Penn, subj: letter of invitation to serve on NAS/ARDC study group, 14 July 1957, NAS 7; Minutes, National Academy of Sciences/National Research Council Governing Board, 9 December 1956, item: proposed study of scientific and technological future of the Air Force, w/attchs: a report on the 9 December 1956 meeting; memo to Dr. John S. Coleman, NAS, from unknown correspondent, subj: luncheon meeting between Dr. Bronk, Gen Power, and Lt Gen Doolittle, 3 December 1956; voting records of NAS Council with respect to the NAS/ARDC Summer Study, NAS 9; Memo, Coleman to Louis Jordan, subj: study for ARDC on long-range planning for R&D, 14 January 1957, NAS 9;

Ltr, Bronk to possible participants in NAS/ARDC Summer Study, subj: NAS/ARDC Summer Study, 22 April 1957, NAS 11.

8. Attch to Bronk ltr, 22 Apr 57, "List of Persons... Contacted Regarding the Air Force Special Study," 3 May 1957; von Karman, Theodore, Summary Report of the NAS/ARDC Study Group Relating to the Long Range Scientific and Technical Trends on Interest to the United States Air Force, 1958, pp. 66-72; Harris, "Origins of the von Karman Study,"; Ltr, Doolittle to Dr. Charles S. Draper, Ivan A. Getting, et. al., subj: assistance on ARDC long-range plans, 2 April 1957, w/attch: draft of letter by von Karman to Advisory Council participants, n.d., NAS 11; von Karman, Science, the Key to Air Supremacy, p. xvii; Ltr, Coleman to Dr. Allen E. Puckett, subj: 1957-1958 NAS Report, 28 May 1957, NAS 5; Ltr, von Karman to Getting, subj: NAS/ NAS/ARDC Advisory Council, 4 June 1957, NAS 11; Ltr, Lt Col Floyd J. Sweet to von Karman, subj: copies of Science the Key to Air Supremacy, 26 April 1957, TVK 90.11; Ltr, von Karman to Lt Col Sweet, subj: Wattendorf participation in NAS/ARDC Summer Study, 10 May 1957, TVK 90.11; von Karman, Wind and Beyond, p. 306.

9. Ltr, Coleman to Puckett, 28 May 1957; Anon., "Woods Hole Conference...Air Force Plans"; Contract, HQ ARDC and NAS, #AF 18 (600)-1661, for "Scientific Investigatory Group to Conduct Long Range Studies," 15 March 1957, NAS 1; Form, "Proprietary Rights-NAS/NRC," NAS 11.

10. Ltr, Gen Thomas D. White, AF Chief of Staff to Bronk, subj: NAS/ARDC Summer Study, 25 April 1957, NAS 9; Ltr, Bronk to White, subj: NAS/ARDC Summer Study, 6 May 1957, NAS 9.

11. von Karman, Wind and Beyond, p. 305; News Release, HQ ARDC, "Nation's Foremost Scientists to Forecast Future Air Force Research and Development Needs," 24 June 1957, NAS 2; Speech, Dr. H. Guyford Stever to the NAS/ARDC Study Group, 24 June 1957, NAS 11; Speech, Hon. James H. Douglas, SECAF to NAS/ARDC Study Group, 24 June 1957, NAS 11.

12. Speech, Lt Gen Putt, DCS/R&D to NAS/ARDC Study Group, 24 June 1957, NAS 11; Speech, Maj Gen Howell M. Estes, Jr. to NAS/ARDC Study Group, 25 June 1957, NAS 11.

13. Ltr, Ofc of the Pres, NAS, to all members of the NAS/ARDC Study Group, subj: activities for July and August, 5 July 1957, w/attchs: agenda for week of 15-21 July, (partial) committee membership, accessions list of studies available at Woods Hole, NAS 9; Ltr, Coleman to Dr. Hudson Hoagland, subj: letter of invitation to NAS/ARDC Study Group, 5 July 1957, NAS 5; Ltr, S.D. Cornell to Mr. Peregrine White, subj: workings of NAS/ARDC Study Group, 21 October 1957, NAS 9; Ltr, Gen Samuel E. Anderson, ARDC Commander, to Stever, subj: 22 November 1957 briefing of NAS/ARDC Study Group, 12 September 1957, NAS 5.

14. von Karman, Wind and Beyond, p. 306; Perkins, Courtland D., Recollections (unpublished memoirs), vol 3, chapter 7, pp. 7-8; Interview, Dr. H. Guyford Stever with M. Gorn, NAS offices, 20 February 1987.

15. Ltr, Coleman to Dr. William R. Sears, subj: Woods Hole accommodations, 9 December 1957, w/attchs: memo to Sears, 9 December 1957; Ltr, Sears to Coleman, subj: reimbursement for Woods Hole, 6 December 1957, NAS 5; Ltr, Dr. Richard S. Cesaro to Dr. Frank Wattendorf, subj: propulsion panel, 23 December 1957, NAS 2; Ltr, Cesaro to Wattendorf, subj: propulsion panel, 23 January 1958, NAS 2.

16. Ltr, B.J. Driscoll to Bronk, subj: February meeting at ARDC, 5 February 1958, NAS 8; Ltr, Driscoll to Walkowicz, subj: Woods Hole II, 31 January 1958, NAS 5; Ltr, Driscoll to Dr. Fred E. Fiedler, subj: schedule for week one, Woods Hole II, 6 June 1958, NAS 11; Ltr, Driscoll to unknown correspondent, subj: accommodations at Woods Hole, 3 March 1958, NAS 11; Ltr, Driscoll to von Karman, subj: reception of Woods Hole I, 4 March 1958, TVK 7.25; Driscoll to Dr. William J. Harris, Jr., subj: Woods Hole schedule, Mar-June 1958, 26 February 1958, NAS 11.

17. Supplemental Agreement, NAS/ARDC Contract #AF 18(600)-1661, 3 March 1958, NAS 1.

18. "List of Invitation Letters" to potential Woods Hole II participants, June 1958, NAS 11; Memo, Driscoll to Bronk, subj: status of NAS/ARDC Study Project, 14 May 1958, NAS 8; Ltr, Driscoll to Coleman, subj: committee chairs at Denver meeting, 15 April 1958, w/attch: "Notes for Denver Meeting, 27 April 1958," NAS 2; Ltr, Lt Col Sol Ernst to Driscoll, subj: administration of Woods Hole II, 28 March 1958, NAS 2; "Technical Secretaries--1958" to NAS/ARDC Study Group, n.d., NAS 11.

19. Memo, von Karman to members of the 1958 study group, subj: objectives of Woods Hole II, March 1958, NAS 11; Ltr, von Karman to Dr. Courtland Perkins, subj: objectives of Woods Hole II, 21 May 1958, NAS 11; Ltr, von Karman to Sears, subj: Woods Hole II preparation, 16 May 1958, NAS 11; Ltr, Sears to von Karman, subj: preparation for Woods Hole II, 3 June 1958, NAS 11.

20. Memo, Sears to all summer study participants, subj: work schedule, 26 August 1958, NAS 11; Memo, von Karman to study group membership, subj: schedule for remainder of year, 20 August 1958, NAS 11; "Program Outline for Committee 1-2" of 1958 Woods Hole Study, 1 July 1958, NAS 11; Memo, Director's Office to summer study membership, subj: content of final report, 25 July 1958, NAS 11; Schedule, NAS/ARDC study schedule for 26 and 27 June 1958, 25 June 1958, NAS 11; Memo, Director's Office to committee chairmen, subj: program for preliminary briefing of USAF officials, 12 and 14 August 1958, NAS 11.

21. Perkins, Recollections, v.3, p. 9; von Karman, Wind and Beyond, pp. 306-307; Supplemental Agreement, #AF 18(600)-1661, NAS/ARDC, 22 September 1958, NAS 1; Supplemental Agreement, #AF 18(600)-1661, NAS/ARDC, 19 November 1958, NAS 1.

22. Summary Report of the NAS/ARDC Study Group 1958 (S/RD), pp. 1-3 (U); Ltr, Coleman to Sears, subj: wrap-up of the NAS/ARDC study, 27 October 1958, NAS 11; Ltr,

Driscoll to Dr. Frederick C. Frick, subj: NAS briefing to ARDC, 27 October 1958, NAS 11; Agenda, "Preliminary Agenda for USAF Briefing on Results of Study Project, December 15-16 1958," 23 October 1958, NAS 11; Agenda, "Preliminary Agenda for USAF Brief-ing on Results of Study Project, December 15-16 1958," 18 November 1958, NAS 11.

23. Summary, NAS/ARDC Study Group Report (S/RD), pp. 4-10 (S), 47-49 (S).

24. Ibid., 11-19 (S).

25. Ibid., 20-27 (S).

26. Ibid., 28-31 (U).

27. Ibid., 32-35 (S).

28. Perkins, Recollections, vol.3, chapter 7, p. 10; von Karman, Wind and Beyond, pp. 306-307; NAS/ARDC Study Group Report (S/RD), pp. 51-52 (C).

Commanding General of the Army Air Forces
Henry H. Arnold

Dr. Theodore von Karman

Gen. James H. Doolittle

Gen. Thomas S. Power

Dr. H. Guyford Stever

Lt. Gen. Donald L. Putt

CHAPTER THREE

CONFORMING SCIENCE TO MILITARY NECESSITY, 1959-1966

The aftermath of the Woods Hole Summer Study had a profound impact on science forecasting for the Air Force. At a time of national crisis, USAF leaders felt the civilian scientists contracted by the National Academy of Sciences had let them down. They not only neglected the question of space, but produced a report which concentrated on relatively near-term weapon systems rather than the far reaches of scientific exploration. Dissatisfaction with the findings of the Woods Hole study group hastened a revolution in the way in which the Air Force picked the scientific brains of the nation. Ultimately, full control would be exercised by military scientists and engineers over all activities related to long-range forecasting. During the 1960s, however, a partnership evolved between academic and corporate science on the one hand, and scientifically trained officers who guided research toward military ends.

The emergence of a large cadre of officers with scientific, engineering, and technical backgrounds took years to come to fruition. As Table 1 illustrates, after a postwar surfeit of engineering officers, during the 1950s

Table 1
USAF Officers in Research, Development and Acquisition
1948-1985[*]

Year	Total RDA	Total USAF	% RDA
1948	4,696	53,948	8.7
1955	3,640	132,484	2.7
1960	4,637	129,689	3.6
1965	7,916	126,058	6.3
1970	9,311	135,475	6.9
1975	6,497	105,161	6.2
1980	7,029	97,901	7.2
1985	9,878	108,400	9.1

[*]Figures for 1948 to 1975 represent the assigned force.

the numbers declined, both as absolute figures and as percentages of the total officers corps. Only when Air Force Systems Command (AFSC), dedicated solely to weapons acquisition, came into being in the 1960s, did the situation change appreciably. Between 1960 and 1965, when the number of Air Force officers fell by over 3,500, the ranks of military personnel in the R&D fields swelled by 42 precent. Even during the Vietnam buildup (1965-1970), when pressure mounted to send men into active combat, the increase among R&D categories rose proportionally to the rise in the rest of the commissioned force. The post-Vietnam downturn, which by 1975 resulted in 20,000 fewer officers than 5 years before, affected military scientists and engineers much less severely. During the succeeding 10 years, aggregate numbers of R&D personnel achieved an all-time high of almost 10,000 people, an unprecedented 9.1 percent of the USAF officer corps.[1]

The tremendous surge in the number of highly qualified military men and women with research and development educations—particularly strong in the early 1960s—made possible the new cooperation among academics, corporate scientists, and engineering officers. General Bernard A. Schriever, ARDC and later AFSC Commander, did more than anyone to forge this alliance among civilian and military representatives of the many R&D fields. Schriever infused these links with considerations of national policy issues and overall military strategy, being careful not to limit interchange to purely technical considerations. To achieve these ends in his report on future aerospace technologies--known as Project Forecast—Schriever carefully selected the roster of contributors, blending military and civilian participants. His circle of friends included a wide array of distinguished scientists and engineers, and he called them from academia, non-profit institutions, and aerospace corporations to join his project. Most importantly, he carefully formulated the report to balance the classic "push" and "pull" factors of weapons development, giving the scientists the freedom to exercise their imaginations (technology push), but making sure creativity served the hard military realities (requirements pull). Using these basic principles, he and his staff produced a highly influential report.

* * *

As the foremost Air Force agency devoted to long-range scientific ideas, the SAB was directly affected by Schriever's reinterpretation of the role of USAF science. The board's substantial, but informal, involvement in the unpopular Woods Hole Study accelerated its problems and made it subject to critical Air Staff scrutiny. When General Doolittle retired as the SAB chairman in November 1958, Air Force Chief of Staff General Thomas White named Donald Putt to succeed him. Putt had retired from the Air Force earlier in the year and brought to the new job a desire to improve the military utility of the SAB's operations. Almost immediately, Putt asked the board's members to review its organization and consider creation of a new set of panels, along the lines of military mission (strategic, tactical, etc.) rather than scientific discipline. Only strongly negative comment among the members persuaded Putt to shelve the concept for the time being.

Nonetheless, the underlying idea of making the SAB more responsive to USAF needs continued to simmer. Two years after the Woods Hole Study, one of Putt's "Junior Indians" became the leading figure in Air Force science and weapons development. No longer "junior", Lt. Gen. Bernard A. Schriever assumed command of ARDC in April 1959. The son of emigrant parents, Schriever was born in Bremen, Germany, in September 1910. Seven years later his family moved to the United States and established themselves in San Antonio, Texas. After attending public schools there and becoming a naturalized citizen in 1923, Schriever enrolled at Texas A&M University and in 1931 received a Bachelor of Science degree. His military career began just after graduation when he accepted a reserve appointment in the field artillery. The following year he entered flight training at Randolph Field, Texas, and was commissioned a second lieutenant in the Air Corps Reserve at Kelly Field, Texas. Assigned as a bomber pilot at March Field, California, in September 1937 he assumed inactive reserve status and became a pilot with Northwest Airlines. But Schriever missed the military life and in 1938 reentered the service as a second lieutenant assigned to the 7th Bomber Group, Hamilton Field, California. A turning point in General Schriever's life occurred during 1939 when he reported to Wright Field, Ohio, for duty as a test pilot. There, in the heart of the Army Air Corps R&D facilities, he found his military calling. He attended the Air Corps Engineering School, following which he enrolled at Stanford University for advanced work in his chosen subject. Schriever graduated in June 1942 with a master's degree in mechanical (aeronautical) engineering.

During World War II he saw varied service. As a major, he served with the 19th Bomb Group in the campaigns of Bismarck Archipelago, Leyte, Luzon, Papua, Northern Solomons, the South Philippines, and the Ryukyus. Early in 1943 he served with the 5th AAF Service Command as Chief, Maintenance and Engineering Division and toward the end of the war commanded, with temporary rank of colonel, the advanced headquarters, Far East Air Service Command.

Every one of Schriever's postwar assignments involved various phases of the weapons acquisition process. At USAF Headquarters he served as Chief, Scientific Liaison Branch, Deputy Chief of Staff for Materiel, until 1950, when he attended the National War College. Shortly after the position of Deputy Chief of Staff for Development was created, he acted as Deputy Assistant for Evaluation and Assistant for Development Planning. During mid-1954, he left the Pentagon to become Assistant to the Commander, ARDC. That summer, he undertook the greatest challenge of his life, command of the Western Development Division (WDD) in Los Angeles, California. Raised to the rank of brigadier general, at the Western Development Division Schriever directed the nation's highest priority military project: the USAF ballistic missile program. In this capacity he also supported the initial phases of the U.S. space program. After almost five years of achievement, he returned to Washington to command ARDC with the rank of lieutenant general.[*] [2]

Shortly after assuming his duties as ARDC Commander, Schriever met with another of Putt's "Indians,"

---

[*]The establishment of Air Force Systems Command (AFSC)--brought about by Schriever and other USAF R&D people who felt research, development, testing, pro-

Col. Vincent T. Ford. Together they puzzled over the best way to bring science to bear on such vital technical programs as missiles and the military uses of space. One answer came from another of Putt's friends, Prof. Samuel T. Cohen, who would later invent the neutron bomb. Cohen decided after talks with Mr. Chester Hasert, Technical Director of the SAB, and Col. Clyde Gasser and Lt. Col. Billy C. Gray, SAB Executive Secretaries, that the Air Force needed military representation on the board. He told Putt that "military science" deserved the same status on the SAB as the physical, natural, and social sciences. A partnership should be forged, he argued, in which technical advice might be tempered by men who understood military requirements and operational factors. Cohen proposed a consulting group to the SAB Chairman composed of "military science" experts drawn from the ranks of retired Air Force officers, "think tank" analysts, and appropriate academicians. The essential drawback of the present SAB, Cohen said, was the members' stubborn ignorance of military matters. Even worse, an "unconscious degree of prejudice" toward the profession of arms permeated the minds of most scientists. Because they spent long years mastering the complexities of their subjects, they assumed they would be able to grasp the problems of military operations with ease. The inexactness of the art of war confirmed for many SAB members that it was an inferior field of endeavor, one which they could readily master. Cohen warned that their hasty suppositions about military imperatives actually undermined the value of their scientific advice because it led them down paths irrelevant to the objectives of the Air Force.[3]

General Schriever and Colonel Ford saw much merit in Cohen's ideas, but they agreed, like many others, that before the board underwent a basic change in character, "an objective, critical examination should be made of the SAB itself...its role, mission and purpose in life, as the individual to whom the SAB reports sees it—the Chief of

---

curement, and production should be consolidated in a single command—resulted in a fourth star for Schriever, who led AFSC from April 1961 to August 1966.

Staff [of the Air Force]." A number of measures calculated to add the military dimension to the board—and to Air Force science in general—occurred during 1961 and 1962, despite resistance from some senior SAB members. The board's secretary, Colonel Gasser, proposed methods to bring SAB projects into closer conformity to Air Staff and ARDC requirements. Gasser was only anticipating reforms, however. Both Dr. Alexander Flax, Assistant Secretary of the Air Force for Research and Development, and Lt. Gen. Roscoe C. Wilson, Air Staff Deputy Chief of Staff for R&D, asked Air Force Chief of Staff LeMay to begin an internal study of SAB operations and determine whether the best use was being made of science for Air Force purposes. A new Deputy Chief of Staff for R&D, Lt. Gen. James Ferguson, acting on the advice of General LeMay, persuaded the Executive Committee of the SAB in January 1962 to form a steering committee comprised of its chairman, vice-chairman, Military Director, as well as the Chief Scientist of the Air Force, and the Air Force Assistant Secretary for R&D. As a governing body, it would 1) review requests to the SAB for research and determine whether the board or some other agency should undertake the work; 2) designate which portion of the SAB should do the project; and 3) decide the extent of dissemination of completed reports. These steps, General LeMay noted, provided "more intimate guidance to day-to-day activities" of the SAB.[4]

Further changes were forthcoming. Shortly after assuming office, Secretary of Defense Robert S. McNamara instructed his deputy, Roswell Gilpatric, to initiate a review of all DOD advisory committees. While this was taking place, a December 1961 article in The New York Times raised questions about Donald Putt's simultaneous service as SAB chairman and President of United Technology Corporation. The award of a large research contract to United Technology triggered the Times's suspicion. Although Putt had resigned the SAB post two months before the story appeared, Secretary McNamara cancelled all appointments to the board until conflict of interest charges were reviewed. For the time being, the SAB was virtually out of business. It resumed operations with the publication of DOD Directive 5500.8 on March 12,

1962, which standardized the terms of employment of Department of Defense advisory committees. Unfortunately for the SAB, the investigations related to the Putt case brought to McNamara's attention the disproportionately large number of SAB participants. He instructed Air Force Secretary Eugene M. Zuckert to slash the combined membership and consultant rolls "to no more than half [the present 160] and preferably to approximately 20." After discussions among McNamara, Zuckert, and LeMay (in which it was pointed out that the last four Assistant Secretaries of the Air Force for R&D—Gardner, Horner, Perkins, and Charyk—had been SAB members), a compromise was agreed upon. Effective January 1, 1963, 90 members and consultants would be removed from the board's roster, leaving only 70. Zuckert was forced to concede a 56 percent reduction in the total list of SAB scholars.[5]

These two changes--the establishment of a steering committee and a massive reduction in the board's manpower --sapped the SAB's institutional autonomy and vigor, leaving it open to additional reform. Early in spring 1961, General Schriever suggested ways in which the board could be harnessed for specific Air Force needs. He discussed with Putt and his SAB successor, Dr. H. Guyford Stever, the idea of autonomous mini-SABs to provide on-the-spot scientific advice for the ARDC product division commanders. Until now, the board had answered ARDC research requests through its Pentagon offices. Schriever, however, had become accustomed to working intimately with top civilian scientists during his years as Western Development Division Commander and liked the direct contact. At first, many SAB members opposed the concept which seemed to suggest wholly independent SABs, but a May 26, 1961 board report on "Air Force Utilization of Scientific Resources" expressed a willingness by the SAB to provide personnel and guidance for division commanders interested in organizing groups of scientific advisers. Schriever accepted the compromise. The SAB Executive Committee approved it and quickly named the new entities Division Advisory Groups (DAGs). By July 1962 the DAGs had been organized at six product divisions: Electronic Systems, Space Systems, Ballistic Missile Systems, Aeronautical Systems, Foreign Technology, and the Atlantic

Missile Range. The DAGs acted in a purely advisory capacity for the division commanders, each of whom selected the members of his DAG from the SAB roster, academia, RAND, or any other institutions. Through this mechanism, the SAB continued to focus attention on advising the Chief of Staff of the Air Force, at the same time providing scientific insight to the Air Force commands. As one early participant in the DAG process observed, it had the beneficial effect of eliminating the bureaucratic delays inherent in working up through Air Staff channels to the SAB calendar, and down the chain of command once a study had been completed. Despite the occasional need for adjustments in DAG membership (such as those resulting from the drastic reductions in the SAB rolls late in 1962), the DAGs proved to be a highly useful institutional adaptation.[6]

General Schriever initiated other actions aimed at placing long-range science at the service of the weapons acquisition community. He established on January 15, 1960, a new product division devoted solely to basic research. Known as the Air Force Research Division* and commanded by Brig. Gen. Benjamin G. Holzman, a former SAB member, it would supervise basic science contracts through the Air Force Office of Scientific Research (AFOSR); keep abreast of European aerospace developments at ARDC's European Office in Brussels, Belgium; oversee internal aerodynamics R&D at the facilities of the Aeronautical Research Laboratory in Dayton; direct the research programs of the geophysics and electronics directorates of the Cambridge Research Laboratories; and administer basic science projects underway at various ARDC centers. Schriever had high expectations for the new division. As coordinating agency for all Air Force basic research, it promised a more cohesive laboratory program, better funding, and more informed leadership. Most important of all, the Research Division would provide "the most enlightened operating and procurement policies in our relations with university

---

*Redesignated, April 1, 1961, the Air Force Office of Aerospace Research (AFOAR) as a separate operating agency. AFOAR was inactivated on July 1, 1970.

research," undertaking a broad program of study grants to institutions of higher learning.[7]

Perhaps more than any other deed, Schriever's success in transforming ARDC into a total weapons acquisition command reinvigorated the role of Air Force long-range science. He relied on a previous SAB study to carry out his plan. A board report published in June 1958, under the chairmanship of Dr. Stever, provided the basis for Schriever's contention that ARDC must control the weapons acquisition process from conceptual phase to full-scale production. Most importantly, the Stever committee recommended breaking the stranglehold on R&D funds held by the Air Staff Deputy Chief of Staff for Materiel and the Air Materiel Command (AMC). Rather than allow the procurement and logistics people to control 80 percent of the R&D budget, the panel suggested that the Headquarters USAF Deputy Chief of Staff for Research and Development and ARDC regulate appropriations requests. Stever's group also called for streamlining procedures related to approving, designing, funding, and constructing R&D facilities. They also proposed that operating R&D agencies determine their own long-term budget priorities to provide greater stability for exploratory research. Finally, they would allow contractors more generous incentives to undertake research, and assign to ARDC the budgetary authority to procure—not just develop—weapon systems. In short, all of the major AMC functions would be absorbed by ARDC.[8]

Naturally, radical recommendations such as these invited strong resistance. But hard pressed by Soviet advances in space boosters and satellites, General LeMay felt the points raised by the Stever committee must not be allowed to fade into oblivion. He therefore appointed a Weapon Systems Study Group to review the applicability of ICBM concurrent development practices to "the entire spectrum of weapon system management." Institutional relationships between the Air Staff, AMC, and ARDC were high on the agenda. A working group of colonels quickly concluded that if concurrent development required planning the entire life cycle of a weapon system in the conceptual phase, the whole acquisition process must be vested in one command. Since ARDC already managed the preliminary phases of development, the colonels recommended the R&D command absorb all AMC functions related to procurement and budgeting.

No one on the study group supported these views — except General Schriever. After years of debate about the correct course of action, the general decided to make a decisive statement. He drafted his own proposals and on April 26, 1960, submitted them to General Samuel E. Anderson* , chairman of the study group. Schriever urged establishing one command for weapons acquisition and one for logistics, thus ending the struggle for precious resources between the future Air Force and the present Air Force. This plan, too, was shelved, but revived in April 1961 when the U.S.S.R. launched the first manned orbiter in space. Deputy Secretary of Defense Roswell L. Gilpatric† informed Secretary Zuckert that when the USAF put its R&D organization in good order, it would receive the military space mission. Dusted off hurriedly, the Schriever plan went forward for Secretary McNamara's and President Kennedy's approval, which it received in a matter of days. As a consequence, effective April 1, 1961, ARDC and AMC were redesignated the Air Force Systems Command (AFSC) and the Air Force Logistics Command (AFLC), respectively. General Schriever, who pinned on his fourth star with the advent of AFSC, now led a major command in charge of its own scientific destiny, as well as that of the Air Force as a whole.[9]

Despite the organizational overhaul, for months after the formation of AFSC, Secretary Zuckert had a nagging feeling that the USAF lacked the vision and vitality it ought to have. Whether true or not, he felt an "intellectual staleness" had overcome Air Force thinking, and groped for a way to remedy it. He did not want to involve the OSD since oversight was becoming the byword

---

*General Anderson was the AMC Commander and had preceded General Schriever as head of ARDC.
†Gilpatric had close ties to Schriever, dating back to Gilpatric's service as Under Secretary of the Air Force from 1951 to 1953.

of the McNamara years; an Air Force technology forecast might easily mushroom into a drawn out, department-wide analysis. Neither did Zuckert want his own Secretariat involved in the process, fearing delays and endless staffing. At the same time, the undertaking must enjoy the "understanding and leadership...and the enthusiastic participation" of the Air Force Chief of Staff. The answer came to Secretary Zuckert one night as he lay in bed. He would ask General Schriever—who had an "uncanny knack for projecting ideas into the future"—to lead from Headquarters AFSC a comprehensive study of long-range technologies for the USAF.* Zuckert first tried out the idea on Gen. William F. "Bozo" McKee, the Vice Chief of Staff and a man he considered to be "the broadest gauged Air Force officer he dealt with." General McKee encouraged the plan and suggested it be raised with General LeMay. LeMay conceded there was something to it, and gave the project his full support.

Zuckert invited McKee and Schriever to lunch to discuss the undertaking. After lengthy conversation, the Secretary turned to Schriever and asked him to initiate an in-depth survey of the existing state of U.S. air power technology, and to predict where these discoveries might lead in the following five or ten years. Specifically, what did science have to offer to improve the ability of the Air Force to do its mission? He suggested the general include representatives of industry and the other services in order to make the report as comprehensive as possible. Schriever agreed to do it, provided he received a directive signed by Zuckert and LeMay verifying its high priority and authorizing him to use whatever resources needed. The Secretary approved these requests, and General Schriever promptly began one of the most ambitious reviews of aerospace science and technology ever undertaken. Zuckert placed full confidence in Schriever and, except for an occasional progress report, divorced himself from the study during the entire period of its preparation.[10]

Schriever initiated the study upon receipt of a letter from General LeMay dated March 9, 1963, empowering him

_____

*Colonel Ray E. Soper, Deputy for Programming during the study, stated in a 1966 interview that the report

to start the project and act as its director. The Chief of Staff directed him, on a priority basis, to concentrate on the pace of technological change as it related to the principal planning activities of the Air Force during the 1965-1975 time period.

The AFSC Commander and his staff quickly expanded this directive to include the theme of USAF weapons in the context of global realities. In a few weeks they had decided on the essential features of the report. They set as its major objective forecasting the USAF mission five to ten years in the future and linking it to technologies available at that time. The study would concentrate on deficiencies in defense aspects of national policy, strategy, and interservice relationships, prescribing correctives from emerging scientific discoveries. "It was really aimed," remarked General Schriever, "at improving the posture of the U.S. Air Force to do its mission within the framework of U.S. policy and national security objectives."[11]

The practical work of organization went forward at high speed. By mid-April, Major General Charles H. Terhune, Jr.,* Commander of the Electronic Systems Division and Schriever's choice for project manager, had laid on Schriever's desk an organization plan for the study. The report issued by Terhune and his planning group referred to General Schriever's undertaking as <u>Project Forecast</u>, the name by which it has been known ever since. Scheduled for completion in four to five months, Forecast was publicized as an Air Force-wide review, not just an AFSC study. At the working level it consisted of: 1) panels whose members served on a full-time basis; 2) outstanding scientists from industry and academia; and 3) contract researchers for the exploration of special subjects. Schriever, the project director, controlled the proceedings through two deputy directors and a small staff.

---

was initiated "to get the Air Force back into the airplane business" after a decade of preoccupation with missiles. Secretary Zuckert dismissed this as a motive for the study.

*Charles H. Terhune had a distinguished career in Air Force R&D. He earned a bachelor's degree in aeronautical engineering from Purdue University and after com-

His project manager, General Terhune, exercised "full responsibility for the total operational activities" of the working panels, and integrated the technical community into the study through the work of a scientific director. The panels treated Technology; Threat; Policy and Military Considerations; Capability; Costing; and Analysis, Evaluation and Synthesis. Diagram One, "Project Forecast Organization Chart," illustrates the framework of Schriever's study, while Diagram Two, "Project Forecast Flow Chart," provides a schematic of the process by which the panels acted upon one another to achieve consensus.[12]

As a dozen technology panels churned out almost every conceivable scientific breakthrough on the horizon, the members of the threat group reviewed each candidate relative to the potential and existing weapons of hostile powers. The policy committee also sorted all the

---

missioning in the Army Air Corps, reported to the Wright Field Materiel Division, where he helped test the first bullet-proof aircraft fuel tanks. Just before WWII Terhune attended Cal Tech, earning an advanced degree in aeronautical engineering. During the war he worked at Wright Field in the Aircraft Laboratory, and later, in the Fighter Branch of the Engineering Division, where he contributed to the P-59 and P-80 jet programs. Much of the remainder of Terhune's career involved missile development. Between 1947 and 1953 he served on the Air Staff and OSD in the guided missile field. Promoted to colonel, he left Washington for New Mexico to become Director of Development at the Air Force Special Weapons Center. Terhune then went to Los Angeles where he served under General Schriever for six years at the WDD. From 1960 to 1964 he was associated with AFSC's Electronic Systems Division as Deputy Commander and Commander, attaining the ranks of brigadier and major general, respectively. Finally, General Terhune commanded the Aeronautical Systems Division from 1964 to 1967 and, receiving his third star, ended his service as Vice Commander, AFSC.

DIAGRAM 1
Project Forecast Organization Chart

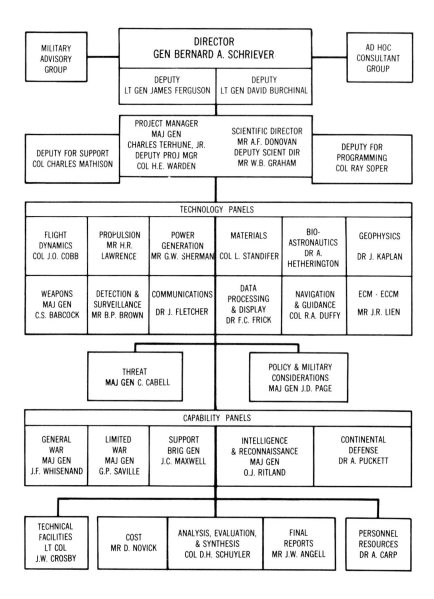

100

DIAGRAM 2
Project Forecast Flow Chart

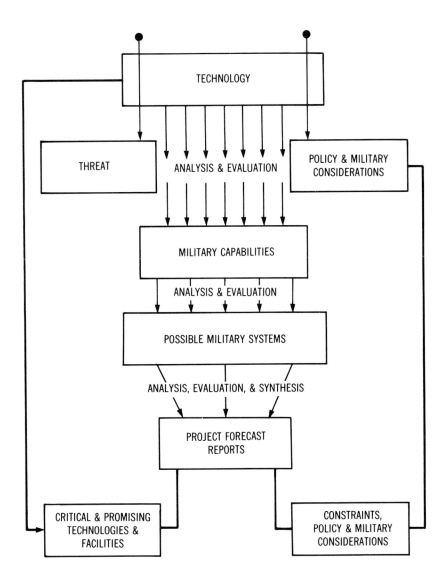

technological possibilities but based its selections on U.S. foreign policy imperatives. Five capability panels examined the proposals which survived the threat and policy screening processes and translated them into weapons and support systems. Finally, the analysis, evaluation, and synthesis committee chose the preferred weapon systems based on cost effectiveness data supplied by the cost panel.

One of General Schriever's most important contributions to the success of Project Forecast was the elaborate network of scientific friends and colleagues whom he had met over the years and could persuade to participate in the study. Schriever enjoyed a fine rapport with most scientists, and his presence alone convinced many to join the project. Ultimately, between 400 and 500 people contributed to the study for various lengths of time. They represented 28 separate Air Force organizations, 13 major government agencies (including the Army, Navy, and Marine Corps), 49 subordinate government agencies, 26 colleges and universities, 70 corporations, and 10 non-profit institutions. The largest such study ever attempted in the DOD, it seemed to one participant "so big...that you just couldn't see how anybody could get their arms around it."[13]

Nonetheless, the same skeptic admitted that Schriever and Terhune did a masterful job of enlisting, organizing, and guiding toward a coherent set of conclusions the huge parade of scientific, military, and technical experts. They exercised direct control over the selection of personnel, picking "sharp guys from...everywhere in the Air Force, Navy, Army." Although directed through AFSC, there were as many officers from SAC, TAC, and the Air Defense Command as there were technical men in uniform. While the project's Military Advisory Group consisted solely of the commanders of all the major Air Force commands, Schriever carefully balanced military and civilian representation on all other panels. Four of six capability committees were chaired by officers, but three-fourths of the technology panels had civilian chairmen.

Schriever relied heavily on his old friends at the SAB for technical advice. Not only were the technology panel chairs of Geophysics and Communications[*] distinguished board members, but almost 60 percent of the Ad Hoc Consultant Group was staffed by men who sat on the SAB, including such top scientists as Gen. (retired) James Doolittle (Director, Thompson, Ramo, Wooldridge, Inc.); Dr. John S. Foster (Director of the Lawrence Livermore Laboratory); Dr. Ivan Getting (President of the Aerospace Corp.), Dr. Charles C. Lauritsen (Prof. Emeritus, Physics, Cal Tech); Maj. Gen. (retired) James McCormack (Vice President, MIT); Dr. Simon Ramo (Vice Chairman, Thompson, Ramo, Wooldridge); Dr. Herbert York (Chancellor, University of California); and Dr. H. Guyford Stever (Chairman, Department of Mechanical Engineering, MIT, and chairman of the SAB).

General Schriever also enlisted the help of the National Academy of Sciences to provide "a committee of distinguished scientists to advise him and his senior staff on scientific...questions of...long-range importance to the Air Force." This the NAS agreed to do through June 1964.[14]

Schriever chose familiar ground on which to conduct the study. He located it at AFSC's Space Systems Division, Inglewood, California, where proximity to Cal Tech and many of the nation's great aerospace firms afforded the same advantages he had found when he commanded the Western Development Division from the rooms of the Little Red Schoolhouse. A portion of the west coast organization was located at the Santa Monica facilities of the RAND Corporation. General Terhune assumed program management responsibilities on April 15, 1963, and the initial task force cadre held its first sessions in California during the last week of the month. Schriever spent most of the peak study months of June and July in Los Angeles, during which time the committees assembled in full strength. The general participated in briefings to the Ad Hoc Consultant Group and the Senior Military Advisory Group, and directly guided the panels in

_____

*Respectively, Dr. Joseph Kaplan, Prof. of Physics, U.C.L.A., and Dr. James C. Fletcher, Vice President, Aerojet General.

their early deliberations. A gradual phase-down began in August, and by the last week in September a Forecast special staff of twenty drawn from the California contingent began operating at Headquarters Air Force Systems Command with the nickname "Forecast East." Organized in a hangar on the Andrews Air Force Base flight line, this group served on the commander's staff. It formed the panels' raw findings into a final report and prepared oral presentations for a number of audiences. The Forecast East group also introduced the conclusions into the Systems Command programming and budgeting process and monitored Headquarters AFSC activities to achieve conformity with Forecast recommendations. Despite the original intention of concluding Forecast by September or October 1963, the special staff continued working through winter 1963-1964.[15]

With the informal approval of the top Air Force leadership, Generals Schriever and Terhune decided in fall 1963 to elicit public support by prematurely releasing some of its preliminary findings to the media. In speeches and press coverage Americans began to hear what the future held for aerospace research. Sifting the California phase of Forecast, Schriever proclaimed in print and before audiences that, contrary to some prevailing scientific thought, aerospace science had not yet reached a technological plateau. Many in the OSD believed that after the brilliant successes of the ballistic missile program, the manned aircraft and its entire technology had become passe. Not only had the F-108 interceptor been cancelled, but steady pressure had been applied to cancel the mach -three B-70 bomber. To make his point, Schriever presented evidence from Forecast which indicated the potential for enormous strides in a number of piloted aircraft; indeed, one panel identified over forty possible new systems. The main areas of improvement envisioned greater range and endurance, larger payload-to-weight ratios, and more efficient propulsion. High payoff technologies in the fields of materials, engines, flight dynamics, guidance, and computers promised significant advances during the 1970-1975 period, especially in logistics operations, VTOL and STOL transports, and bombers.[16]

General Schriever carried these and other conclusions of the Forecast panels with him to an AFSC Commanders' Conference, held at Maxwell Air Force Base, Alabama, on November 13 and 14, 1963. Attended by General LeMay and all AFSC field commanders, it featured two days of briefings by the project's committee chairs. Schriever told his listeners at the end of the sessions that the Pentagon had so far supported the Forecast interpretation of national policy goals, based upon the principle of "limited and balanced deterrence through flexible and controlled response." This framework, he believed, provided "plenty of license to build the kind of Air Force which will implement [the policy goals]." He stressed that neither Zuckert nor LeMay wanted the panel reports to serve as "action" or implementation documents, but only as "blueprints" for the future. Hence, Schriever said firmly, "there will be no [organizational] end runs; everything is going to go through the system, through established channels; no surprises; the actions will be ground into the [existing] machinery [of AFSC]."

The general could afford to speak firmly. He had already presented Forecast briefings to Zuckert and LeMay on September 3; to Deputy Secretary of Defense Roswell L. Gilpatric and the Defense Director for Research and Engineering (DDR&E), Harold Brown, on September 23; and to Secretary McNamara on October 24. Every listener liked what he heard. In fact, based on the preliminary Forecast results, McNamara invited Schriever to submit appropriate adjustments in the fiscal year (FY) 1965 RDT&E budget. To allow the opportunity, the Secretary delayed printing the proposed DOD budget until late November, by which time the President would have to see it. Schriever's amendments reached McNamara's desk on November 22, 1963, the day of President Kennedy's assassination. Government activity ground to a standstill, and the Project Forecast recommendations failed to enter the 1965 budget, an unfortunate setback for its implementation.[17]

Nonetheless, as the Forecast East staff readied the report for publication, early in 1964 it was briefed before the House of Representatives and the Senate. Assistant

Secretary of the Air Force for R&D Dr. Alexander Flax first brought it to the attention of Congress. Testifying on January 22, 1964, before the House Armed Services Sub-Committee on Research and Development, Dr. Flax praised the project's scope and complexity and stated that aspects of it were being incorporated into the planning process. He also promised future budget requests for the C-X (later C-5) heavy transport aircraft. Secretary Zuckert expressed genuine satisfaction with Forecast during a February 4, 1964, hearing before the House Armed Services Committee. Schriever's study represented "a concerted attempt to step back and, against the background of the basic problems of national security, try to assess how advancing technology of the next decade could affect the Air Force in meeting these problems." Zuckert told the Congressmen that Forecast provided an objective analysis of long-term requirements, avoiding "pat recommendations" and clearing the way for significant changes in USAF R&D activities. In an era of hard choices involving limited funding, high cost, and long delivery dates for weapon systems, Forecast painstakingly selected those technologies from which the Air Force could expect optimal returns for each dollar invested.[18]

Finally, on February 26, General LeMay, appearing before the House Committee on Appropriations Sub-Committee on DOD Appropriations, explained the link between strategy and weaponry. The chief reason for Forecast, he said, was "to see whether our strategy matched up with the hardware that we now have and foresee coming forward...." [19]

When Project Forecast was at last released in final form, the Congress, the DOD, and the Air Force knew a good deal about its contents. After a half year of intense labor, in the early days of March 1964 the Forecast East Final Report Working Group presented the Director's Report to General Schriever. On March 12—almost one year to the day since the Chief of Staff's initial directive—the AFSC Commander forwarded copies of the study to Secretary Zuckert and General LeMay.

In its structure and conclusions, Schriever had tried to incorporate national policy questions into evaluations of appropriate technology. After careful review of strategic thinking, the Forecast staff decided that no single doctrine accounted for existing or projected weapon systems. Discarding the prevailing view that massive retaliation or mutual assured destruction safeguarded the world from war, Schriever endorsed the idea that major conventional or tactical nuclear wars might have to be fought, and could be won. Moreover, the general felt both types of conflict could be prosecuted without the onset of global nuclear war. He pointed out that Soviet advances in propulsion, aircraft, missiles, and space, had increased their capacity to fight prolonged conventional wars and tactical nuclear engagements. Their advanced technology programs, stated the Forecast Director's Report, could lead the U.S.S.R. to new military capabilities beyond those of the United States.[20]

Based on this analysis of Soviet science and the potential for entirely new categories of military action, Forecast argued the necessity of preserving the superiority of the strategic deterrence force. At the same time, its authors stated the case for a genuine flexible response policy, capable of repelling all acts of aggression short of total nuclear war. Under the thermonuclear umbrella, unpredictable local or regional situations might involve the U.S. in a variety of military engagements. Recognizing that American leaders might not be in a position to choose the weapons of future wars, development of "controlled nuclear response" technology would provide protection should the need present itself. Successful use of such weaponry depended on a manned bomber system with full command and control; pinpoint delivery accuracy to minimize the strength of nuclear yields; and warheads which caused minimal collateral damage. The ability to wage war after a tactical nuclear encounter implied improved theater air mobility using highly mobile VTOL aircraft and a logistics apparatus independent of fixed bases.[21]

To achieve these objectives during limited conflicts, the technology panels reviewed scientific progress with four criteria in mind: direct usefulness to national security, a high chance of practical success, the likelihood of a major advancement over presently projected systems, and reasonable cost. A number of technologies met all four qualifications. Revolutionary improvements in materials science--particularly in high strength boron filaments and oxide-dispersion strengthened metals--opened new vistas for aircraft construction. Boron filaments, ten times stronger than steel and with far less density, could be combined with plastic binders to reduce vehicle dead weights by as much as three-fourths. Drastic increases in heat resistance of up to several hundred degrees appeared likely using a technique in which thorium oxide particles were microscopically dispersed in the chemical structure of various metals. In practical terms, these two technologies might result in large cargo transports able to carry perhaps four times the tonnage of existing models; cargo planes up to two million pounds gross weight; and high performance VTOL aircraft.[22]

The materials breakthroughs had far-reaching implications for engine designs. Increased operating temperatures and higher speeds on the tips of rotating machinery might lead to turbofan engines with radically reduced fuel consumption. Both global transports and long-endurance combat aircraft would profit greatly from such advances. Turbofan engines might also be used for flexible performance aircraft which could fly high/low, subsonic/supersonic missions, yet avoid the instability inherent in varying wing geometry in flight. High thrust-to-weight ratio propulsion systems made possible very survivable VTOL engines for conventional warfare. Liquid hydrogen power plants held for next generation reconnaissance aircraft the promise of extremely high altitudes and speeds of up to mach six. A practical, reusable space launch vehicle only awaited a solution to the cooling problems of high pressure oxygen-hydrogen rocket engines. Flight dynamics research also revealed path-finding discoveries. Improved laminar flow control could reduce aerodynamic drag as much as 50 percent in subsonic vehicles. If used selectively, the variable geometry wing would permit heretofore impossible combinations of flight characteristics: subsonic cruise, high speed penetration at low levels, supersonic dash at high altitudes, and STOL. Finally, research suggested that the operating temperatures of high-speed engines might be reduced by injecting a thin film of coolant into the boundary layer of an aircraft's wings, thus cutting drag and improving engine efficiency.[23]

Like swept wing technology, the study of tactical nuclear weaponry had matured. Included in this category were enhanced radiation weapons, that is, fission-fusion devices which emitted a flash of radiation against enemy personnel with very little blast, heat, or radiological damage. Suppressed radiation warheads also fell under the category of fission-fusion weaponry, but drastically reduced radioactive contamination by lowering the yield of the fission component and reducing the output of neutrons from the fusion component. The most promising of the tactical nuclear weapons, known as pure-fusion bombs, would release very low yields and be more effective, cheaper, and cause less collateral damage than the others.[24]

Guidance technology kept pace with warhead improvements. Optical image matching techniques promised to make possible air-to-ground missiles with a circular error of probability (CEP) of only ten feet. Demonstrations suggested that ICBMs, aided by better inertial instruments and more accurate geodetic information, could be guided to targets within a CEP of one-tenth of a nautical mile. In addition, extremely advanced computers were being developed to guide missiles and do a number of other high-speed, precision tasks necessary for a controlled and flexible response policy.[25]

What did these discoveries foretell for new weapon systems? An Advanced Manned Precision Strike System (AMPSS) was recommended for "highly discriminate nuclear operations under stringent command and control conditions." As a complement to the long-range ballistic missile, AMPSS offered the advantage of operation independent of forward basing conditions. Advanced turbofan engines and the variable geometry wing allowed long range, STOL, and large load-carrying capacity. To enhance AMPSS stand-off capability over enemy skies, the Forecast staff proposed developing extremely accurate air-to-surface projectiles known as Hitting Missiles. Fired ten miles from its target,

the Hitting Missile would strike within ten feet of its
objective. It would deliver very low yield nuclear devices
on such sites as bridges, missile launchers, and underground
command posts.[26]

Two roles were envisioned for VTOL aircraft:
strike-reconnaissance and light transport. The high
thrust-to-weight lift engine endowed VTOL aircraft with
the most important capabilities for limited war and
counterinsurgency operations: ground survivability; flight
over enemy territory at low altitude and high speed; and
extensive ferry range for rapid, global deployment. Light
transport with VTOL would satisfy intra-theater operations.
The same new engines which powered strike-reconnaissance
aircraft would also provide propulsion for high-speed
transports able to lift several tons of material from points
of embarkation directly to areas of engagement. Allowing
pinpoint dispersal of supplies to many distant and remote
sites, the VTOL light transport would also improve theater
survivability by reducing the number of large
concentrations of materiel and aircraft.[27]

Paramount among Project Forecast recommendations
was development of the CX-X large cargo transport. It
too fit the mold of quick response to sub-nuclear military
emergencies. The CX-X exploited advances in propulsion
and aerodynamics, resulting in an aircraft of vast range,
enormous capacity, and independence from intermediate
bases. By transporting large numbers of personnel, as well
as such heavy and odd-shaped cargo as helicopters and
tanks directly to the war zone, in a matter of hours
American air and ground power could be projected to
almost any region on earth.[28]

Finally, the Forecast staff pointed out five potential
programs which might benefit from emerging technologies
and radically improve existing aerospace capabilities:
better ICBM accuracy; mobile air defense (basing advanced
radars on long-range aircraft such as the CX-X); a manned
orbiting laboratory (MOL) to test man's usefulness in
space-based surveillance and launch procedures; a reusable
space launch vehicle using new materials and high
temperature chamber rockets to greatly reduce take-off

costs; and hypersonic aircraft, a by-product of hydrogen-fueled engines which would sustain flight inside and outside the earth's atmosphere.[29]

Taken as a whole, Project Forecast kept clearly in view the fundamental presuppositions of American military strategy. Working from these bases toward technological solutions, it presented a highly focused, clear agenda for improving U.S. military security. The report admitted the United States had already taken steps to improve its aerial capabilities "in the higher and lower end of the conflict spectrum," defined respectively as all-out nuclear attack on the one hand, and counterinsurgency on the other. Between these poles, Forecast proposed technologies to strengthen the large middle area between nuclear holocaust and 'brushfire' engagements, suggesting a broader range of response to potential aggression. Specifically, air power for tactical nuclear and prolonged conventional warfare must be developed. A dangerous lack of deterrence in this middle zone of conflict demanded the U.S. fill the void with appropriate new weapon systems.[30]

From the outset, Schriever faced the problem of adapting USAF thinking to the Forecast process. He worked with the Forecast East staff to accustom the Air Force to the project's methodology. Indeed, since the course of scientific exploration could not be predicted and new discoveries having military applications might be uncovered at any time, Schriever felt Forecast "should not begin and end with...a single summary report. Rather, it should be an open-ended, live, and continuing effort...updated at periodic intervals to reflect important changes in technology, the world environment, and national policy objectives." In pursuit of this goal, the general once more took the Forecast message to the public. He again identified a number of promising technologies, and warned in articles and speeches that the security of the nation depended on capitalizing on these possibilities, turning projections into weapon systems. His work paid off. The beneficial effects of the study seemed apparent; it not only shaped popular attitudes toward air power research, but focused the collective Air Force mind on the future. Almost immediately, AFSC laboratory activity intensified in the fields of materials, propulsion, navigation and guidance, and electronics/computers.[31]

On the strength of these hopeful early signs, General Schriever initiated several highly visible development programs based on the Forecast recommendations. During March 1964, the same month in which the Forecast Director's Report was published, the Aeronautical Systems Division (ASD) began airframe, propulsion, and program definition studies for the CX-X (later C-5A) heavy cargo aircraft. So confident was Schriever of its technical feasibility that even before the CX-X engines had been fabricated or tested, he shortened the time of its initial operational capability (IOC) by almost three years, from late 1971 to early 1969. A half year after the completion of Forecast, the USAF approved procurement of three squadrons of C-5A transports. Forecast also resulted in the opening of AFSC program offices for the Manned Orbiting Laboratory and the medium-sized VTOL cargo aircraft.

General Schriever also undertook development of the Hitting Missile. Highly accurate and lethal in a single pass, this next generation air-to-ground weapon offered the capability of striking fixed targets from stand-off distances, well outside the range of defensive weapons. The Hitting Missile would improve close air support and interdiction and deliver either low yield nuclear or high explosive warheads. General Schriever got the Hitting Missile underway in April 1964, when he established an ASD office to design, develop, test, and acquire the new weapon.* [32]

Not content just to initiate major programs, Schriever directed periodic Forecast implementation reviews from his staff. Establishing program offices was one thing; quite another to bring advanced technologies to fruition. The first major implementation review, entitled "Project Forecast Program Status," dated November 30, 1964, simply

---

*At the same time Schriever inaugurated the Hitting Missile office, he also initiated the AGM-X Short Range Attack Missile (SRAM) program, also at ASD.

concentrated on projecting schedules for Forecast-related systems and plotting budgets. During the summer of 1965 the twelve Forecast panel chairmen met with General Schriever to discuss progress in fulfilling the goals of the report. They found that, despite lack of progress in some areas for technical or management reasons, there was generally "good progress" in implementing the Forecast proposals and "many examples of technical advances" which underscored the validity of the original study. The panel chairs did not feel a mass updating of the scientific content of Forecast had become necessary, but some did suggest drafting specialized, ad hoc reports to account for new technical knowledge.

One year later, this positive outlook had all but vanished. Expenditures for U.S. military involvement in Southeast Asia, as well as prolonged administration efforts to bring to bear management efficiencies in the DOD, resulted in severe reductions in the budgets of Forecast programs. A Forecast Situation Report of July 1966 traced a pattern of funding cuts in Air Force R&D dating back to 1961. Contrary to published reports of a threefold increase in these outlays, a steady decline characterized the 1961 to 1966 period. Vietnam War costs and tighter management controls were not the only problems; General Schriever sensed in the top DOD leadership an unmistakable technological conservatism, a reliance on "off the shelf" R&D. Consequently, scientists and engineers working on the most advanced projects envisioned by Forecast felt little incentive to strive for the far reaches of the state of the art. Worse still, weapon system programs in development, many of which also had their origins in Forecast, had been so stunted by fiscal malnourishment that Schriever began to talk of a "technologically stagnant force." The general lamented an American air power establishment based upon the F/B-111, the product of current technology; a C-5A, which grossly compromised the very long range and composite materials character of the original CX-X; a low risk C-142B program rather than Forecast's CV-X, the advanced V/STOL transport; and a technically conservative V/STOL fighter developed cooperatively with West Germany, in place of a more effective American-made close-support, vertical/short take-off and landing aircraft.[33]

HARNESSING THE GENIE

An AFSC Task Force Report on Technology Program Trends issued in August 1966—the month in which General Schriever retired—condemned even more sharply these and other dilutions of the original intent of Forecast. Complaining of a "series of strictures on its military R&D effort which inhibit technological progress," it reported that the 1966 research and development funding level represented a ten-year low. The task force endorsed wholeheartedly the DOD policy of diverting most of its wherewithal toward Southeast Asia requirements. But it also recognized the current crash efforts to adapt technically to the war as the "result of prior short-term thinking", which characterized R&D funding between 1961 and 1966. Future crash programs were already in the making as crucial Forecast technology programs had almost ground to a standstill. The filaments/composites projects had suffered severe funding reductions. Within three years, eight separate composites development plans had been submitted by AFSC, only to be whittled down by higher DOD authorities to an insignificant seventeen percent of the proposed budgets. Forecast's projection of a highly accurate ICBM guidance system had also fallen on hard budgetary times. The next generation ballistic missile guidance development program was disapproved in 1964. Development of the scramjet, a manned hypersonic vehicle with expected speeds of between mach four and eight, had been all but stopped when a coordinated technology plan to develop its combustion, materials, and flight dynamics was slashed to less than twenty percent of proposed funding. Consequently, completion of these three Forecast brainchildren had been effectively postponed from the 1970s to the 1980s. The task force foresaw grave dangers to long-term national security should the trend continue. Development programs approved for funding in 1965-1966 depended on technologies at least five years old, far behind those recommended by Forecast. The report warned that "continual funding restrictions, [and] procedural and policy limitations mitigating against bold new proposals will impose a technological plateau on USAF military technology where none exists among potential opposing forces." The real dangers of technological surprise followed by costly and ill-conceived crash programs loomed larger the longer Schriever's agenda was not implemented.[34]

Despite the apparent cloud of pessimism shrouding General Schriever's departure from AFSC and the Air Force, most observers and participants agreed that Project Forecast was a highly significant and effective undertaking. The Director of the Air Force Avionics Laboratory, Mr. Peter R. Murray, was deeply involved in drafting and implementing Forecast. He argued that regardless of budget cutting in such programs as boron composites, hundreds of people had been exposed to this and other ideas during the Forecast sessions. When the scientists and engineers returned to their own offices after making their contributions to the project, they brought zeal and new insights down to the lowest levels of the Air Force, industry, and academia. Murray recalled that their enthusiasm for the new research prompted them to insert monies into local budgets to follow-up on the most promising lines of inquiry. Hence, while advanced technology funding stagnated during the McNamara years, Forecast stimulated basic research at the working level, which would manifest itself in practical terms when R&D outlays increased during the mid-1970s. But even by the most concrete standards, Forecast did achieve some remarkable successes.

Dr. Alexander Flax, Assistant Secretary of the Air Force for Research and Development from 1963 to 1969, attributed three major weapon system breakthroughs to General Schriever's project. The high bypass engine for the C-5 aircraft introduced a new core structure which opened up hitherto unknown thrust and range capabilities in atmospheric propulsion. Dr. Flax called the high strength composite findings of Forecast a radical advancement for aerospace technology and the principal reason these materials were eventually incorporated in aircraft design. Finally, he praised the development of the Hitting Missile as one of the greatest accomplishments of the Forecast team.[35]

Ten years later, reflecting on his tenure as AFSC Commander, General Schriever adopted the views of Flax and Murray. He admitted a decade after the study that the portions on exploratory development had been faithfully carried out. He also saw hope for intra-theater airlift in the Advanced Medium Range Short Take-Off-and-Landing (AMST) aircraft, conceded great improvements in ICBM guidance, and spoke optimistically about production of tactical nuclear weapons. The A-X (later A-10) close air support program and the "smart" bombs used late in the Vietnam War likewise had their origins in Project Forecast. Calling the report "a hell of an exercise," Schriever proposed that the Defense Director of Research and Engineering* periodically undertake like studies to impart clearer direction to Air Force R&D. He hoped thus to curb the existing practice of "the guy who squawks the loudest and gets the most contacts...gets something going."

Eugene Zuckert agreed with the general's assessment of Forecast's importance, and attributed its success to Schriever's freedom of action. The Secretary may have contributed the essential idea of Forecast, but he gave Schriever a totally free hand to determine its direction and methodology. He received occasional progress reports from the AFSC Commander, but otherwise kept the Secretariat out of the picture. "Schriever outdid himself," he said later, combining a profound knowledge of the development process with wide-ranging contacts among civilian scientists. Indeed, the general's friendly ties to the scientific community, more than anything else, persuaded the Secretary that he should be the catalyst to revitalize USAF thinking.

Forecast pleased Zuckert for several reasons. Its participants had reviewed thoroughly the existing state of air power science. They charted a new course for USAF R&D based upon a rigorous process of selecting the most appropriate emerging technologies. More important, the study helped the Air Force view its mission in a global perspective. Rather than any single proposal, Zuckert felt Forecast proved its worth by engendering a true institutional self-examination. Looking back on his achievements as Secretary of the Air Force, Zuckert was proudest of Project Forecast and considered it his greatest accomplishment in office. Though he spent no more than

---

*Since renamed the Under Secretary of Defense for Research and Engineering (USDR&E).

twenty hours and General LeMay devoted as little as fifteen minutes to it, Zuckert called Forecast a great success. He attributed its effectiveness to Schriever's skill and to full USAF support at the highest levels. Most important, it was "a good idea which was followed through."[36]

* * *

Ironically, but unintentionally, Project Forecast contributed to the diminution of the status of the USAF SAB. More precisely, Forecast served to draw attention to the progressive narrowing of the board's focus. During the 1940s and 1950s, the SAB's reports generally concerned themselves with the broad science issues of the Air Force: ten year forecasts of aircraft technology, turbo-propulsion, atomic weapons, boundary layer control, and so on. But starting in 1960 the board began to investigate increasingly detailed subject matter. During the SAB's first fifteen years, on average only five percent of its reports dealt with specific weapon systems; after 1959 about thirty percent of all studies involved advice on particular weapons. The change was truly sudden. In 1959 the board wrote one such report; in 1960 it wrote six. Persistently over the next twenty-five years it devoted much of its time to very specific subjects, rather than broader reports. As the Air Force asked more detailed questions, the SAB found itself less able to answer the large ones.

The problem of shorter focus, then, began to affect the SAB just a year or two before the highly influential Forecast was completed. The von Karman heritage of SAB preeminence in the long scientific view seemed challenged by Forecast, a study produced wholly under the auspices of Air Force Systems Command. Early in 1964 the SAB was given an opportunity to win back some of its lost prestige. While the Forecast East staff was busy preparing the Director's Report for Schriever, at a January 7 SAB Steering Committee meeting LeMay asked the board to report on the long-range capability and potential of USAF tactical warfare. Secretary Zuckert supported the undertaking. Adhering to General Schriever's emphasis on improving the Air Force's capability to fight conventional wars, the SAB panel hoped to augment Forecast's work on tactical air technology. In doing so, the authors would break what had become the common SAB practice of writing reports on specific, rather than general, technological subjects. In a sense, the project for LeMay represented an opportunity for the SAB to return to the Toward New Horizons model.

Soon after the board's January meeting, Dr. Leonard S. Sheingold, member of the SAB Executive Committee and electronics panel, was named director of the Tactical Air Capabilities Task Force. During February and March 1964 he canvassed the Office of the Defense Director for Research and Engineering and visited Air Force officials--including Secretary Zuckert--for insights into the tactical air problem. After also taking SAB suggestions at the spring meetings, Sheingold began to assemble panels from among his colleagues on the board, as well as representatives from the Army, Navy, Atomic Energy Commission, academia, RAND, IDA, MITRE, the Lincoln Laboratory, and industry labs. During the summer, eight working groups were established: Aircraft, Logistics, Reconnaissance, Command and Control, Navigation and Strike, Weapons and Munitions, Test and Evaluation, and Support (Meteorology and Engineering Geology). Added to the eighty panel members (thirty-seven of whom were drawn from the SAB rolls), were forty officers selected from the Air Staff, TAC, AFSC, AFLC, and the Office of Scientific Research. Despite the diversity, all but one of the working group chairs were SAB members. Both General Schriever, who sat on the board's Executive Committee and advised Sheingold on conducting the study, and Secretary Zuckert, praised the composition of the panels. They especially liked the inclusion of military personnel, who added an operational perspective.[37]

The Steering Group of the Tactical Air Capabilities Task Force (comprised of Dr. Sheingold, Mr. James F. Healey, and the working group chairmen)[*] held its first meeting in May 1964 at TAC Headquarters with the TAC Commander, Gen. Walter Sweeney, in attendance. Aware

---

*The panel chairs included Dr. Murray Geisler of RAND, and these SAB members: Prof. Courtland D. Perkins, Dr. Jack Ruina, Dr. William H. Radford, Dr. Seymour W.

of the group's interest in the low and middle spectrum of conflict, General Sweeney suggested they concentrate on four areas: improved night and weather capability; V/STOL applications to assault airlift; an advanced tactical air control system; and support equipment of reduced weight and size. Thirty-five meetings and twelve months later, these issues were reflected in the findings of the task force. The panel members closely followed Dr. Sheingold's advice to seek practical, rather than highly technical solutions, and to couple these ideas to factors of timeliness and cost effectiveness. But unlike Project Forecast, whose methodology emphasized comprehensiveness and the widest possible integration of scientific, military, and national policy issues, this study remained faithful to the traditional SAB approach. The task force simply divided into technological categories the various tactical air problems. While the Steering Group did attempt to recast the panel findings into groups of weapon system families, the report essentially reflected the technical backgrounds of the SAB members.[38]

The Aircraft Working Group predicted the greatest breakthroughs for tactical air power in the field of propulsion. High thrust-to-weight ratios, specific fuel consumption, and volume efficiency provided the basis for new capabilities such as operational V/STOL and lightweight fighters. Logistics for the tactical mission required improvement by incorporating in field test exercises relevant factors like supply, repair, and maintenance. More importantly, logistics considerations must be evident in the design phases of fighters and transports, taking into account deployment and dispersal requirements. Tactical reconnaissance operations were found lacking in two respects: field testing of visual—and visually aided—detection needed to be more realistic to take into account speed, altitude, visibility, weather, and geography; and better cooperation between reconnaissance users and the R&D community was required in order to determine at the earliest point in the development process mutual objectives and standards of performance. Lacking a

---

Herwald, Dr. Albert Latter, Mr. Richard Horner, Dr. William Kellogg, and Dr. John C. Reed.

coherent national policy, command and control of tactical operations required an "unambiguous national doctrine" which dictated missions and command and control capabilities. Existing command and control redundancies and technical incompatabilities in off-the-shelf equipment would end when policy dictated components, rather than the reverse. The Navigation/Strike Working Panel offered a number of important technological avenues, including countering the surface-to-air missile threat by developing stand-off missiles of greater than fifty miles range. Multipurpose avionics development, as well as accelerated exploration of improved infrared sensors for night operations, ought to be given the highest priority.

Among the more promising technologies uncovered by the Weapons and Munitions panel were controlled fragmentation area weapons and high accuracy projectiles guided by electro-optical homing methods for use against hard targets. Both weapons would "greatly improve" tactical strike effectiveness. The Test and Evaluation Working Group found that the Air Force relied too heavily on tests, which "alone will rarely provide a measure of combat effectiveness." Instead, the interactive process of analysis, simulation, and testing must be undertaken, from which a repository of reliable results may be compiled as a guideline for future tests. Finally, the effects on tactical air power of weather and geological surveys was reviewed by the support panel. The Meteorology Working Group proposed intensive research on overflights of bases on TAC deployment routes, aerial refueling, and visibility over combat zones. Geological reconnaissance surveys promised dividends to tactical air by taking into account the nature of soils, vegetation, and terrain in planning the locations of forward operational bases.[39]

The Tactical Air Capabilities Task Force Report had a far different reception than Project Forecast. Although praised warmly both by Secretary of the Air Force Harold Brown[*] and Air Force Chief of Staff General John P. McConnell,[†] it was consigned to a wide-ranging process

---

[*]Brown succeeded Secretary Zuckert on October 1, 1965.
[†]McConnell succeeded General LeMay on February 1, 1965.

of review and comment by the Air Staff. Its contents were briefed to Secretary Brown, General McConnell, and select staff members on June 29, 1966, and 1 month later given broad distribution. The SAB and Deputy Chief of Staff for Research and Development distributed some 374 copies of the 9-volume study. With the approval of General McConnell, the Deputy Chief of Staff for Research and Development, Lt. Gen. James Ferguson, initiated a "careful examination" of the report to prepare a unified Air Force position on its findings.

A group of nine Air Staff officers, each expert in the subject matter of one of the Tactical Air Task Force volumes, assembled in early September to write the USAF's corporate viewpoint. But contributors to the review were not limited to representatives of interested directorates; major Air Force commands, as well as several Army and Navy agencies, all added inputs. Indeed, a total of seventy-five separate organizations were asked to submit critiques.

Directions issued by the Headquarters Air Force Directorate of Operational Requirements spelled out the desired format: for each SAB recommendation a parallel Air Force reply was requested, in which the USAF stated how it would comply or why it should deviate from the report. To promote free discussion, these remarks would "be for Air Force use only and...not be sent to the SAB." A strict schedule paced the review, the final product of which would be scrutinized by General Ferguson before being sent to General McConnell and Secretary Brown. However, delays in receiving replies from some of the participants hampered the progress of the compilers in Operational Requirements. After two extensions of Ferguson's August 31 deadline for directorate submissions, the Air Force reply was finally briefed to him on December 15, 1966.[40]

The presentation General Ferguson heard and the final Air Force response to the task force report praised the SAB study; but in much greater proportion, it argued that the USAF had already undertaken most of the recommended actions. In several instances, the Air Force respondents disagreed sharply with the board's findings. The tepid reaction to the report might be explained in part by the struggle the Air Force had been waging to adapt to the war in Southeast Asia. In this context, news that the service was not well prepared to fight a conventional war might not be well received. On the other hand, the task force did not seem to recognize the most recent tactical warfare improvements. For example, the Air Force reply to the logistics volume stated explicitly that the Vietnam conflict had already produced "a shift in emphasis in tactical capabilities towards conventional warfare." The reconnaissance review wondered why the task force called for better exploitation of existing intelligence data, yet at the same time suggested research on new hardware and sensors. Those who studied the command and control recommendations admitted that in the past the field did lack clearly defined objectives; but "in recent months," said the Air Force rebuttal, reduced interservice differences had resulted in better unity of operation. Similarly, the navigation/strike proposals to develop night flight, foliage penetration, stand-off air-to-air missiles, and multipurpose avionics all met with a discussion of on-going and parallel USAF activities. Likewise, references to existing programs—area weapons and electro-optical homing devices—were made in answer to the weapons and munitions volume. Only in the fields of aircraft, test and evaluation, and support did the SAB report and the USAF review substantially coincide.

As Secretary Brown hinted in a letter transmitting the Air Force comments to Dr. Stever, the Tactical Air Capabilities Task Force had produced a conservative document with few doctrinal, organizational, or technological initiatives not already undertaken by the USAF. He agreed with its conclusion that in the past the Air Force had not concentrated sufficiently on preparing for "middle and lower levels of conflict." But he argued that as a result of new concepts, equipment, and training, a "marked increase" had occurred lately in the ability of U.S. air power to fight conventional wars.[41]

* * *

Inevitably, the report of the SAB Task Force suffered in comparison to Project Forecast. But the fault did not lie entirely—or even mainly—with the board. The political climate of the Vietnam War rendered academic service to the Air Force a highly unpopular activity, and many who might have contributed their insights were warned off by the fear of campus harassment. Moreover, while the SAB underwent reorganization, retrenchment, and a narrowing of focus during the early 1960s, General Schriever was consolidating his power at ARDC and AFSC. As commander, he had at his disposal far more human and financial wherewithal than the SAB could muster. He also had the personal support of Secretary Zuckert, who fathered the Forecast idea, as well as the blessing of General LeMay. Perhaps more important than these factors, General Schriever had long stood at the forefront in attempting to reinvigorate long-range Air Force science. Within months of the last Woods Hole meeting, the mantle of USAF basic science fell from the aging hands of Dr. von Karman to the waiting grasp of General Schriever. Through Donald Putt, the ARDC Commander had come to know von Karman and many of the original SAB members. Here Schriever learned firsthand what the scientist could do for the Air Force, how he approached problems, and what he needed to succeed. Schriever's answer to the sluggish state of Air Force science was simple, but brilliant: combine in one institution civilian science and military objectives, and strike an appropriate balance between the two. While maintaining the visionary spirit of von Karman, Schriever connected science to national policy and practical military requirements. In transforming ARDC to AFSC, he provided the institutional framework for rejuvenation. On one hand, he added production and procurement—weapons acquisition functions—to the command. On the other, he strengthened its scientific base by adding the Division Advisory Groups and the Air Force Research Division.

Having begun the job of linking science to weapons acquisition, Schriever had the chance to widen his influence with Zuckert's invitation to do Project Forecast. He made the very most of this opportunity. Under his direct supervision, Forecast assembled the largest and most

diverse body of aeronautical scientists and engineers ever
assembled for a single report. His long-standing contacts
in academia, the SAB, industry, and government paid off
handsomely. Just as significant, he and General Terhune
organized the project so that the most advanced scientific
ideas were measured against the "real-world" standards of
cost-effectiveness, national policy aims, and military
utility. The results received the best praise of all:
eventual implementation.

The Tactical Air Capability Report, completed toward
the end of the Schriever era, gave the USAF Scientific
Advisory Board the opportunity to prove it could still
provide the Air Force with broad-based, long-term
technical advice. Its panels included academics and
military people, and its final report attempted to link
technological progress to such factors as organization and
tactics. Unlike Forecast, however, the study lacked a
military sponsor who would encourage the exercise of
scientific imagination, but at the same time test the
findings against potential weapon system applications.
Unfortunately, the product offended none, pleased few, and
lacked a strong supporter to "sell" its case. The report's
lukewarm reception on the Air Staff raised a question
lurking since Woods Hole times: should civilian scientists
hold only highly circumscribed roles in the counsels of the
Air Force. Unluckily for USAF science forecasting, the
idea of a limited role for independent science gained
credence about the time of Schriever's retirement. The
problem in the 1970s and 1980s then became one of
keeping alive the spirit of Forecast. With no clear
successor to the von Karman-Schriever tradition, the
answer to the dilemma was found in a corporate approach
to USAF long-range science, a solution in which no "great
man" dominated the process and almost all study was
undertaken internally.

NOTES

1. Chart and accompanying narrative derived from the USAF Statistical Digests, 1948 (Restricted) , FY 1955 (C), FY 1960 (C), FY 1965 (C), FY 1970 (C), FY 1975 (S); and the USAF Summary, FY 1988/1989 (U).

2. Sturm, SAB, p.2; USAF Biography, "General Bernard A. Schriever."

3. Ltr (draft), Dr. Samuel Cohen to Donald L. Putt, subj: increasing military influence on the SAB, 5 May 1959, w/atchs: Notes by John Stokes, Vincent T. Ford, and Gen Bernard A Schriever; Ltr, Vincent T. Ford to Gen Bernard A. Schriever, subj: a military group in the SAB, 19 May 1959, SP 168.7171-141.

4.   Ltr, Ford to Schriever, 19 May 1959, as above; Ltr, Col Clyde D. Gasser to Lt Gen Donald L. Putt, subj: modernization of SAB, 27 February 1961, SAB 2; Ltr, Col Clyde D. Gasser to Dr. H. Guyford Stever, subj: improved SAB operating procedures, 31 January 1962, SAB 2, w/atch: draft of form requesting SAB assistance; Ltr, Gen Curtis LeMay to Lt Gen R.C. Wilson, subj: altering SAB operational procedures, 8 June 1962, SAB 2.

5. Sturm, SAB, pp. 110-113; Extract, revised DOD Directive 5030.13, April 1962, "Advisory Committees," SAB 2; "Recommendations for Continuance of Advisory Committee," 8 May 1962, SAB 2; Memo, SECAF to SECDEF, subj: extension of Air Force Advisory Committees, 2 June 1962, SAB 2; Memo for SECAF from Robert S. McNamara, subj: reduction of SAB, 21 June 1962, SAB 2; Memo, SECAF Eugene M. Zuckert to Air Force Chief of Staff Gen LeMay, subj: SAB reduction, 22 June 1962, SAB 2; Ltr, Lt Gen James Ferguson to AFCCS, subj: SECDEF directive on SAB, 21 June 1962, w/attch: "Notes on the SAB," SAB 2; Ltr, Lt Gen James Ferguson to Gen Curtis LeMay, subj: SAB reductions, 29 June 1962, SAB 2; Ltr, Gen Curtis LeMay to SECAF Zuckert, subj: SAB reductions, 3 July 1962, w/attch: "Resume of the Mission, Growth, and Productivity of the SAB," SAB 2; Memo (FOUO), Eugene M. Zuckert to SECDEF, subj: SAB reductions, 17 July

1962, SAB 2; Ltr, Gen LeMay to SECAF, subj: SAB reductions, 13 August 1962, SAB 7; Ltr, Lt Gen James Ferguson to SECAF, subj: reconstitution of SAB, 7 November 1962, SAB 8; AFR 20-30, "Organization and Mission—General, USAF SAB," 23 November 1962, SAB 11; Memo, Col Clyde Gasser to SAB Steering Committee, subj: Current Action Items, 8 November 1962, SAB 7, w/attch: "List of Members/Consultants to be Dropped from the SAB Roster," a/o 1 January 1963.

6. Sturm, _SAB_, pp. 102-105; Interview, Dr. Getting w/Gorn, 12 March 1986; Report, "Report of the SAB Committee on Air Force Utilization of Scientific Resources," 26 May 1961, AFSC; Ltr, Col Clyde D. Gasser to Lt Gen Donald L. Putt, subj: modernization of SAB, 12 July 1961, SAB 2; Memo, C.S. Irvine to AF/CV subj: SAB, 14 July 1961, SAB 2; Ltr, Lt Gen James Ferguson to AFIIS, subj: management inspection of AFSC, 27 July 1962, SAB-7; Lt Gen James Ferguson to Gen Bernard A. Schriever, subj: SAB and DAG reconstitution actions, 2 November 1962, SAB 2.

7. Sturm, _SAB_, p. 97; Ltr, Lt Gen Bernard A. Schriever to Dr. Detlev V. Bronk, subj: formation of ARDC Research Division, 8 January 1960, NAS 11.

8. Stever, H. Guyford, Report of the USAF Scientific Advisory Board Ad Hoc Committee on R&D, June 1958, pp. 5-7, 8-21, 22-40, 105; HQ ARDC Annual History, 1 July-31 December 1959, pp. 107-117.

9. ARDC/AFSC Annual History, 1 January-30 June 1961, pp. 1-19, 30-36; [General Samuel E.] Anderson Committee Report of the Weapon Systems Study Group, August 1960, pp. 1-11; [Lt Gen Mark E.] Bradley Proposal for ARDC Reorganization, March 1960; Interview, General Bernard A. Schriever with Major Lyn Officer and Dr. James C. Hasdorff, 20 June 1973, AFHRC Oral Interview #676, pp. 21-27; [General Bernard A.] Schriever Plan for ARDC Reorganization, 26 April 1960, pp. 1-13.

10. Interview, Mr. Eugene M. Zuckert with M. Gorn, 15 July 1986; Interview, Schriever with Maj Officer and Dr. Hasdorff, p. 55; Interview, Col Ray E. Soper with unknown

interviewer, 29 November 1966, AFSC; Interview, Putt with Hasdorff, p. 44.

11. Ltr, Gen Curtis LeMay to Gen Bernard A. Schriever, subj: authority for Project Forecast, 9 March 1963 in Annex B, "Project Information," of Project Forecast Director's Report (S/RD), SP K168.154-14; Interview, Schriever, p. 56.

12. Article, Anon., "Air Force Inaugurates 'Project Forecast,'" Armed Forces Management, July 1963, vol 9, p. 13; Project Forecast Organization and Mission Planning Group Report, 13 April 1963, pp. 1-2, 8-10, SP 168.7171-223; Forecast Director's Report, Annex B, pp. B-2 and B-4; USAF Biography, "Lieutenant General Charles H. Terhune, Jr."

13. Futrell, Concepts and Doctrine, p. 438; Forecast Director's Report, Annex B, pp. B-5 to B-12; Interview, Peter R. Murray with Hugh N. Ahmann, 10-11 July 1973, AFHRC Oral History Interview, pp. 37, 40, 45.

14. Interview, Zuckert, 15 July 1986; Futrell, Concepts and Doctrine, p. 438; Forecast Director's Report, Annex B, pp. B-5 to B-12; Interview, Lt Gen James H. Doolittle, 23 June 1965, AFHRC Oral History Interview #623, p. 29; Interview, Murray with Ahmann, pp. 37, 40, 45; Ltr, Frederick Satz to Dr. Charles H. Townes, subj: AFSC Contract, 27 October 1962, NAS 12, w/attch: Minutes, NAS Division of Physical Sciences, 10 February 1963. 1963.

15. History of Air Force Systems Command, 1 January-30 June 1963, vol I, p. 2; History of Air Force Systems Command 1 July-31 December 1963, vol I, pp. 14-15; Forecast Director's Report, Annex B, p. B-12; History of Air Force Systems Command, 1 January-30 June 1964, vol I, pp. 29-30.

16. Article, Anon., "First Details Issued on 'Forecast' Secret Study on Weapon Systems," Air Force Times, vol 24, 9 October 1963, p. 5; Article, Anon., "Schriever Disputes 'Plateau' Theory," Aviation Week and Space Technology, 11 November 1963, p. 31; Article, Anon., "Air Force

"Forecast" Studies Reveal Manned Aircraft on Threshold of Big New Advances," Army, Navy, Air Force Journal, 16 November 1963, vol 101, pp. 12-13.

17. Commander's Conference Notes, Maxwell AFB, AL, 13-14 November 1963, pp. 58-59, SP 168.7171-197; Forecast Director's Report, Annex B, p. B-12; Interview, Murray, pp. 41-42.

18. U.S. Congress, Hearings Before A Committee on Armed Services of the House of Representatives, Subcommittee on Research and Development, 22 January 1964, 88th Congress, 2nd session, p. 7814; U.S. Congress, Hearings Before A Committee on Armed Services of the House of Representatives, 4 February 1964, 88th Congress, 2nd session, pp. 7412-7413.

19. U.S. Congress, Hearings Before A Subcommittee of the Committee on Appropriations, 26 February 1964, 88th Congress, 2nd session, pt.4, p. 527.

20. History of AFSC, 1 July-31 December 1963, p. 17; Ltr, Gen Bernard A. Schriever to Eugene M. Zuckert and Curtis E. LeMay, subj: Forecast Director's Report, 12 March 1964, in Forecast Director's Report, pp. i-v; Forecast Director's Report, pp. 2-3; Interview, Schriever, pp. 56-59.

21. Forecast Director's Report, pp. 4-6.

22. Ibid., pp. 7-9.

23. Ibid., pp. 9-10.

24. Ibid., pp. 10-11.

25. Ibid., pp. 11-12.

26. Ibid., pp. 13-14.

27. Ibid., pp. 14-15.

28. Ibid., pp. 14-15.

29. Ibid., pp. 15-17.

30. Ibid., p. 18.

31. Ibid., pp. iv-v; Article, Gen Bernard A. Schriever, "Forecast," Air University Review, vol 16, March-April 1965, p. 12; Speech, Gen Bernard A. Schriever to Rotary Club of Los Angeles, CA, 10 July 1964, AFHRC 35252, p. 1220; Article, Gen Bernard A. Schriever, "Schriever Urges Bold Approach to Future," Armed Forces Management, vol 11, May 1965, p. 37.

32. Article, Schriever, "Bold Approach," p. 37; History of AFSC (S), 1 July 1964-30 June 1965, vol 2, pp. 13, 29-30, 100-101.

33. "Project Forecast Program Status" (S/RD), a/o 30 November 1964, SP 168.7171-223; "1966 Forecast Situation Report" (S), July 1966, w/attchs: Ltr (draft), Schriever to SECAF Harold Brown, subj: "Role of R&D in National Security," 12 July 1966; Ltr (draft), Schriever to SECAF Harold Brown, subj: military technology and the R&D program, 8 July 1966, SP 168.7171-226.

34. "Technology Program Trends--AFSC Task Force," (S/NOFORN), August 1966, SP 168.7171-227, pp. 3, 7-10, 23.

35. Interview, Peter R. Murray with Hugh N. Ahmann, p. 43; Interview, Dr. Alexander Flax with M. Gorn, 18 August 1986, NAS Building, Washington, D.C.

36. Interview, Gen Bernard A. Schriever with Major Officer and Dr. Hasdorff, pp. 60-63; Interview, Mr. Eugene Zuckert with M. Gorn.

37. Sturm, SAB, pp. 126-128; USAF SAB Report of the Tactical Air Capabilities Task Force, vol 1, Executive Summary (S/RD), pp. 1-1 to 1-5, 42-43, June 1965, SAB 13; "USAF Scientific Advisory Board Reports, 1949-Present," n.d., SAB files.

38. Tac Air Capabilities Report, pp. 1-1 to 1-5, 42-43.

39. USAF SAB Report of the Tactical Air Capabilities Task Force, vol 2, "Aircraft," p. 2; vol 3, "Logistics," pp. 51 & 53; vol 4, "Reconnaissance," pp. 54-55; vol 5, "Command and Control," p. 37; vol 6, "Navigation/Strike," p. E-1; vol 7, "Weapons and Munitions," p. v; vol 8, "Test and Evaluation," p. 38; vol 9, "Support (Meteorology and Engineering Geology)," p. iv.

40.   Ltr, Col Robert J. Burger to all members and military representatives of the SAB, subj: Final Report, USAF SAB Tactical Air Capabilities Task Force, 27 July 1965, SAB 12; Ltr, Dr. H. Guyford Stever to Gen John P. McConnell subj: submission of SAB Tac Task Force Report, 28 July 1965, SAB 12; Memo, Maj Robert H. Howard to Col Woodward, subj: distribution of SAB Tac Task Force Report, 28 July 1965, SAB 12; Ltr, Gen John P. McConnell to Dr. H. Guyford Stever, subj: distribution of SAB Tac Task Force Report, 10 August 1965, SAB 12; Ltr, Col Milton Collier to Maj Robert H. Howard, subj: distribution of SAB Tac Task Force Report, 20 August 1965, w/atch: distribution list, SAB 12; Ltr, Maj Richard Campbell to file, subj: USAF SAB Tactical Air Capabilities Task Force Report, 9 September 1965, w/attchs: "Team to Construct AF Position on SAB-TTF Report," "Proposed Structure and Schedule for AF Reply to SAB," "Distribution List for TTF Report," "Replies Not Yet Received," SAB 12; Ltr, Maj Richard H. Campbell to file, subj: USAF SAB Tactical Air Capabilities Task Force Report, 15 October 1965, w/atch: Schedule, SAB 12; Ltr, Col Geoffrey Cheadle to Col Robert Burger, subj: USAF SAB Tactical Air Capabilities Task Force Final Report, 17 December 1965, SAB 12; Ltr, Maj Robert Howard to SAB, subj: SAB Tactical Air Capabilities Task Force Final Report, 9 June 1966, SAB 12; "Air Force Review of the USAF SAB Tactical Air Capabilities Task Force Final Report,"(S/RD), December 1965, p. vi, SAB 6.

41. AF Review of SAB Tactical Air Capabilities Task Force, pp. 28-38; Ltr, SECAF Harold Brown to Dr. H. Guyford Stever, subj: SAB Tactical Air Capabilities Task Force Report, 27 January 1966, SAB 12.

CHAPTER FOUR

SCIENTISTS IN UNIFORM, 1966-1986

During the years following Project Forecast, USAF science forecasting drifted farther afield from the SAB. After Woods Hole and the Tactical Air Capabilities Task Force Report, the Air Force seemed to doubt the Scientific Advisory Board's capacity to undertake these broad-scale analyses. The board contributed very little to the Project Forecast sequels of the 1970s and 1980s, in part because its participation was circumscribed. Consequently, the SAB increasingly confined itself to subjects of limited scope. Though very useful as a trouble-shooter for thorny technical problems, the board ceased to look—and was no longer asked to look—to the far horizon as it had in the days of von Karman and Schriever. Some SAB members hoped the inclusion of younger scientists and engineers would equip it to again project technologies into the future. But other members were less sanguine. They felt the era of the SAB's face-to-face communal sessions had passed, eclipsed by computerized models and statistical analyses of the future of air power science. Indeed, from the mid-1960s to the mid-1980s the SAB ceased to be an organization dominated by scholars. When its overall numbers were reduced as a result of the McNamara cuts, the losses occurred among university professors, not representatives of private laboratories or aerospace firms. The balance between academic and non-academic was almost even in 1970; thirteen years later those outside the universities accounted for about eighty percent of the membership. The SAB thus found itself at odds with von Karman's model—a body of senior academic generalists conferring mature judgements on the future of aerospace science.

While the role of the SAB was changing, science forecasting, lacking a distinct home, became an institutional orphan. The death of Theodore von Karman in May 1963 and the retirement of Bernard Schriever in

August 1966 contributed to the drift in long-term scientific advising. Lacking a powerful figure to represent it and an institutional affiliation to give it stature, the practice of undertaking periodic reports on the future of aerospace science became an in-house function, the work of the scientist in uniform. Not only was the officer with extensive technical education commonplace as early as the mid-1960s; clear rewards existed for the technologically trained. A coherent and carefully conceived program had been established for military scientists and engineers to assure career progression within their field, assuring a steady influx of technical minds for the Air Force.[1]

* * *

The SAB quickly fell victim to these trends. No sooner had the ink dried on the <u>Tactical Air Capabilities Task Force Report</u> than the board underwent yet another reorganization. Recognizing some deficiencies in the report, as well as in the board's structure, SAB Chairman Dr. H. Guyford Stever solicited ideas early in 1967 for improving its service to the USAF. The board's executive secretary, Col. Robert J. Berger, proposed a drastic restructuring. The ten existing panels, all of which were scientifically oriented,* would be recast into four mission area committees: strategic, tactical, defense, and support.

Stever was willing to go even farther. In March he asked Air Force Chief of Staff General John P. McConnell to review SAB operations with the goal of improving its utility to the Air Force. General McConnell asked his R&D deputy, Lt. Gen. Joseph R. Holzapple, for suggestions. Holzapple presented six recommendations, including appointment of a special SAB advisory committee composed of one military representative from each of the R&D directorates; clearer definition of problems submitted to the board for study; verbal answers—rather than written reports—to staff questions of minimal complexity; a system of tracking the effectiveness of SAB studies; increasing the awareness of members of operational considerations, particularly regarding Southeast Asia; and submission by

---

*The existing panels included aeromedical/biosciences, aerospace vehicles, electronics, geophysics, guidance and control, information processing, 'Open Ear', pro-

Air Staff offices of a priority list of scientific problems requiring attention. General Holzapple also suggested a number of substantive new roles. For example, the board might review regularly the Air Force exploratory development program as it related to the nation's technology base. It could also act as a sounding board for weapon system ideas during the conceptual phase of development, or act as devil's advocate for any scientific controversy.[2]

These bold proposals did not cause a SAB renaissance. Rather, they resulted in greater military oversight of its affairs. Headquarters Operating Instruction 80-5 established on May 20, 1968, a SAB Staff Review Group to decide which projects the board should undertake. Comprised of the Air Staff Deputy Chief of Staff for Research and Development, the Chief Scientist of the Air Force, members of the SAB Secretariat, and two senior Air Staff representatives, the review group would appoint for each study one general officer to act as "task monitor." He would attend SAB panel meetings and participate in his assigned study by explaining the military side of technological questions. Each draft board report would be seminared by the task monitor and his panel associates "to insure that [it] is clear, concise, and not subject to misinterpretation."[*] [3]

Despite its circumscribed role,[†] the board did continue to serve the Air Force well. During 1971 and 1972 it undertook two useful ad hoc summer studies, on aircraft technology and space, respectively. In fact, the ad hoc panels, which drew membership from all the appropriate technology committees, had really proven their value. Their good work suggested further SAB reorganization. If board members from diverse fields of

_____

pulsion, psychology/social sciences, and information processing.

*The details of the new seminar process, as well as the procedures for AFSC and AFOSR review of SAB papers, were outlined in Air Staff Operating Instruction 80-7, July 1968.

†Asked in 1970 to list its most significant achievements during the past three years, the board's leadership cited twelve accomplishments. Only one of

science could sit successfully on the summer panels, should not the existing committee structure, based on technological specialty, be supplemented with panels whose themes cut across scientific disciplines? The question was answered in 1972 when the board found itself with twelve vacancies. The new chairman, Dr. Robert G. Loewy,[*] initiated discussions on reforming the panels. Averaging fifty years of age, the members also discussed the problem of attracting younger people to their ranks. After a vigorous exchange of letters on these subjects, on January 17, 1973, Dr. Loewy, vice chairman Dr. Gerald Dineen, Air Force Chief Scientist Dr. Eugene Covert, and the eight panel chairs convened in the Pentagon to restructure the board. They "strongly favored," and finally approved the establishment of cross-matrix panels to cover three operational areas: strategic, tactical, and mission resources. Their membership would be drawn from the existing technology committees, resulting in panels double the size of the present ones.[4]

This step represented an attempt by the SAB to remake itself in the image of the Air Force, and to better serve its master. Regardless of the sincerity of the reform, however, when the USAF decided once again to initiate a long-range science study, the SAB was not selected to do it. Indeed, it participated only to a very limited extent. Ten years after the completion of Project Forecast, on August 10, 1974, Air Force Chief of Staff General David C. Jones[†] directed the Headquarters Assistant Deputy Chief for Plans and Programs, Maj. Gen. Foster Lee Smith, to act as executive agent in conducting a review of long-range scientific trends. Two factors contributed to the timing of the undertaking. The January

---

the studies--the USAF portion of a DOD proposal for national space objectives—dealt with broad scientific issues. The rest treated incremental improvements in existing systems or subsystems. This outlook, so different from that envisioned by Dr. von Karman, had gradually come to charactarize the modern SAB.

*SAB chairman from November 1972 to October 1975.

†Air Force Chief of Staff from July 1, 1974, to June 20, 1978.

1973 peace treaty between the United States and Vietnam hastened a reappraisal of American defense policy. The central focus of U.S. military interests shifted from Southeast Asia to Europe, and it became clear that a different theater of war demanded new weaponry and fresh scientific innovation. Also influencing the decision to update Forecast was the realization that in the wake of the Vietnam drawdown, USAF resources would be pared. The Middle East oil embargo of 1973 likewise pointed up the fragility of natural resources. These facts—a new defense emphasis and a drastic scarcity of money and fuels—led Air Force leaders to turn to science for long-term solutions.

General Jones launched the study by directing all parties concerned to concentrate their energies on a few crucial subjects. He wanted to know the effect of the existing state of international affairs on USAF general purpose and mobility forces. He also wondered about the future of the Air Force in space, the potential of laser technology, and the possibility of all-weather/night capabilities for the tactical forces. The group was charged to explore these, as well as other scientific opportunities of extraordinary promise.[5]

General Smith and Dr. Michael I. Yarymovych, Chief Scientist of the Air Force and co-chairman of the study, began quickly to establish committees. Taking their cue from von Karman's Toward New Horizons, they named their project New Horizons II. The chairmen convened the steering group in fall 1974 to determine goals and policies. Along with Smith and Yarymovych, its members included Maj. Gen. George J. Keegan, Jr., Assistant Chief of Staff for Intelligence; Maj. Gen. George P. Loving, Director of Plans, and his successor, Maj. Gen. Richard L. Lawson; Maj. Gen. Robert P. Lukeman, Assistant Chief of Staff for Studies and Analysis; Maj. Gen. Otis C. Moore, Director of Operations; Maj. Gen. Alton P. Slay, Director of Operational Requirements; and Brig. Gen. Lovic P. Hodnette, Director of Reconnaissance and Electronic Warfare. The steering group turned for expert advice to such diverse sources as the six Air Staff Deputy Chiefs of Staff, the Air Force Board Structure, AFSC planning and laboratory personnel, the SAB, RAND, the intelligence community, several of the major Air Force commands, "and other agencies or individuals, public or private," able to shed light on the subjects under discussion.

To oversee daily operations, the steering group appointed Brig. Gen. John E. Ralph, Director of Doctrine, Concepts and Objectives, to act as study director. General Ralph led a study group of six to twelve people, drawn selectively from his directorate. They served as a permanent staff for the project. The formal analysis of technical subject matter occurred in seven study panels, including Alternative Strategies; Foreign Military Potential; Technology Emphasis; Space; Lasers; Night and Adverse Weather Operations; and General Purpose and Mobility Forces. A total of forty-nine men—every one of whom served on the Air Staff at the time—sat on the steering group, study group, and study panels. All but Dr. Yarymovych were military men, and almost half (including co-chairman Smith and study director Ralph), came from the Air Staff Deputy Chief of Staff for Plans and Operations. Surprisingly, perhaps, for a report involving USAF science, fewer than twenty-five percent of the participants were assigned from the Deputy Chief of Staff for Research and Development.[6] Diagram 3 illustrates the New Horizons II organizational structure.

Before the panels started their deliberations, the exact purpose of the study was set forth for them. Concerned with technology during the period 1985 to 2000, the report would relate scientific opportunity both to the predicted foreign threat and to evolving U.S. foreign policy. Four areas would dominate study panel discussions: space, from the viewpoints of technical advances and possible USAF roles; laser technology, for offensive and defensive purposes, and the extent to which the United States should pursue it; night and all-weather fighter capabilities, which became imperative as the U.S.S.R. sought to develop tactical aircraft capable of operating twenty-four hours a day in all climates; and other technological possibilities, the utility of which must be balanced against the scarcity of natural resources and post-Vietnam cuts in exploratory development funding.

DIAGRAM 3
New Horizons II Organization Chart

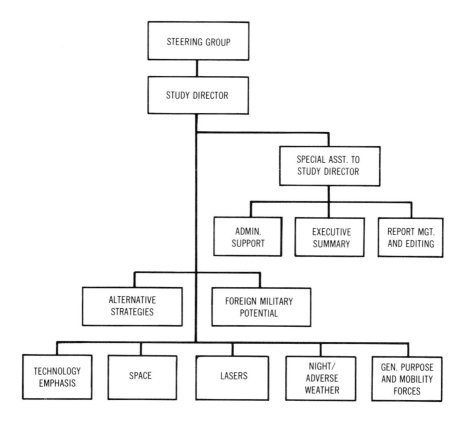

"The final report," the panelists were told, "should reflect broad Air Force objectives, directions, and relative priorities [and]...identify near term actions." [7]

Never before had a group about to forecast scientific trends for the USAF received such specific instructions on what it should cover.[*] The task was even categorized in five phases, beginning with a survey of the likely national and international military and economic developments between the years 1985 and 2000. Phase two would be devoted to deciding the probable concepts, missions, and technological needs of mobility and general purpose forces late in the century. The next section concerned itself with scientific projections in the fields of space, lasers, and night/all-weather flying, including the ways in which Air Force missions, operational concepts, and development processes affected the usefulness of these technologies. While phases one to three were underway, Dr. Yarymovych and the technology emphasis panel would undertake the fourth step, surveying all applicable scientific endeavors, visiting laboratories, consulting with the SAB, drafting a list of innovative projects, and rating them in order of probable effectiveness. Fifth and last, New Horizons II would conclude with a summary of the main points, recommendations for the most promising avenues of research, an assessment of Air Force long-range planning practices in general, and proposals for implementation.[8]

The small New Horizons II staff prepared the report while coping with the normal load of Air Staff duties. As a result, the December 31, 1974, deadline had to be postponed, and the report did not reach General Jones's office until May 1975.[†] The study recommended, in order

---

[*]General Ralph limited the scope of New Horizons II on the mistaken belief that Theodore von Karman had warned against undertaking full-scale long-range studies, such as his own Toward New Horizons. In fact, von Karman never expressed this opinion. He stated only that the SAB, lacking the resources to write a new report, should not by itself do a sequel to the famous study.

[†]Along with Volume One, the Executive Summary, General Jones received six detailed reports, entitled Alternative Strategies, Foreign Military Potential,

of significance, eight steps by which the USAF could maximize technological progress. First, and most important, full advantage should be taken of signal and data processing advances as applied to command and control of forces. Although the USAF developed, operated, and supported aircraft "superbly," better control systems needed to be incorporated into weapon systems from the outset of the acquisition process. The panel members suggested, secondly, that the Air Force draft a coherent plan to introduce and operate space systems, recognizing that comprehensive planning in the development stages would be repaid later by lower operating and maintenance costs. The third of the study's conclusions emphasized the need for survivable military satellites, ground control, and ground launch stations. Panel members suggested that the cost of arming satellites and providing launch alternatives, such as mobile basing on land and in the air, be included at the start of space development programs. Conclusion four recommended accelerated research on directed energy (laser/particle beam) weapons, first in the areas of increased power and fire control, and later in airborne and space-based applications. Funding at 1975 levels was deemed sufficient to sustain existing studies on reducing the weight and improving the firing accuracy of these systems.[9]

Point five of New Horizons II proposed a development dear to Theodore von Karman: tactical air power capable of operating fully despite factors inhibiting visibility. To be fully effective, however, night and adverse weather flying would require highly complex technologies linking aircraft, munitions, remotely piloted vehicles, space systems, and support equipment. A digitalized, worldwide cartographic memory bank comprised the sixth recommendation. The satellite-based Global Positioning System (GPS) promised all-weather precision coordinates for ground and air forces operating below, on, or above the

---

Technology Emphasis, The Role of the Air Force in Space, Laser Technology Applications, and Future Operational Concepts (Part A: Night and Adverse Weather Operations; Part B: General Purpose and Mobility Forces).

surface of the earth. Seventh, they asked General Jones to support the development of a heavy lift, global range aircraft which, at the same time, satisfied late twentieth century demands for cost effectiveness and energy efficiency. The committee members envisioned a transport capable of flying unrefueled to any point on the globe and back, using propulsion, materials, and aerodynamics breakthroughs anticipated by the turn of the century. The last item on the New Horizons II agenda forecasted a space defense system which shielded American satellites from attack by hostile orbiters and denied access to space to enemy forces. Based on progress in laser research, these anti-satellites might be either airborne or space-based, but had to be capable of launch on short notice.[10]

Despite the guiding hand of several Air Staff general officers, New Horizons II cast a small shadow. Not only did it have little influence on USAF research and development outlays, it was all but forgotten in a short period of time. New Horizons II lacked impact for a number of reasons. Though initiated as a scientific forecast, the SAB, AFSC, and independent civilian scientists participated only as expert "consultants," not as part of the decision-making machinery of the study. Not only did this oversight result in a report deficient in the broadest possible scientific content; it also reduced the extent to which people in positions to affect its implementation might actually do so. In addition, New Horizons II lacked a well-known figure to actively promote the maximum support for its findings. Dr. von Karman and General Schriever both had the reputations and personal appeal to bring their reports to the attention of prominent people inside and outside the Air Force. Undertaken with very low visibility, New Horizons II received a corresponding degree of notice when it was completed. Finally, the report suffered from bad timing. Hard on the heels of the Vietnam War, the Air Force may have wanted to look to the technological future. But Congress and the public were not in a mood to forget the immediate past, and this was reflected in fiscally constrained DOD budgets in the postwar period.

*   *   *

A decade passed before the Air Force undertook a sequel to New Horizons II, but intervening events proved the latter was not an isolated example of the ascendancy of scientists in uniform. Late in 1979 AFSC Commander Gen. Alton D. Slay[*] and SAB Chairman Dr. Raymond L. Bisplinghoff[†] signed a Memorandum of Agreement (MOA) which shifted the balance of power in the Division Advisory Groups (DAGs) from the SAB to Systems Command. Henceforth, the AFSC Commander exercised greater control over the activities and membership of the DAGs. Slay appointed a Headquarters AFSC DAG Secretary to oversee all command relations with the SAB; empowered his Product Division commanders to choose their own DAG secretaries; and, most importantly, enjoyed the final word on which members of the board would sit on the DAGs. In a second instance of the growing prominence of military men in the process of science and technology forecasting, during the command of Slay's successor, Gen. Robert T. Marsh,[**] an ad hoc panel of colonels whom Marsh called the "Seven Man Group," was chosen from the Product Divisions to survey the Air Force for "innovative concepts and new ideas that could fundamentally change the nature of warfare." The colonels were selected by Brig. Gen. Robert D. Eaglet, Headquarters AFSC Deputy Chief of Staff for Plans and Programs, who called them among "the most creative, iconoclastic thinkers" in the USAF. During the summer of 1983 the Seven Man Group visited every Air Force four-star general and many of the Air Staff Deputy Chiefs of Staff, as well as DOD, NASA, and Department of Energy (DOE) in-house laboratories. Seeking "truly revolutionary, long-term concepts," they discovered a number of promising technologies which might result in cost-effective weapon systems or sub-systems.

The Seven Man Group did not constitute an updating of New Horizons II, serving instead as an interim attempt

---

[*]Gen Slay was AFSC Commander from 14 March 1978 to 1 February 1981.

[†]Dr. Bisplinghoff served as SAB Chairman from 1 September 1978 to 19 July 1982.

[**]Marsh commanded AFSC from February 1, 1981, to August 1, 1984.

to survey advanced science and relate it to weapons development. But two years after its completion, Systems Command did launch a new, full-scale exploration of future technology trends.[11] Gen. Lawrence A. Skantze,[*] who succeeded General Marsh at AFSC, conceived of the undertaking. Educated in science and engineering, Skantze had spent most of his career as a weapons program manager. One of his formative experiences involved participation in Project Forecast.[†] As a major he had shuttled back and forth between the Pentagon and Andrews Air Force Base, dividing his time between executive officer duties in the Office of the Secretary of the Air Force and General Schriever's team of scientific prognosticators. The latter left a lasting impression. Even before assuming command of AFSC in summer 1984, Skantze had decided there should be an update of Schriever's twenty-year-old study. He quietly raised the idea with his staff in January 1985 at the Joint Logistics Conference at Patrick Air Force Base, Florida, and defined it more clearly in the succeeding weeks. By the following April, General Skantze had decided on the broad approach to the follow-on Forecast, and asked a group of trusted colleagues to go again to Patrick and hammer out a blueprint for the project. The sessions included Brig. Gen. Eric Nelson, HQ AFSC Deputy Chief of Staff for Plans and Programs; Brig. Gen. (selectee) Charles F. Stebbins, HQ AFSC Deputy Chief of Staff for Science and Technology; Col. Alan Gropman of the Air Staff Deputy Chief of Staff for Plans and Operations; Col. John Friel, Air Force Space Technology Center (AFSTC) Commander; Col. James M. Walton, Commander of the Air Force Weapons Laboratory (AFWL); and Mr. Alan Goldstayn and Lt. Col. Donald Neireiter from General Nelson's office. When their talks ended they had agreed on one crucial point: the new report would adhere to the structure and format of Project Forecast.[12]

The next month, before any briefings or formal discussions outside AFSC, General Skantze approved their

---

[*]The AFSC Commander from August 1, 1984 to July 17, 1987.

[†]Skantze served prominently in a number of important program offices, including the Manned Orbiting Laboratory (MOL), 1966-1969; Short Range Attack

blueprint, and preliminary planning began on a study that would project technological capabilities 20 years in the future. About 50 Air Force officers, enlisted personnel, and civilians were assembled for the secretarial, editorial, and staff work-load. Additionally, later in the year, between 100 and 150 scientists, engineers, and military experts would take part in the study. Total budgeted support costs were $3.3 million. By May 1985, then, a clear picture of the study's technical course had been set. So had its name. In honor of its predecessor, staff members called it Project Forecast II.

On May 9, 1985, at his monthly meeting with Air Force Chief of Staff Gen. Charles Gabriel,[*] General Skantze raised the subject of Forecast II and asked that it be assigned high priority. Gabriel gave a verbal go-ahead, but delayed issuing a formal directive pending further details from AFSC. The process went forward speedily. Chairmen for several of the projected panels were selected and they, in turn, began to sift the names of possible committee members and choose topics of discussion. After meeting with General Skantze, the chairmen convened to discuss panel interaction and prepared an overall working plan for the program managers, whom Skantze designated to be Generals Nelson and Stebbins. In describing his candidates to General Gabriel, the AFSC Commander stated that he had no higher priority than completing Forecast II and pledged to supervise it personally.[13]

By late May, the basic outline of Forecast II had been sketched in significant detail, allowing General Nelson to brief a joint meeting of the Air Force Council/Air Staff Board on the goals of the project. With General Skantze

---

Missile (SRAM), 1971-1973; Airborne Warning and Control System (AWACS), 1973-1977. He was program manager for SRAM and AWACS. He later became the Deputy Chief of Staff for Systems at HQ AFSC, Commander of ASD, the Air Staff Deputy Chief of Staff for Research, Development, and Acquisition, and Vice Chief of Staff, USAF.

*Air Force Chief of Staff from July 1, 1982, to June 30, 1986.

in attendance, he described the work and conclusions of Forecast I and admitted the new study's close kinship to it. Forecast II, initiated to match war-fighting capabilities to anticipated technologies, would propose innovative weapon system concepts based on the latest scientific trends. Nelson assured his listeners that such factors as maintenance of a balanced force structure and the role of the Strategic Defense Initiative (SDI) would be of paramount importance during the deliberations. Nonetheless, no good ideas, however unorthodox, would be rejected without lengthy consideration. Nelson estimated the study to cost $4 million. The salaries of Air Force participants would be paid by the organizations for which they normally worked.[14]

The likeness of Forecast II to Forecast I was most evident in its panel structure. The bulk of the project's analysis would be undertaken by three sets of committees: ten technology panels (propulsion and power, materials and producibility, vehicles and structures, electronics and sensors, information and processing, armaments and weapons, communications, life sciences, environmental sciences, and reliability/maintainability); five mission panels (strategic offense, strategic defense, theater warfare, low intensity warfare, and battle management); and three analysis panels (systems analysis, systems cost, and threat/readiness). Similar, too, to Forecast I methodology, a Military Advisory Group and a Senior Review Group would advise General Skantze both from the military and scientific viewpoints on the applicability and practicality of the proposed weapon systems. Nineteen distinguished generals—one-, two-, and three-star—had been asked to serve on the Military Advisory Group. The Senior Review Group candidates included nine retired USAF general officers and an equal number of civilian scientists and former DOD officials.[15]

General Nelson explained that panel interaction operated in much the same way as Forecast I. The threat committee, which equated foreign capabilities to Air Force missions, fed its findings to the technology panels. They, in turn, weighed this information during the process of selecting technologies with high potential, and recasting them as possible weapon systems. Armed also with the threat assessment, the mission panels reviewed the choices of the technologists, adding considerations of military utility and necessity. Those candidate weapon systems that survived the appraisal were sent on to the analysis panels for cost-effectiveness studies. When the surviving technologies/ systems reached the Military Advisory and Senior Review Groups, they received a priority ranking, following which General Skantze evaluated their worth.[16] Diagram 4 illustrates the Forecast II organizational structure.

Nelson presented his Pentagon audience with a precise schedule for the far-reaching endeavor. In June and July 1985 office space and staffing would be seen to; from August through October the technology and mission panels would work almost simultaneously to ferret out the most suitable candidates; the analysis panel would operate from September to December; and after a mid-term summary in November, a final report would be issued in February 1986, in time for the next Air Force Chief of Staff's Commander's Conference. Once the report was presented to the USAF and the public, AFSC and the other commands would develop jointly a Program Objective Memorandum (POM) strategy which funded the exploitation of Forecast II technologies designated as likely weapon systems of the future. Meantime, the Major Commands were expected to program funds for concept definition and demonstration/ evaluation of these select ideas.[17]

The Board Structure reacted favorably to General Nelson's briefing, giving the Forecast II team a hopeful start to long months of hard work. First, official sanction had to be given. On June 11 General Nelson repeated his briefing for Dr. Thomas E. Cooper, Assistant Secretary of the Air Force for Research, Development and Logistics. At the same time, General Skantze presented the Forecast II blueprint to General Gabriel. The following day, Skantze covered the same ground for Secretary of the Air Force Verne Orr. All reviews were highly positive and on June 12, 1985, Secretary Orr and General Gabriel signed a letter, approving Forecast II to begin. It called for a "comprehensive study to identify emerging high-leverage

DIAGRAM 4
Project Forecast II Organization Chart

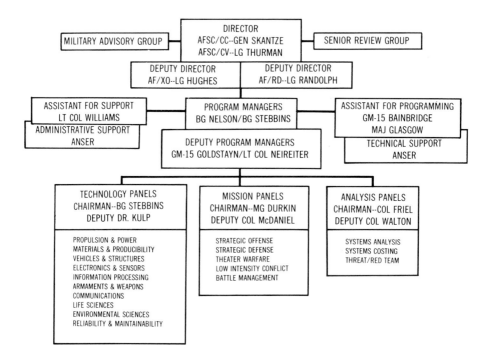

technologies...over the next twenty years." Pledging the "assistance and support" of the Air Staff and all USAF field organizations, they conjured up the images of Theodore von Karman and Bernard A. Schriever in urging Skantze to "break away from conventional thinking." [18]

Taking another leaf from General Schriever's book, the Forecast II staff decided early on to encourage public interest in and support for the project by giving it the widest possible publicity. They compiled a list of sixteen leading newspapers and periodicals whose editors would welcome interviews with the study's leaders and piqued their interest with a news release outlining the intent of the undertaking. In one published discussion, General Skantze explained that the purpose of Forecast II was to find technologies which had high potential as future weapon systems and speed up their development with extra funding. Other breakthroughs might have obvious utility as modifications of existing systems. The main value of the report, he said, was to break out of the tyranny of the budget process and do some genuine forward thinking.*
"What I'm saying," he told one interviewer, is that "there's got to be some vision that says now where we could be 10, 15, 20 years from now." [19]

The first order of practical business was establishment of project offices. Since it would be funded from Systems Command accounts, General Skantze expressed a desire to minimize costs. To reduce TDY outlays, the staff decided to locate Forecast II in the Washington, D.C., area, just south of the Pentagon in Crystal City, Virginia. Since the Air Staff Directorate of Operational Requirements had a long standing support contract with a local think tank—Analytic Services, Inc. (ANSER)† of Crystal City—Forecast II was incorporated into the existing agreement. The terms provided that ANSER supply office space and equipment; secretarial,

---

*Skantze also publicized the project from the speaker's podium, in such forums as the National Contract Management Association, which he addressed on July 18, 1985.

†AFRD OI 20-1, May 19, 1983, defined ANSER as an "independent, non-profit research corporation" which since 1958 provided technical assistance to the Air

graphics, and scientific/technical assistance; and generally facilitate "data gathering, synthesis, refinement, and presentation" of Forecast II. The ANSER people would not act in an advisory capacity; clearly, this was to be an internal study by the USAF, whose ideas and policies ANSER would only support. Their services would span several phases:

> Site preparation (June 16 to July 14).
> Initial study (July 15 to August 18).
> Transition (August 19 to September 30).
> Full study (October 1 to November 21).
> Presentation (November 25 to February 16, 1986).
> Wrap-up (February 17 to March 16, 1986).
> Producing an interim report (due in November 1986).
> Editing and producing the draft and completed
>   versions of the final report.
> Preparing an administrative analysis, in addition to
>   providing all briefing materials.

As the Directorate of Operational Requirements contract expired at the end of Fiscal Year 1985, the Air Force and ANSER negotiated a new agreement. Submitted on July 15, 1985, it covered the period July 1, 1985, to March 30, 1986, and satisfied all terms requested by the Forecast II staff at a cost of $2,032,000.[20]

During early summer, in preparation for the official start of the project on August 1, Generals Skantze, Nelson, and Stebbins worked to fill in the panel membership. They also enlisted the cooperation of serving and retired Air Force leaders, as well as private citizens, to support the undertaking and encourage fresh ideas. General Skantze persuaded Air Force Vice Chief of Staff Gen. Larry D. Welch to sign a memo drafted at AFSC soliciting the assistance of all Air Staff Deputy Chiefs of Staffs, Major Commands, and Separate Operating Agencies (SOAs) in Forecast II studies. Skantze also sent letters to fifty-five retired Air Force four-star generals—including every living Chief of Staff, Vice Chief of Staff, and ARDC/AFSC

Staff Deputy Chief of Staff for Research and Development.

Commander—apprising them of the goals and methods of the project and soliciting their "significant observations and comments." Most applauded it as a chance to break out of incremental progress and make broad technological advances. He canvassed all of his Product Division commanders for the "full support of your organization and some of your best people as participants." Beyond this, the AFSC Commander took his campaign to the private sector. By correspondence, he solicited ideas for the study from thirty of the top corporate chief executive officers, numerous industry and trade associations, the deans of fifty universities receiving OSR contracts, as well as all sitting and retired members of the SAB and the Defense Science Board. Finally, Skantze continued to schedule interviews with the press.[21]

The last weeks before the formal launching of Forecast II involved frantic activity. Lists of panel members went to the panel chairs for preliminary selection, and on to Nelson and Stebbins, who approved the final choices. The chairmen then drafted methods of operation and schedules, and met together for the first time at ANSER on July 29-30. Meanwhile, the technology panel members began to arrive for their initial discussions, and on the 30th listened to suggestions submitted by the AFSC field and a Soviet threat briefing.[*] The following day, all of the panelists were welcomed officially to the Crystal City project headquarters by General Nelson, General Stebbins (chairman of the technology panels), Brig. Gen. Robert F. Durkin[†] (Air Staff Deputy Director of Operations and head of the mission panels), and Col. John Friel (Commander of the Air Force Space Technology Center and chair of the analysis committees).

Every person whom these four men addressed that morning was an Air Force employee. While this fact may have raised doubts whether the USAF would receive completely detached expert advice, it did serve a fourfold purpose. It brought to bear individuals intimately involved

---

[*]The analysis panels also held their first meeting on July 30.

[†]Durkin was promoted to major general on December 2, 1985.

with the subject matter. It reduced contractor anxieties about losing proprietary information to other contractors. It lessened Air Force concerns about appearing too closely connected with defense industries. Fourth, and perhaps most important, it provided an opportunity to infuse USAF laboratories with new concepts and projects, thus correcting a deficiency recognized by a former AFSC commander: the "tendency to decreasing incremental progress and eventual stagnation unless bold efforts are taken."

In sharp distinction to the all-military New Horizons II, a majority (63) of the 107 Forecast II panelists were civilian Air Force personnel. Most of the civilians (55) worked for the AFSC laboratories as scientists and engineers, 22 of whom had doctorate degrees. They comprised the vast majority of the technology panels. The remainder of the civilians sat on the analysis panels, where they also constituted well over 50 percent of the membership. By contrast, every mission panel seat but one was occupied by a military man. Systems Command employees -- especially those from the Air Force Wright Aeronautical Laboratories (AFWAL)--dominated the proceedings. Seventy-three of the panel members worked for AFSC, and almost one-third were assigned to AFWAL. The next largest contributors included the Air Staff with 10 officers and SAC with 8.

Rounding off Forecast II personnel, General Skantze made the final selections for two important panels: the Military Advisory Group (MAG) and the Senior Review Group (SRG). The SRG, empanelled to give the corporate insights of retired general officers and provide a "sanity check" to the proceedings, included such distinguished men as Generals Bernard A. Schriever, Lew Allen, Jr., William W. Momyer, and Brent Scowcroft. The MAG, by contrast, was assembled to enlist Major Command support for the project's recommendations, advise on existing programs that paralleled or affected Forecast II, and facilitate overall Air Force acceptance. It consisted mainly of the names General Nelson listed in his first Forecast briefings: the Air Staff Deputy Chiefs Of Staff and the Major Command vice commanders.[22]

Project Forecast II began officially on August 1, 1985. To mark the occasion, General Skantze came to Crystal City to speak to the panel members and answer some of their questions. "I want this study to be a major factor in influencing tomorrow's Air Force," he said. "I expect great things." He asked for open minds, and the pursuit of paths both traditional and unorthodox to arrive at great ideas. "The past hints at what's ahead," and General Skantze wanted them to remember the far-seeing Theodore von Karman and infuse Forecast II with the thrill of discovery evident in Toward New Horizons. Indeed, he called it a study "progressing in the style of von Karman." Skantze praised the first-class talents of the panelists, and asked them to forget for the next half year the day-to-day problems, the bureaucratic grind, and the normal evolutionary approach to research. Instead, he wanted them to open the floodgate of ideas, drawing from military, scientific, academic, and industrial sources.[23] That evening, the general attended a social for panel members, at which he answered many questions and clarified his outlook on the report.[24]

Six months of hard work lay ahead. To maximize the return on the time expended, General Nelson briefed the participants on the study's operational and administrative procedures. The program managers decided that regardless of which panel germinated an idea, or if a concept originated outside the Forecast II offices, the technology panels would guide all technical suggestions through the process. The analysis and mission panels would likewise assume leadership for systems and capabilities, respectively. Once the chairman of the technology panels (General Stebbins) approved a candidate technology suggested by the contributors, it would enter the master technology matrix and be tracked by computer as it passed from hand to hand (see Diagram 5).

The mission panels then would review the proposed technology, deciding whether the systems and capabilities ascribed to it were realistic and useful. Having passed on these (or added their own systems or capabilities), the mission panelists would send their findings to General Durkin. With his approval, candidate capabilities would

DIAGRAM 5
Project Forecast II Matrix

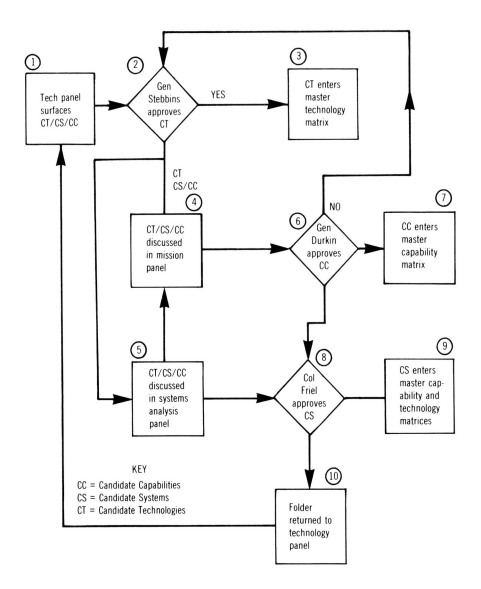

1. Tech panel surfaces CT/CS/CC
2. Gen Stebbins approves CT
3. CT enters master technology matrix

CT
CS/CC

YES

NO

4. CT/CS/CC discussed in mission panel
5. CT/CS/CC discussed in systems analysis panel
6. Gen Durkin approves CC
7. CC enters master capability matrix
8. Col Friel approves CS
9. CS enters master capability and technology matrices
10. Folder returned to technology panel

KEY
CC = Candidate Capabilities
CS = Candidate Systems
CT = Candidate Technologies

enter the master capabilities matrix. Should Colonel Friel and his associates on the analysis panels agree that a candidate system met the tests of cost-effectiveness and relevance to the threat, they would approve it, add new ones if needed, and enter them into the technology and capability matrices. Finally, the whole package would be returned to the technology panels where additional technical concepts would be inserted to conform to the new capabilities and systems. The process did not necessarily originate in the technology panels. If an idea arose in the mission or analysis committees, it would be channeled into the other two panel groupings following the same pattern.[25]

In what form would these proposals make their way through the labyrinth? Generals Nelson and Stebbins relied on a "tried and true" format, the white paper. Preferably one page in length, but no more than five, each candidate technology would be summarized in seven categories:

A short title.

A narrative paragraph stating the nature of the concept.

Its practical payoff(s).

A single sentence explaining its applications.

A listing of potential military capabilities.

Performance charactaristics which would demonstrate its feasibility.

A programmatic description, including engineering manpower, costs and schedule for demonstration; the number of competing contractors or laboratories; the quantity of expensive test items; the type of testing/demonstration required; any special facilities; and supporting technologies.

Ninety percent of the final Forecast II recommendations would evolve from the technology panel white papers. Candidate system and candidate capabilities white papers would include much the same information as the technologies, except the capabilities would discuss operational considerations rather than developmental factors, and the systems would stress such programmatic points as procurement/production scheduling and funding.[26]

This ad hoc AFSC think tank was not the only source of white paper innovation. Newspaper and magazine articles generated an outpouring of scientific ideas, and the Forecast staff stimulated still more response by placing notices in the Commerce Business Daily and The Federal Register calling for white papers on technologies, systems, and capabilities relevant to USAF needs in the twenty-first century. White papers were also solicited from all Air Force organizations. Warning that General Skantze wanted no institutional "filtering" of suggestions, Deputy Program Manager Lt. Col. Donald Neireiter suggested these submissions be sent directly—not through the chain of command—to the Crystal City project offices. In particular, he asked the Systems Command scientists and engineers to take the opportunity to propose system concepts based on the anticipated state of aerospace technology in twenty years time. The authors of these and other "outside" white papers would be contacted by the Forecast II staff should their proposals prove useful.[27]

In practice, these organizational methods functioned effectively. The project office conceived of the process in two sequential parts: a divergent phase, followed by a convergent phase. During divergence, the panelists sought to amass as many new and radical scientific ideas as possible; in convergence, the process worked in reverse, paring down thousands of suggestions to a few dozen practical proposals. Divergence lasted roughly from August to early October 1985, during which time potentially useful technical concepts were collected from academia, government laboratories, think tanks, and contractors. Care was taken not to pre-judge or eliminate suggestions which at first seemed improbable. During this investigatory period, everyone associated with Forecast II encouraged "real free thinking [and] true innovation." In the second, or convergent half, which lasted from about early October to mid-December, brainstorming sessions ranked the white papers and gradually reduced them to a manageable number. These months, characterized by compromise and consensus, marked the decision-making period of the project.

The main theme during late summer and early fall involved "technology push," as opposed to "requirements pull." As General Nelson explained, normal Systems Command planning concerned itself with gearing scientific discoveries of the next twenty years to the needs of the operational commands. In other words, requirements usually governed the selection of preferred technologies; but in Forecast II science came first. Consequently, the technology panels were the center of project activity, and the structure of their meetings encouraged a powerful synergy among members. Each technology panel, which had seven to nine participants, met in cramped conference cubicles in the Crystal City offices. Purposely packing together mixed groups of colonels and high-ranking civilian employees (all of whom knew of General Skantze's six month deadline) the Forecast II leadership hoped for a deluge of ideas. They were not disappointed. The panels threw up for debate thousands of possibilities called "one liners." After frank discussions involving military utility and cost effectiveness, the most likely ones were committed to a master list and fed into the review process as white papers. Altogether, about 900 of them entered the system from the panels, and 1,100 from outside sources, including universities, defense industries, think tanks, and private citizens. Most of the surviving white papers originated in the panels. About 90 percent of the 1100—the preponderence of which sprang from DOD contractors—were deemed ineffectual; in an effort to assure profit, their proposals tended to be too evolutionary, conservative, and short-termed. Other white papers submited from outside the Forecast II offices were rejected because they were too advanced to be practical, too costly to procure, or lacking in potential military capability.[28]

Another question hampered the contribution of private industry: that of proprietary rights. During Forecast I, industry representatives sat on the various panels. But Generals Skantze and Nelson felt that the prevailing climate of the 1980s, in which "horror" stories about contractor overpricing and spare parts costs attracted front page news, demanded more circumspection than in the past. They decided to allow corporate representatives to brief the panels on the proposals, but not to serve on the committees themselves. This would reduce the reluctance of individuals to disclose their ideas, but at the same time greatly restrict who could hear them, and what could be done with them. Thus, even though some thirty-two contractor presentations were briefed in just one week in August, their impact might have been reduced due to internal precautions against the inadvertant disclosure of proprietary data. Caveats stamped on all such material warned that without the approval of the originating corporation, it could not be revealed outside the government, nor used for any purpose except Forecast II evaluation. The project staff could not discuss the proprietary proposals of one firm with any other without the permission of its authors. No briefings of company-owned concepts could be undertaken outside of the government. Indeed, case-by-case approval had to be obtained for each proprietary idea presented to the Senior Review Group, whose members were compelled to sign a non-disclosure statement. Whether evolutionary or revolutionary in character, the white papers submitted by the private sector were at a distinct disadvantage compared to the internally generated concepts.[29]

The role of the ANSER Corporation reached peak stride during the divergence phase of Forecast II. It too had to accommodate itself to the proprietary data requirements of the project, securing a separate access agreement with each company desiring protection for its information. More important still, ANSER was directed by Deputy Program Manager Alan Goldstayn to provide a scientific categorization for Forecast II, that is, comprehensive lists of all the major branches of the natural sciences and applied engineering disciplines. This ANSER supplied within two weeks, suggesting the subject groupings of the National Technical Information Service (NTIS). Goldstayn also asked ANSER to identify American centers of scientific/ engineering excellence so that the Forecast II staff could tap particular fields of study to the fullest extent. He asked ANSER to review the NTIS breakout for avenues of research which held special promise for the Air Force in the twenty-first century, and draft a time-phased development plan for them. Finally, ANSER would assist in the preparation of a computer program to rank the Forecast II white papers numerically, help flesh out some of the panels' findings, and submit an independent assessment of project results.[30]

As the white papers shuttled back and forth among the committees, the AFSC public affairs office asked the Forecast II staff to provide unclassified but substantive findings for the press. To create the maximum impact on public awareness and maintain high credibility, requests were made for materials on specific technologies, projections, and applications. Systems Command public affairs offices distributed Forecast II stories to the local media. Their Headquarters AFSC and Secretary of the Air Force counterparts wrote and distributed news releases and arranged print and electronic interviews with project leaders. As well as AFSC and Air Force publications, Forecast II stories appeared in government agency periodicals, industry magazines, scientific and technical journals, newspapers, and on television and radio. At least twenty-three magazines and newspapers, nine industry publications, three trade association periodicals, and three government agency newsletters picked up the story. The coverage not only provided Forecast II with favorable publicity—associating it with science and progress—but accustomed the public to the idea that promising future weapon systems depended upon Congressional support and funding.[31]

During October 1985 the hum of white paper production and revision slowly began to merge with the sound of debate as the second, or convergence phase took hold. Hard choices had to be made. The first hurdle was a mid-term progress report to the Air Force Chief of Staff. Due the first week in November, the Forecast staff decided to meet the deadline by briefing the Chief on the fifty best candidates among the hundreds of white papers. This list would not represent Forecast's final system and technology selections; rather, it would reflect the most promising prospects at the project's half-way point. The panel chairmen met at ANSER to pare down the numbers and, after intense discussion, reached consensus on the top fifty general technology and system concepts. Their choices were then presented to the Senior Review Group and the Military Advisory Group. The chairmen selected the fifty based on numerical rankings, which took into account factors like cost, military usefulness, relationship to force structure, and likelihood of successful development.

Subjective evaluations of high potential concepts also played a part in the deliberations. Once the Senior Review Group and the Military Advisory Group were satisfied with the content and presentations of the fifty systems and technologies, they were briefed to the Chief of Staff's Commanders Conference by General Skantze and the Forecast II staff. Skantze brought back valuable suggestions from the Chief's meeting, which the panel chairs evaluated at the ANSER offices. General Stebbins and his associates then faced the daunting task of applying the criticisms of the fifty sample candidates to the hundreds of white papers still awaiting review.[32]

Despite the size of the job, the momentum to complete the study did not lessen. General Nelson scheduled weekly "all hands" staff meetings to spur progress and work out significant problems. He also encouraged the production of additional white papers as fresh insights occurred. But the main order of business from early November to early December—the "big push" as the staff called it—entailed panel brainstorming sessions. During these dialogues the participants consolidated some ideas, eliminated others, and constantly changed and debated the likely candidates. As late as the first week in November, General Stebbins discovered that of 970 staff-generated white papers in circulation, only 200 had been discarded and 155 still awaited action. Probably without much hope of success, he asked the panelists to process and return in 2 days the remaining 615 still in their possession![33]

To hasten the selection process, a number of criteria were applied to the candidates. First, ANSER personnel had written a computer algorithm for the initial rankings, which reduced the extent of simple counting needed to determine the relevance of each idea in the matrix. Secondly, the process of reducing some 2,000 white papers to a manageable level—set at 400 by the Forecast II managers—was not really too difficult. Measured by the standards of utility to the Air Force mission and potential for meeting the threat anticipated from foreign powers, the leading proposals were self-evident. In addition, General Skantze's firm 6-month deadline, the "reality checks" of the cost analysis panels, and the in-depth reviews of promising technologies by special investigative teams, promoted consensus. In the end, General Stebbins reviewed and approved each of the 400 candidates—of which 250 described technologies and 150 involved weapon systems.

The real difficulty began when it came time to narrow them to the target number of 70. "The blood letting," said one participant, "came in boiling the 400 down to keepers." An executive committee composed of the AFSC Chief Scientist, Dr. Bernard Kulp; the 10 technology panel chairs; General Stebbins; and Deputy Program Manager Maj. David Glasgow was asked to make these hard choices. They met in closed session, and, in essense, locked the door behind them until they agreed on which of the 400 would survive. At this point, their subjective evaluations dominated the discussions, and the exchanges were frank, sometimes sharp. Since most of the members of this executive panel were AFSC laboratory commanders or directors, they argued with special passion when projects related to their organizations came to a vote. On the other hand, the debates centered ultimately on weapon system capabilities in relation to the threat, which limited digressions and raised the level of discourse. Not without pain and dissent, the numbers gradually fell.[34]

By mid-December, the "smoke had begun to clear." The divergence/convergence process was at last yielding definite finalists in fully articulated form. By December 11 the list had been pared to forty-one systems and thirty-seven technologies; to reach seventy only eight more had to be cut. Consequently, the preparation of top-level briefings and the final report (due in March) could be undertaken. The ANSER staff, responsible for writing and editing Forecast II, suggested following the Forecast I format, which General Nelson approved with minor changes. Panel members and chairs, meanwhile, received instructions to consider for the final report "what we did, why we did it, how we did it, conclusions, recommendations," and implementation. They were also asked by Nelson to compile "lessons learned," stating positive and negative aspects of Forecast II for those who would one day undertake Forecast III. Most important of all, by December 17 the panelists had agreed upon the seventy white papers. Exactly one month later, these write-ups (all formatted in the prescribed style) were in the hands of the project's program control office. So the ANSER editors could begin work at the earliest possible date—and in light of the anticipated departure of the Forecast II study team at the end of January -- panel members began to submit some of the finished summaries before December 17.[35]

Meanwhile, the major briefings went forward. After "dry runs" for General Skantze and the panel members, on January 13, 1986, Generals Nelson, Stebbins, and Durkin gave a two-hour presentation to the Military Advisory Group. The next day, much the same talk was heard by the Senior Review Group. Scheduling allowed a month to sift and incorporate the MAG and SRG comments and prepare for Skantze's second Forecast II briefing to Corona (February 14), an AFSC Product Division/laboratory commanders presentation (February 19), and an HQ AFSC staff briefing (February 24). All of the discussions sought to impress on the audiences four essential ingredients of Forecast II: the methodology of the project; the seventy technologies and systems selected; a sampler of the more accessible and promising of the seventy; and the process of implementation.[36]

The briefings had the desired effects: to stimulate positive reaction to the project and build support for funding new laboratory programs. The Forecast II managers, who had begun to pack up the Crystal City offices and assemble an implementation staff at HQ AFSC, were eager to capitalize on the strong support they had helped to encourage. They rewarded generously those who served on the panels, awarding a total of 112 medals to civilians, officers, and enlisted personnel. Recognition of their achievements bolstered the participants' pride in the undertaking, and sent them back to their laboratory benches eager to implement the fruit of their hard work. To maintain a comparable level of morale among the Forecast II leadership, General Nelson asked Major Glasgow and his associates to organize a contributors' conference at ANSER for the panel chairmen. Two sessions of 2 days duration each were organized from April 14 to 18. Here the chairmen reviewed and edited drafts of the final report, allowing, as General Skantze said, "meaningful feedback" to the project's most important contributors. The findings were likewise scrutinized by 350 industry representatives, who were also invited to the conference.

Once internal consensus for Forecast II had been forged, other organizations were canvassed for support. The leadership of the Air Force Institute of Technology hosted a visit by the AFSC Chief Scientist, Dr. Bernard Kulp, who came there to persuade them to modify their curriculum to reflect the new emphases of Forecast II. General Stebbins made a similar visit to the Air Force Academy. Additional briefings of the project results, tailored specifically to each audience, were heard by the Defense Science Board, the Aerospace Industries Association of America (AIAA), the USAF major air commanders, and a Chief Executive Officer conference hosted by General Skantze.* [37]

The AFSC Commander realized that the Air Force faced leaner budgets than it had known in the first six years of the defense-oriented Reagan administration. Hence, he acted on his own initiative to back Forecast II ideas with funding and manpower. Skantze directed the laboratory commanders to restructure their organizations with the goal of implementing the Forecast II agenda. During the fiscal 1988 to 1993 time period, the general instructed them to convert ten percent of their programs to Forecast II work, using the project recommendations as a blueprint for investing these funds. Finally, he told his Product Division commanders to join with the laboratories to produce development plans which supported the Forecast II systems initiatives, inserting specific program planning in the fiscal year 1988 Budget Estimate Submission. These policies not only injected the latest long-range scientific study into the basic science program planning processes, but served to terminate dead-end laboratory projects and improve their quality of output. [38]

---

*Some 400 audiences heard Forecast II briefings during the life of the project.

HARNESSING THE GENIE

The publication in June 1986 of the Project Forecast II Director's Report quickened the implementing activities. For a cost of just under $2 million (less salaries), an impressive and far-reaching study had been produced. The seventy technologies and systems were divided into six broad categories: Propulsion and Power; Vehicles, Structures, and Materials; Electronics and Optics; Weapons; Information, Computation, and Displays; and Systems Acquisition and Support. As Table 2 illustrates, the Forecast II staff suggested a number of ways to radically improve the means of propelling vehicles through the atmosphere and into space.

Table 2

PROPULSION AND POWER

High-Energy-Density Propellants
Antiproton Technology
Particle-Bed Nuclear Propulsion
Combined-Cycle Engine
Space Power
High-Performance Turbine Engine

A few of these six offered particular promise. New air-breathing propulsive systems held the possibility of power for an aerospace plane, capable of horizontal take-off, orbital flight, and horizontal landing. From conventional runways it could provide worldwide interceptor, transport, and space rescue capabilities. Three avenues appeared especially hopeful for a new age of space propulsion. First, high energy chemical propellants--such as tetrahydrogen—might allow conventional engine designs to propel ten times the current space payloads. Antiprotons, combined with protons, formed the most powerful energy source known and safely harnessed, could reduce travel from earth to Mars from the present two to three years to two to three months. Atomic propulsion, consisting of nuclear fuel encapsulated in small ceramic pellets, could be mated in space with hydrogen to form a controlled reaction of great intensity. One such load of fuel might propel fifty space vehicles from low earth to geosynchronous orbit.[39]

Vehicles, Structures, and Materials, outlined on Table 3, offered many useful insights into the future Air Force.

Table 3

VEHICLES, STRUCTURES, AND MATERIALS

Hypervelocity Vehicle
Advanced Heavy-Lift Space Vehicle
Manned Space Station
Reusable Orbit Transfer Vehicle
Intratheater VSTOL Transport Aircraft
Special Operations Aircraft
Supersonic VSTOL Tactical Aircraft
High-Altitude, Long-Endurance, Unmanned Aircraft
Multimission Remotely Piloted Vehicle (RPV)
Multirole Global Range Aircraft
Hypersonic Interceptor Aircraft
Tactical Low-Cost Drones
High-Temperature Materials
Cooling of Hot Structures
Ultralight Frames
Ultrastructured Materials
Hypersonic Aerothermodynamics
STOL/STOVL/VTOL Technology

Collectively, they presaged a time of more maneuverable aircraft, reduced dependence on fixed basing, cheaper access to space, and the capacity to launch larger payloads into orbit. The most important single technologies needed to undertake these achievements--to operate at temperatures up to 4,000 degrees--embraced titanium and aluminum alloys, lightweight metallic compounds, heat resistant carbon materials, and damage-tolerant ceramic composites. Also crucial were ultralight and ultrastrength materials structured in the laboratory at the molecular level for particular mechanical, electrical, and thermal characteristics. These breakthroughs, as well as improved understanding of hypersonic aerodynamics, would result in a new family of aircraft, ranging from high-altitude, long-endurance reconnaissance vehicles able to stay in flight two weeks or more, to the transatmospheric aerospace plane. In addition, fast aircraft with VTOL offered great potential for search and rescue operations, permitting full capabilities in normal circumstances and landings without runways in adverse conditions. Gigantic space structures would take long steps toward realization thanks to light materials and new structural and control technologies.[40]

Electronics and Optics (Table 4) offered a world of increased capability affecting almost every weapon system of tomorrow. Four technologies were thought to offer the biggest rewards. First, by substituting electronic with

Table 4

ELECTRONICS AND OPTICS

Fail-Soft, Fault-Tolerant Electronics
Full-Spectrum, Ultraresolution Sensors
Smart Skins
Acoustic Charge Transport
Wafer-Level Union of Devices
Non-Linear Optics
Photonics
Distributed Sparse Array of Spacecraft
Bistatic Radar System
Artificial Ionospheric Mirror
Space-Based Surveillance System
Imaging System
Space Object Identification System
Airborne Surveillance System

photonic devices--using photons instead of electrons to sense, compute, transmit, and read signals--it would be possible to overcome electromagnetic pulse, radio frequency interference, and electronic warfare threats. These goals would be realized by pursuing a variety of photonic technologies including optical communication, sensors, computing, signal processing, and kill mechanisms. Second, non-linear optics, capitalizing on many different phenomena which defied conventional concepts of the behavior of light, promised many applications to electro-optical systems. Third, artificial intelligence (AI) computers could operate as "managers" in what were termed fail-soft, fault-tolerant systems. Able to combine the hardware and software of many computers, the AI brain would override the effects of battle damage or electronic failure and allow the system to remain operational. Fourth was the concept of distributed sparse arrays in space for communications and surveillance systems. Such constellations would experience a very gradual deterioration of capability and a degree of military survivability impossible in monolithic structures.

The practical implications of these four technologies were profound. The Forecast II staff predicted photonics would revolutionize present thinking about strategic, tactical, and space battle, and negate the dangers of electronic warfare. Phased array radar could be embedded under the outer shells of aircraft, providing a kind of "smart skin" which would be highly survivable, allow optical communication in all directions, and eliminate easily detected pods and domes. Phased array radars might also be placed in space over enormous distances, enabling excellent survivability and ease of system improvement (by simply adding new units to the existing constellation). Fiber optics held out for aerospace vehicles the prospect of "fly by light," resulting in an unlimited number of channels for in-coming and out-going signals. Non-linear optics provided opportunities for highly precise navigation and non-mechanical pointing and tracking of targets.[41]

Weapons would also undergo significant change and redefinition in the years to come. As Table 5 shows, a long list of possibilities existed. The most fruitful ones

Table 5

WEAPONS

Autonomous Antiarmor Weapons
Autonomous High-Value-Target Weapons
Long Range Air-to-Air Missile
Multirole Conventional Weapons
Long-Range Boost-Glide Vehicle
Hypervelocity Weapons
Advanced Antisatellite System (ASAT)
Direct-Ascent Antisatellite System
Spacecraft Defender
Brilliant Guidance
Directed-Energy Technology
Antiterrorism Technology
Plasma Defense Technology
Satellite Protection

involved means to penetrate densely defended enemy ground targets, and development of space-based weapons. For modern air-to-ground operations, the so-called "smart" bomb was indispensable, but costly to produce. Worse still, the "smart" bomb required communication after take-off, making its launch platform vulnerable to attack. Forecast II proposed a way to procure an almost infinite number of them, and at the same time provide autonomous operation. Using monolithic integrated circuits, single computer chips programmed with electrical, optical, analog, and digital information could transform "dumb" bombs to "smart" ones. Moreover, by combining recent discoveries in sensors (infrared, millimeter, and laser radar) with acoustic, optical, and pattern recognition advances, a new generation of weapons could be developed to detect, identify, lock on, and navigate to targets without operator intervention. Directed energy weapons were also on the verge of quantum improvements. Long-range, high-altitude, and very high velocity microwaves and lasers would have devastating effects against hardened targets, and provide excellent defensive space applications as spacecraft defenders and on-orbit anti-satellites (ASATs).[42]

Forecast II also suggested a number of steps to lengthen the existing American lead in computer technology. Table 6 highlights fifteen candidates with high potential in this field. Of this number, three main lines of inquiry stood out: AI computers to control massive amounts of information (i.e., battle management); man-machine interaction, in which the latter reacted reliably to such subtle human actions as speech and eye movements; and virtual displays, capable of translating all-source sensor data into natural-looking electronic images.

Table 6

INFORMATION, COMPUTATION, AND DISPLAYS

Low-Cost, High-Speed Military Computer Technology
Ultrahigh Software Quality and Productivity
Knowledge-Based Systems
Advanced Deception
Broad Spectrum Signature Control
Distributed Information Processing
Survivable Communication Networks
Adaptive Control of Ultralarge Arrays
Robotic Telepresence
Virtual Man-Machine Interaction
Rapidly Reconfigurable Crew Station
Aircrew Combat Mission Enhancement
Super Cockpit
Battle Management Processing and Display System
Theater Air Warfare Command, Control, and
Communications Intelligence

These technical improvements would lead to radical new controls for pilot information, known collectively as the Super Cockpit. Rather than relying on conventional displays, the Super Cockpit would project images directly into the pilot's eyes, transmit aural signals, monitor his head and eye movements, sense voice commands, and link all of the above straight to the fire control and flight systems. Also on the horizon were relatively unsophisticated robots whose "limbs" and "eyes" would be controlled by the gestures of human operators. This application could yield robotic manipulators capable of repairing satellites in space, operating in chemical/biological environments, making microchips, and doing heavy construction work. Finally, the information-computation–display revolution would permit the comprehensive integration of all significant intelligence data in a total battle management information system for strategic, tactical, and space warfare. From theater to squadron operations, this network would provide heretofore unmatched data, displays, and communication capabilities.[43]

Systems Acquisition and Support, the last of the six Forecast II categories, entailed three principal advances: the smart built-in test (BIT); unified life cycle engineering; and advanced manufacturing technology. The smart BIT idea involved the ingenious use of very high-speed integrated circuits (VHSIC) and very large –scale integrated (VLSI) chips. Coupling them integrally with environmental sensing devices and designing them into electronic systems, malfunctions in the most complex pieces of electronic equipment would be automatically detected, diagnosed, repaired, and tested. Life cycle engineering was also about to enter the age of total computerization. A system incorporating computer-aided design (CAD), computer-aided manufacturing (CAM), and computer-aided support (CAS) promised the cability to analyze trade-offs in performance, support, and production during the design phase of the weapons acquisition process. Finally, advanced manufacturing technology could be applied in an effort to reduce paperwork associated with present industrial practices. It would also enlist AI to develop the highest quality software for mission critical defense uses, making more efficient, standardized, and repairable the computer systems crucial to USAF operations.[44]

* * *

Forecast II took just one year from inception to completion of the final report. An equally formidable task lay ahead during summer 1986: institutionalizing the seventy proposals. General Skantze had already directed the Product Division and laboratory commanders to divert part of their energies to the Forecast II projects, but much remained to be done. For twelve to eighteen months a skeleton staff at HQ AFSC would attempt to implement as much of the report as possible, hoping to prevent the good ideas being tabled and forgotten. The chief aims of

Forecast II—revitalizing Air Force R&D, terminating "dry well" activities at the labs, and shifting present research off comfortable plateaus—still required considerable ingenuity.

As the implementation staff geared up, the SAB was asked by General Skantze to investigate the Forecast candidates and suggest which of them deserved top funding priority. The board had declined to become involved in the project because its role, determined by the Forecast II staff, was too circumscribed. Its members first heard the Forecast II conclusions in briefings at their 1986 annual meeting. For the first time in its history, the SAB was asked to review a completed USAF science forecast in which it had not participated as an organization.* Once the opportunity presented itself to make comments on the finished product, the SAB leadership quickly began an informal review. They divided the seventy technologies and systems among the five standing committees: Weapons, Electronics, Sciences, Biosciences, and Aerospace Vehicles. The findings were mixed. Chairman Robert W. Lucky† [20] reported to General Skantze that some of the seventy, like directed energy weapons and the super cockpit, had good potential. But in many other cases his reviewers "saw not new and emerging...tecnnologies, but rather old programs into which program managers were trying to breathe new life." Some of the panelists felt the project turned out to be "a forecast of...perceived future requirements around which technologies were gathered—rather than a forecast of technical growth which...could satisfy...future requirements." Others found many of the Forecast offspring to be too speculative, too costly, or too time-consuming.[45]

Since the Forecast II implementation schedule proceeded independently of the SAB evaluation, work went forward on inserting the seventy finalists into the fiscal year 1988 Budget Estimate Submission despite the board's misgivings. Meantime, General Stebbins and his associates

---

*Dr. Eugene Covert, SAB chairman until summer 1986, sat on the Forecast II Senior Review Group. He was the only SAB member who participated in the project.
†Chairman of the SAB beginning July 1, 1986.

continued their efforts to lay a solid groundwork of
Forecast II support. They briefed the project to the Air
Staff, the Air Force Secretariat, OSD, other government
agencies, and Congress. Attendance at trade conferences
and university symposia allowed one-to-one dialogue. The
Systems Command Public Affairs offices also continued to
attract attention for the project by pouring out
information to the national and local press, the electronic
media, and a variety of industry and popular magazines.
In association with the remaining Forecast II organization,
they produced a colorful, unclassified Executive Summary
whose glossy format received wide distribution.

The short-term implementation strategy, formulated
as early as summer 1985, provided different approaches for
the technologies, systems, and capabilities. Candidate
capabilities would be "marketed" to the major commands
and the Air Staff by suggesting concepts of operation and
pointing out acquisition risks, costs, and schedules.
Proposed systems concepts would be re-formulated by
General Nelson's Deputy Chief of Staff for Plans and
Programs, and be presented as structure validation
demonstrations to the using commands and industry, as well
as to the Air Force Board Structure for inclusion in the
fiscal year 1988-1992 POM. Technology implementation
would be developed by General Stebbins and his staff using
such initiatives as reorientation of the existing science and
technology base; working with other government agencies,
industry, and academia to link Forecast II technologies to
parallel, on-going projects; and identifying the new ideas
with potential acquisition programs.

To arrive at a unified investment policy, the staffs
of Generals Stebbins and Nelson, as well as a number of
their AFSC field counterparts, formed concept action
teams to devise detailed plans and budget requests for
Forecast II laboratory research and development activities.
The requests had some hope for approval. But Systems
Command laboratories and product divisions did not
experience the effects of the project in isolation.
Aerospace industries began to restructure their independent
research and development programs according to the
objectives of Forecast II, and new Office of Scientific
Research contracts started to reflect the same themes.[46]

* * *

The implementation phase of Project Forecast II capped a twenty-year period in which Air Force science forecasting experienced a significant change in outlook. It became a thoroughly military enterprise. Through a series of reforms and reorganizations, aimed at making it more responsive to Air Staff requirements, the USAF SAB gradually found itself in a position of supplying specific scientific advice on questions of relatively limited scope. The SAB's standing was further confirmed during the preparation of the USAF's fourth major report on the long-term future of Air Force science, New Horizons II. Initiated by General Jones in 1974, every one of its forty-nine panelists was assigned to Headquarters USAF, and all but one of them—the Chief Scientist of the Air Force, the co-chairman of the project—was in uniform. Though the SAB occupied a prominent organizational position in the Pentagon, its members contributed to New Horizons II only as in-house consultants. Instead of placing SAB scientists on the New Horizons technology panels, Air Staff officers dominated the proceedings. In fact, almost half of the project's participants, including its other co-chairman and the study director, worked in the Headquarters Deputy Chief of Staff for Plans and Operations.

The outcome of New Horizons II reflected its insular character. A conservative study which emphasized readily attainable technologies, it was hamstrung by a number of factors. Its personnel lacked the requisite R&D, as well as scientific, knowledge. Their uniformity of outlook fostered consensus, but also stifled vigorous debate and new ideas. Moreover, it was drafted in 1974, the year after the U.S. withdrawal from Vietnam and the Arab oil embargo. Its authors knew these events would result in severe USAF budget reductions, an expectation which influenced their view of the future. Indeed, the dawning of the "age of limitations" did not augur well for a process whose very usefulness depended on unfettered thinking, breaking through existing scientific barriers, and transforming the most promising new ideas into funded programs. Finally, the New Horizons II staff began their task with a long and detailed list of instructions whose precise requirements curbed the necessary freedom of inquiry.

Project Forecast II fared much better. Conceived at AFSC, it enjoyed wide latitude to seek out the most advanced technological ideas. But despite conscious efforts to recreate General Schriever's model of a scientific forecast, Forecast I and II were only superficially alike. Both were directed by AFSC commanders, who had considerable resources at their disposal. In format and committee structure, they had much in common. Yet Forecast II bore the Systems Command imprint from start to finish. Unlike its predecessor, which drew talent from the whole nation, Forecast II's technical participants came overwhelmingly from the AFSC laboratories and product divisions. An in-house endeavor, it was directed entirely by military figures who dealt solely with technological questions. General Schriever, on the other hand, brought to his panels and panel chairs men of industry, academic science, government science, think tanks, as well as his own laboratories. Schriever organized Forecast I to take into account not only technology, but broad national goals and military objectives. He and his panels effectively related the future of USAF science to the long-term national security and foreign policy interests of the country.

Forecast II, by contrast, concentrated on tomorrow's technologies, systems, and capabilities as ends in themselves. The report reflected System Command's belief in the primacy of technology itself, and the need to turn its laboratories into agents of scientific change. With thousands of military and civilian scientists and engineers on its payroll, AFSC leaders felt the command could generate a top quality long-range forecast primarily out of its own resources. Forecast II achieved a remarkably wide survey of possible avenues of aerospace research and generated a genuine trailblazing spirit among its contributors. Radically different from Toward New Horizons and Forecast I, it offered a third alternative to the models provided by Dr. von Karman and General Schriever.[47]

NOTES

1. Article, Lt Col Harold Steiner, "The Future Role of the USAF Scientific Advisory Board," Air University Review, vol 21, November-December 1969, pp. 62, 67; article, Maj Joseph P. Martino, "Forecasting the Progress of Technology," Air University Review, vol 20, March-April 1969, pp. 12-20; article, James W. Jones, "The Making of an Acquisition Officer: A Career Development Program Ensures an Adequate Pool of Air Force Officers Qualified to Direct the Acquisition of Major Weapon Systems," Government Executive, November/December 1987, pp. 22-30; Sturm, SAB, pp. 136-143; "USAF SAB Members, 1945-," n.d., SAB files.

2. List, USAF SAB membership and panels, a/o 1 July 1966, SAB 5; Memo, Col Robert J. Burger to Dr. H. Guyford Stever, subj: reorganization of SAB, 11 January 1967, SAB 10, w/attchs: Proposed SAB organization table; draft letter, Stever to SAB members, subj: SAB reform, January 1964; Staff review, "Discussion materials for General Holzapple during his meeting with Dr. Stever," March-April 1967, SAB 10; Narrative on SAB-Air Staff relationship entitled "Back-up Details," September 1967, SAB 14.

3. Operating Instruction, HQ OI 80-5, "Staff Review Group and General Officer Task Monitors for the SAB," 20 May 1968, SAB 11; Operating Instruction, HQ OI 80-7, "Processing SAB Reports," 30 July 1968, SAB 11; Report, Col Orlando Manci, "Improving the Operations of the USAF SAB," 17 January 1969, SAB 11; Regulation, AFR 20-30, "The USAF SAB," 14 January 1970, SAB 10; Operating Instruction, HQ OI 80-5, 21 July 1972, SAB 15; Operating Instruction, HQ OI 80-7, "Processing SAB Reports," 15 May 1973, SAB 15; Regulation, AFR 20-30, "The USAF SAB," 23 February 1976, SAB 15; Supplement to AFR 20-30 (AFSC Supplement 1), "The USAF SAB," 31 October 1977, SAB 15; Article, Brooke Nihart, "Scientific Advisory Boards: Bargain or Boondoggle?" Armed Forces Journal, 7 March 1970, SAB 16.

4. Ltr, Col Daniel W. Cheatham, Jr. to Lt Gen Otto J. Glasser, subj: SAB membership, 4 October 1972, SAB 18,

w/attchs: Composition of the SAB, Panel Membership, USAF SAB Rotation Summary, Centers of Excellence, Typical Candidates; Ltr, Dr. Robert G. Loewy to Lysle H. Peterson, M.D., subj: SAB panel structure, 2 November 1962, SAB 18; Ltr, Dr. Robert G. Loewy to Dr. Willis H. Ware, subj: SAB panel structure, 29 December 1972, SAB 18; Ltr, Col Daniel W. Cheatham, Jr. to record, subj: panel chairs meeting with Drs. Loewy and Dineen, 17 January 1973, 26 January 1973, SAB 18; Memo, USAF SAB to Lt Gen Gasser, subj: SAB changes, 6 February 1973, SAB 18, w/attch: memo for the record, subj: discussion between Col Cheatham and Dr. Loewy re: 31 January dinner meeting, 1 February 1963; Memo, Col Daniel W. Cheatham, Jr. to Mr. Hansen, subj: SAB reorganization, 5 April 1973, SAB 18, w/attch: Panel Membership; List, Cross-Matrix Panels, 22 June 1973, SAB 18.

5. Article, Col James E. Strub, "Research Horizons: Where the Air Force Ought to be Going," Air University Review, vol 28, November-December 1976, pp. 16-25; Executive Summary (S/NOFORN), New Horizons II Study, Final Report, June 1975, p. A-3 (ltr, Gen R.H. Ellis, Vice C of S of the AF to AF/CCN, IN, SA, AC, RD, DP, LG, XO, PR, subj: Air Staff Long Range Planning Study, 10 August 1974).

6. Executive Summary, New Horizons II, pp. C3-4 (Study Participants), B-3 (New Horizons II Organization), A8-9 (Terms of Reference—Long Range Planning Study), and V (Forward).

7. Executive Summary, New Horizons II, pp. A4-7 (Terms of Reference—Long-Range Planning Study).

8. Executive Summary, New Horizons II, pp. A9-12 (Terms of Reference—Long Range Planning Study), and V (Forward).

9. Executive Summary, New Horizons II, pp. 29-31.

10. Ibid., pp. 31-32.

11. Memorandum of Understanding, USAF SAB/AFSC DAG Activities, December 1979, SAB 22; Memo, Brig Gen

Robert D. Eaglet to Gen Robert T. Marsh, subj: Seven Man Group, 4 March 1983, AFSC.

12. USAF Biography, "General Lawrence A. Skantze," a/o August 1984; Interview, Brig Gen Eric Nelson with Dr. Perry Jamieson, HQ AFSC/HO, 27 June 1986.

13. Ltr, Martin K. Bainbridge to HQ AFSC/XRB, DA, JA, AC, PK, DL, XR, subj: synopsis and budget for support of Forecast II, 8 May 1985, FII, w/attchs: Project Forecast Support, Contract Options, ANSER Facilities, Market Survey Synopsis; Talking Paper, Forecast II, 6 May 1986, FII w/attch: draft letter for Gabriel/Orr; Memo, Col Charles Stebbins to AFOSR/CC, subj: Forecast II 20 May 1985, FII; Ltr, Gen Lawrence A. Skantze to Gen Charles Gabriel, subj: Forecast II, 21 May 1985, FII; List, "Project Forecast II Panel Pre-study Activities," 13 May 1985, FII.

14. Briefing(FOUO), Brig Gen Eric Nelson to Air Force Council/Air Staff Board on Forecast II, 28 May 1985, FII.

15. Ibid.

16. Ibid.

17. Ibid.

18. Schedule, Forecast II Briefings, May-June 1985, n.d., FII; Schedule, Forecast II Briefings on 11 June 1985, n.d., FII; Memo, Brig Gen Charles Stebbins to Gen Skantze, subj: Forecast II, 6 June 1985, FII, w/attch: draft letter by SECAF Verne Orr and Gen Charles Gabriel; Memo, Col Thomas Honeywill to Alan Goldstayn, subj: draft Orr-Gabriel letter, 10 June 1985, FII; Ltr, SECAF Verne Orr and Gen Charles Gabriel to Gen Lawrence A. Skantze, subj: Forecast II, 12 June 1985, FII.

19. Memo, Mr. Walt Werner to HQ AFSC XR/DL, subj: Forecast II publicity, 11 June 1985, FII, w/attch: media outlets; Memo, Col Alan M. Shoemaker to HQ AFSC/CC,CV,CS, subj: interviews on Forecast II, 25 June 1985, FII; News Release, USAF, "Project Forecast II," n.d., FII; Interview, General Lawrence A. Skantze, n.d., FII;

Questions and Answers, Forecast II, n.d., FII; Aerospace Speeches, Statements Data, USAF, "Defense Acquisition Process," (speech by Gen Skantze to the National Contract Management Association, Los Angeles, CA, 18 July 1985), FII; Article, Walter Andrews, "Air Force Panel Takes Aim at Forecasting Future Weapons," Washington Post, 20 May 1985, p. 4A; Article, Leonard Famiglietti, "Forecast II to Explore Technologies of Future," AF Times, June 1985; Article, Anon., "General Skantze Directs Forecast II," AFSC Newsreview, 28 June 1985, p. 3; Article, Anon., "Air Force to Study Technologies/ Weapons for Next Twenty Years," Defense Daily, 1 July 1985, p. 6; Article, Anon., "General Skantze Directs Project Forecast II," Discovery, 19 July 1985, p. 8; Article, Anon., "New Project Looks Ahead Twenty Years at Technology," Desert Wings, 26 July 1985, p. 8; Article, Robert R. Ropelewski, "USAF Moves to Identify Defense Options of Next Twenty Years," Aviation Week and Space Technology, 29 July 1985, p. 14.

20. Interview, Skantze, n.d.; Ltr, Brig Gen Eric Nelson and Brig Gen Charles Stebbins to Maj Gen D.L. Lamberson, subj: Forecast II support, 12 June 1985, FII; Ltr, Lt Col Richard L. Dickson to Mr. John A Englund (Pres., ANSER), subj: Support of Forecast II, 14 June 1985, w/attch: Tasking for ANSER; Organization and Mission--General: Analytic Services, Inc., (ANSER) (AF/RD OI 20-1, 19 May 1983); Ltr, Maj Gen Harold J.M. Williams to AFSC/XR, subj: Tasking for ANSER, 18 June 1985, FII; Ltr, Mr. Alan Goldstayn to HQ AFSC/CSG, subj: Logistics Support for Forecast II, 19 June 1985, FII; Ltr, Brig Gen Eric Nelson to Lt Gen Charles H. Terhune (ret.), subj: Forecast II Support, 25 June 1985, FII; Ltr, Ms. Joy Murtaugh to Mr. Frank Clark, subj: Cost Proposal to Support Forecast II, 15 July 1985, FII, w/attch: ANSER Cost Proposal, 15 July 1985; Addenda to ANSER Cost Proposal, 5 September 1985, FII; Ltr, Alan Goldstayn to Dr. Mignogna, subj: ANSER Support to Forecast II, ca. 1 October 1985, FII.

21. Interview, Brig Gen Eric Nelson with M. Gorn, 4 March 1986; Ltr, Gen Lawrence A. Skantze to Gen James R. Allen (ret.), subj: Forecast II, 19 June 1985, FII, w/attch: list of four stars who received the letter; Ltr, Gen Robert T. Marsh (ret.) to Gen Lawrence A. Skantze, subj:

Forecast II, 29 June 1985, FII; Ltr, Gen Lawrence A. Skantze to Lt Gen Melvin F. Chubb, Jr., subj: Forecast II, 19 June 1985, FII; Ltr, Col Philip J. Conran to Gen Lawrence A. Skantze, subj: Forecast II, 25 June 1985, FII; Ltr, Lt Gen Forrest S.McCartney to Gen Lawrence A. Skantze, subj: Forecast II, 25 June 1985, FII; Ltr, Gen Lawrence A. Skantze to Gen Larry D. Welch, subj: Forecast II, 21 June 1985, FII, w/attchs: two draft letters on Air Staff DCS, Majcom, SOA participation in Forecast II; Ltr, Gen Larry D. Welch to ALMAJCOM, SOA/CC, subj: Forecast II, 28 June 1985, FII.

22. Interview, Brig Gen Eric Nelson with M. Gorn, 4 March 1986; Interview, Maj David Glasgow with M. Gorn, 11 April 1986; Ltr, Gen Marsh to Gen Skantze, 29 June 1985; Schedule, "Project Forecast II Agenda July 1985," 27 July 1985, FII; Draft Schedule, Technology Committee, 2 July 1985, FII; White Paper Formats, Project Forecast II, 9 August 1985, FII; Memo, Brig Gen Eric Nelson to HQ AFSC/XRB, AC, subj: Col Friel's appointment to analysis panel, n.d., FII; Msg, HQ AFSC/CC to AIG 10865, subj: Forecast II; 181800Z July 1985, FII; Msg, Hq AFSC/CC to AFSC labs, ASD, ESD, SD, AD, HQ MAC, HQ USAF, HQ TAC, ADTAC, SPACECOM, SAC, subj: Forecast II participants, 221900Z July 1985, FII; List, Senior Review Group, 22 July 1985, FII, w/attchs: Senior Review Group Candidates, Notes on Possible Congressional SRG Appointments, Mission of the Review Group; List, Candidate Military Advisory Group Members, n.d., FII, w/attchs: Duties of MAG and Notes; Ltr, Lt Col John C. Williams to all Forecast II panel chairs, subj: panel rosters, 5 August 1985, FII, w/attch: panel rosters; Msg, HQ AFSC/CC to AFSTC, AFWL, AFCMD, ESD, ASD, SD, AD, subj: Forecast II systems analysis panel, 232000Z, July 1985, FII.

23. Schedule, Project Forecast II Addenda, August 1985, FII; Article, Pat Muldrow, "Project Forecast II Kickoff: Study Focuses on Weapons of Tomorrow," AFSC Newsreview, 9 August 1985; Speech, Gen Lawrence A. Skantze, "Project Forecast II," to the Air Force Institute of Technology Association of Graduates 4th Biennial Technical Symposium, 11 October 1985.

24. Memo, Brig Gen Eric Nelson to Gen Lawrence A. Skantze, subj: Forecast II social, 23 July 1985, FII.

25. Schedule, 5-9 August 1985 Forecast II, FII; Memo, Alan Goldstayn to Brig Gen Eric Nelson, subj: Forecast II procedures, 9 August 1985, FII, w/attch: procedures briefing; Procedures, Forecast II Study Progress 24 July 1985, FII, w/attch: Forecast Panel Matrices.

26. White Paper Formats, Project Forecast II, candidate technology, candidate system concept, and candidate capability, 9 August 1985, FII.

27. Ltr, Brig Gen Charles Stebbins to HQ AFSC/PK, JA, subj: Imput of white papers to Forecast II, 7 August 1986, FII, w/attch: proposed Commerce Business Daily, and Federal Register announcements on Forecast II; Msg, HQ AFSC/ CC (Lt Col Donald Neireiter, Deputy Program Manager, Forecast II) to AIG 10866, subj: Forecast II—call for white papers, 231200Z, July 1985, FII.

28. Interview, Nelson with Gorn, 4 March 1986; Interview, Glasgow with Gorn, 11 April 1986; Ltr, Brig Gen Charles Stebbins to Mr. G.V. Neklaitis, subj: white paper submissions, 22 October 1985, FII.

29. Interview, Nelson with Gorn, 4 March 1986; Schedule, Forecast II Industry Presentations, 22-28 August 1985, a/o 25 August 1985, FII; Schedule, McDonnell Douglas Briefing to Forecast II, 19 September 1985, FII; Schedule, McDonnell Douglas Brief, 9 September 1985, FII; Ltr, Alan Goldstayn to HQ AFSC/PK, JA, subj: Proprietary Data, Forecast II, 4 September 1985, FTT, w/attch: AFSC Form 91; Ltr, Maj David Glasgow to all Forecast II panel members, subj: handling of proprietary data, 6 September 1985, FII, w/attchs: worksheet and instructions, Proprietary Data, White Paper Control Sheet; Ltr, Brig Gen Gordon A. Ginsburg to CC-1E (Forecast II), subj: Proprietary Data...Forecast II, 9 September 1985, FII.

30. Memo, Alan Goldstayn to all Forecast II Panel Chairs, subj: disclosure of proprietary data to ANSER personnel, 30 September 1985, FII, w/attch: disclosure agreement; Ltr,

Alan Goldstayn to to Dr. Mignogna (ANSER), subj: ANSER Technical Support to Forecast II, 15 August 1985, FII; Memo, Mr. Tom Macmillan (ANSER) to Brig Gen Eric Nelson, subj: categories of science and technology, 30 August 1985, FII, w/attch: list of sciences and engineering disciplines.

31. Memo, Walt Werner to Alan Goldstayn, subj: Forecast II publicity plan, 3 October 1985, FII, w/attchs: Public Affairs Plan: Project Forecast II Publicity, List of Media Outlets for Project Forecast II Release, assorted articles on Forecast II August 1985-August 1986.

32. Schedules, Forecast II, September 1985, FII; Schedules, Forecast II, 1 October-15 November 1985, FII; Ltr, Brig Gen Eric Nelson to all Forecast II panel members, subj: Project Status Update, 7 November 1985, FII, w/attch: Time-Line Calander.

33. Ltr, Nelson to Forecast II, 7 Nov 85; Memo, Martin K. Bainbridge to all Forecast II panel chairs, subj: weekly Forecast II meetings, 6 November 1985, FII; Ltr, Brig Gen Charles Stebbins to all panel chairs, subj: Forecast II white papers, 6 November 1986, FII.

34. Interview, Brig Gen Nelson with Perry Jamieson, 27 June 1986; Interview, Maj David Glasgow with M. Gorn, 11 April 1986; Schedules, Forecast II, 11 November-29 November 1985, FII; Review Schedules, 25-26 November, 2-5 December 1985, FII; List, Project Forecast II Mission Panel Group Most Needed Aerospace Capabilities, 21 November 1985, FII, w/attchs: Tentative Brainstorming Schedule for Needed Capabilities (21 November 1985), Needed Capabilities Brainstorming Procedures (25 November 1985), Capabilities (2), Strike, Mission Panel Potential Capabilities (9 September 1985), Mission Capabilities; General Information, Project Forecast II folders, n.d., FII; Ltr, Brig Gen Eric Nelson to all Forecast II panel members, subj: weekly meeting, 15 November 1985, FII.

35. Schedules, Forecast II, 2-6 and 16-20 December 1985, FII; Ltr, Brig Gen Eric Nelson to all Forecast II panel members, subj: convergence process, 4 December 1985, FII;

Ltr, Brig Gen Charles Stebbins to R&M panel, chairs, members, and all PT/PS OPRs, subj: explicit R&M comment on Forecast II PT and PS comments, 11 December 1985, FII, w/attch: PT/PS List; Ltr, Martin K. Bainbridge to Forecast II personnel, subj: Forecast II Final Report, 2 December 1985, FII w/attch: sample table of contents page; Ltr, Martin K. Bainbridge to all Forecast II personnel, subj: request for lessons learned, 9 December 1986, FII; Ltr, Maj David Glasgow to Forecast II panel members, subj: documentation of T,S folders, 13 December 1985, FII, w/attchs: Technology Content Format, System Content Format; Ltr, Martin K. Bainbridge to authors of PT, PS, T, and S folders, subj: writings for final report, 18 December 1985, FII w/attchs: document requirements, options; White Papers, final drafts (technology 1-48, systems 1-49), n.d., FII; Memo, Martin K. Bainbridge to all OPRs on PS and PT write-ups, subj: updated fleshout instructions, 23 January 1986, FII, w/attchs: Flesh Out Instructions Update on Project Systems Folders, Flesh Out Instructions for Project Technology folders (PT), Program Plan; Ltr, Brig Gen Eric Nelson to Forecast II staff, subj: lessons learned from Forecast II, 21 February 1986, FII; Ltr, Col Norman A. McDaniel to authors or panel chairs, subj: review of edited PS/PT descriptions, 19 March 1986, FII; Schedules, Project Forecast II Phase-Down Agenda, 31 January 1986-October 1986, and Forecast II Tasking, 7 March 1986, FII.

36. Schedules, Forecast II, 9-15 and 21-24 January 1986, FII; Briefing (S/Working Papers), Project Forecast II Briefing to the Military Advisory Group, 13 January 1986, FII; Briefing (S/Working Papers), Agenda of the Project Forecast II Senior Review Group, 14 January 1986, FII; Msg, HQ AFSC/cc to ALAFSC/XR and AIG 8028/CC, subj: Briefing Results of Forecast II, 301730Z, January 1986, FII; Msg, HQ AFSC/CC to AFSC Product Divisions, subj: Project Forecast II briefing, 141200Z, February 1986, FII; Briefing, Project Forecast II to the HQ AFSC Staff, 24 February 1986, FII.

37. Schedules, Forecast II Phase-Down (Jan-Oct 86) and Forecast II Tasking, FII; Ltr, Brig Gen Eric Nelson to HQ AFSC/CC, subj: Forecast II recognition, February 1986, FII,

w/attchs: Project Recognition/Military, Project Recognition/Civilian; Telephone Directory, Project Forecast II, 20 December 1985, FII; Ltr, Brig Gen Eric Nelson, to ?, subj: Forecast II Contributor's Conference, 17 March 1986, FII; Ltr, Brig Gen Charles Stebbins to unknown correspondent, subj: Forecast II Contributor's Conference, n.d., FII, w/attch: agenda, seminar topics, conference II, security form; Agenda, USAF SAB Spring General Meeting at AFIT, Wright Patterson AFB, OH, 22-23 April 1986, 18 April 1986, FII.

38. Ltr, Gen Lawrence A. Skantze to ALAFSC/CC, subj: Project Forecast II Status Report, 27 January 1986, FII; Ltr, Stebbins to Dixon, effects of Forecast II, FII; Ltr, Brig Gen Charles Stebbins to Dr. Jelle de Boer, subj: Improvement of AFSC Labs, 21 January 1986, FII; Staff Summary Sheet, Brig Gen Charles Stebbins to HQ AFSC/XR, DL, CST, CS, CV, CC, subj: Forecast II Briefings to Product Division CCs, 23 January 1986, FII.

39. Budget (Business Sensitive), Forecast II, a/o 12 December 1985, FII; Director's Report(S), Project Forecast II, HQ AFSC Forecast II Office, June 1986, FII, p. 8i; Forecast II Executive Summary, HQ AFSC Forecast II Office, n.d., FII, pp. 5-6.

40. Director's Report, pp. 8 and 40; Executive Summary, p 7; Interview, Maj David Glasgow with M. Gorn, 11 April 1986; Interview, Brig Gen Eric Nelson with M. Gorn, 4 March 1986.

41. Director's Report, pp. 8 and 40; Executive Summary, pp. 9-10; Interview, Brig Gen Eric Nelson with M. Gorn, 4 March 1986.

42. Director's Report, pp. 8 and 40; Executive Summary, p. 12.

43. Director's Report, pp. 8 and 40; Executive Summary, pp. 13 and 15.

44. Director's Report, pp. 8; Executive Summary, p. 16.

45. Agenda, USAF SAB Spring General Meeting at AFIT, Wright Patterson AFB, OH, 22-23 April 1986, 18 April 1986, FII, w/attchs: Point Paper on SAB study of Project Forecast II, 3 April 1986; Project Forecast II; listing of the candidate technologies and systems; assignments to SAB panels of Forecast II topic areas; list, Forecast II tasking a/o 3 February 1986, 5 February 1986; Ltr, Dr. Robert W. Lucky, SAB chairman, to AFSC/CC, subj: SAB review of Forecast II, 11 February 1987, FII files, w/attchs: Reports of SAB panels on Weapons (S), Electronics, Sciences, Biosciences, and Aerospace Vehicles; Comments on SAB role in Forecast II by Maj David Glasgow, Forecast II Deputy Program Manager, made on a review copy of this study; Interview, Col Gilbert Kelley, SAB Executive Secretary, with M. Gorn, 28 October 1986.

46. Interview, Maj David Glasgow with M. Gorn, 11 April 1986; Interview, Brig Gen Eric Nelson with M. Gorn, 4 March 1986; Briefing, Post [Forecast II] Activities, 23 September 1985, FII; Director's Report, pp. 73-74; Executive Summary, p.17; Annex I, Forecast II Director's Report, "Lessons Learned,"; Briefing (S), Project Forecast II to the Air Council, 31 July 1986, FII.

47. Interview, Col Gilbert Kelley, SAB Executive Secretary, with M. Gorn, 28 October 1986; Agenda, USAF SAB General Meeting with attchs; Interview, Mr. Eugene M. Zuckert with M. Gorn, 15 July 1986; Interview, Dr. Ivan Getting with M. Gorn, 12 March 1986.

Hon. Eugene M. Zuckert

Gen. Bernard A. Schriever

Gen. David C. Jones

Maj. Gen. Foster Lee Smith

Dr. Michael I. Yarymovych

Gen. Lawrence A. Skantze

Brig. Gen. Eric B. Nelson

Brig. Gen. Charles F. Stebbins

CONCLUSION

The five Air Force science forecasts initiated since 1944 reflect four broad themes: institutional wandering of the process; the transformation of the von Karman model; the rise of military scientists and engineers; and the decline of the SAB. But regardless of the organizational ebb and flow, the reports as a whole made a highly significant contribution to the well-being of the USAF. Measured by the standards of conformity to original purpose, general influence, resulting new initiatives, and impact on R&D budgets, none of the five achieved complete success. But the foremost ones—Toward New Horizons and Project Forecast—certainly accomplished what they set out to do. General Arnold asked Dr. von Karman's group to survey the worldwide state of air power science at the end of the Second World War and forecast where the breakthroughs would lead. General Schriever followed Secretary Zuckert's directions to re-focus Air Force thinking on the future, relating technical progress to national security issues. Both attracted tremendous attention in the Air Force, the DOD, and the private sector. The notoriety was due in part to von Karman and Schriever, two men of influence, ability, and reputation who knew how to lead, and how to maximize the effect of their work. Most important, Toward New Horizons and Project Forecast hastened the development of important new concepts, including, respectively, the initial ICBM program and a separate command for research and development; and such technological departures as composite materials, the high by-pass engine, and future aircraft like the C-5, B-1, and A-10.

The ultimate effectiveness of Project Forecast II remains to be seen. Its main objective was to activate Air Force laboratories to comb science and technology for promising new weapon systems. In the process, the project director, General Lawrence A. Skantze, hoped to reinvigorate the labs themselves. The Forecast II organizers utilized public relations techniques to marshal public support for their findings, thus enhancing the influence of the report before critical funding authorities such as Congress, OSD, and Headquarters USAF. Not content to wait for fiscal support, AFSC allocated a small portion of its resources toward laboratory work on the seventy Forecast II systems and technologies. Systems Command also tried to sustain the momentum of the project by establishing an implementation staff whose principal task was to insert the Forecast II agenda into the Budget Estimate Submission and the Program Objective Memorandum. The effectiveness of the project awaits not only the results of research at the AFSC labs, but the impact of budget reductions expected through the mid-1990s.

By most standards, Woods Hole and New Horizons II achieved only minimum impact. The Woods Hole problems were essentially beyond the control of its director and his associates. Drs. von Karman and Stever and their SAB colleagues were asked to undertake a sequel to Toward New Horizons, and they did so faithfully. But their process could not be reconciled with the Air Force's sudden desire to scrap the whole methodology and write a forecast of space activities. Von Karman found himself at odds with USAF authorities. Sputnik had thrust aside the project's original purpose: to inform ARDC how it should balance the ballistic missile program with the total Air Force R&D structure. Because of confusion as to its raison d'etre, Woods Hole failed to spur new programs or initiatives. New Horizons II, on the other hand, did succeed in its purpose of highlighting recent technologies and systems for a future of presumed scarcity, but it had little effect on the introduction of new systems, and still less on budgeting for new weapons. The product of Air Staff officers, many of whom had little or no R&D background, New Horizons II lacked adequate connections to air power science and technology to have a significant impact on the technological future.

* * *

Perhaps the most surprising aspect of Air Force science forecasting is that changes in the processes and styles of the five reports did not result from conscious design or planning. Rather, they were the product of drift and organizational wandering. Except for the early days, when Theodore von Karman erected the SAG to continue the science forecasts begun by Toward New Horizons, the process has suffered from the absence of a fixed address in the USAF. In meandering from the SAG/SAB to the NAS to AFSC to the Air Staff Deputy Chief of Staff for Plans and Operations, and back again to AFSC, science forecasting lost valuable continuity. Disruptions in the process made coherent methodology, personnel practices, and funding impossible. As a result, each of the five began at the beginning, recreated the process anew each time—in short, invented the wheel again and again. Lessons learned from predecessors could not be transmitted.

In light of the organizational instability, it would have been impossible for Toward New Horizons—or any other model—to keep forecasting on a coherent track by virtue of its example alone. Every study team after von Karman paid homage to the great man and his first report and claimed the tradition for their own; they then went about doing the studies as they pleased. The actual von Karman model emphasized such factors as independent civilian advice, strong academic participation, comprehensiveness rather than speed, and connecting scientific and technical trends to overall defense policy. With some exceptions, this pattern prevailed in Woods Hole and in Project Forecast. By the time New Horizons II and Project Forecast II were initiated (respectively, thirty and forty years after Toward New Horizons) the original methods had faded from memory. Both of the last two reports were completed with little independent or academic participation. Neither had much to say about the relationship between proposed technologies and their place in the general defense landscape. Perhaps this fundamental divergence from von Karman's pattern would have occurred whether or not science forecasting was rooted in a definite niche; but as an institutional orphan, the process changed almost unconsciously, rather than by reasoned and informed discussion.

In part, von Karman's example of scientific forecasting was displaced by the rise of Air Force officers with scientific and engineering educations. Ironically, von Karman's suggestion in Toward New Horizons for a cadre of officers with graduate degrees in the physical sciences ultimately eroded the character of the process he inaugurated. Beginning in the early 1960s, these highly qualified people were commissioned in great numbers, and in subsequent years assumed positions of top responsibility in AFSC and the Air Force as a whole. Quite naturally, by the mid-1970s—around the time of New Horizons II—enough scientists and engineers had filled the Air Force ranks to lend credence to the idea of initiating internal science forecasting. Those who organized Forecast II ten years later came to the same logical conclusion. But one element was lacking in enlisting Air Force officers for long-range R&D reports: true disinterestedness toward the subject matter. Despite the tremendous and necessary advances in staffing the USAF with high caliber scientists and engineers, it was still hard to deny von Karman's preference for civilian academics who had no personal attachment to the institution and could perhaps take a broader view than those involved in the daily administration of Air Force science and technology.

Not unexpectedly, the increase in military scientists and engineers coincided with the SAB's retreat from science forecasting. Between the early 1960s, when it participated actively in Forecast, and the mid-1980s, when it was only asked to comment on a completed draft of Forecast II, the SAB lost control of the type of study it was originally designed to undertake. Despite this fact, the board still had within it the seeds von Karman had sown many years before—the capacity to connect the Air Force with the vast pool of scientific talent scattered across the country. Such talent had the potential to complement the cadre of USAF R&D officers with fresh and unencumbered perspectives on the broad fronts of future air power science. During the last days of the Second World War, General H.H. Arnold expressed to von Karman the value of this balance between independent and government science in pursuit of long-range science policy: "the technical genius which could find answers...was not," he warned, "cooped up in military or civilian bureaucracy, but was to be found in universities and in the people at large."[*]

---

[*]From Theodore von Karman, The Wind and Beyond, p.268.

BIBLIOGRAPHIC NOTE

The most important documentary underpinnings of Harnessing the Genie are the five multi-volume science forecasts undertaken by the U.S. Air Force since 1944: Toward New Horizons (1945), The Woods Hole Summer Studies (1957-1958), Project Forecast (1964), New Horizons II (1975), and Project Forecast II (1986). All five are in the collections of the Office of Air Force History, Bolling Air Force Base, Washington, D.C. At the same location are the papers of General Bernard A. Schriever, ARDC and AFSC Commander from 1959 to 1966, as well as a large body of transcribed oral interviews with major Air Force figures. The Pentagon offices of the Air Staff Branch of the Office of Air Force History has in its files a collection of documents from the Forecast II project office, disbanded in Summer 1986. In the Air Force Historical Research Center, Maxwell Air Force Base, Alabama, are the weekly activity reports of the Headquarters U.S. Strategic Air Forces (HQ USSTAF), which describe Dr. von Karman's European missions on behalf of General Arnold.

Outside the Office of Air Force History and Historical Research Center holdings are several depositories with manuscripts relevant to USAF science forecasting. The History Office at Headquarters Air Force Systems Command, located at Andrews Air Force Base, Maryland, has a fine collection of ad hoc reports on airpower R&D dating from the late 1940s. The USAF Scientific Advisory Board, staffed in the Pentagon, houses papers on its membership, policies, and reports from as early as 1944. At the California Institute of Technology archives, the Theodore von Karman Collection, available on microfilm from the National Air and Space Museum, Washington, D.C., provides insight on the life and work of the great scientist. Finally, the National Academy of Sciences in Washington, D.C., preserves and makes available to scholars documents on the relationship between the U.S. scientific community and the airpower establishment.

The secondary literature of Air Force science forecasting is far less ample. Thomas Sturm's The USAF Scientific Advisory Board: Its First Twenty Years (Washington, D.C., 1967) traces the board's development from its beginnings in 1944 to the membership reductions under Secretary of Defense McNamara. Dr. Theodore von Karman's famous autobiography, The Wind and Beyond: Theodore von Karman, Pioneer in Aviation and Pathfinder in Science (Toronto, 1967), written with the assistance of Lee Edson, gives a good-natured account of the man who first introduced civilian science to the Air Force. Robert A. Hanle's Bringing Aerodynamics to America (Cambridge, Massachusetts, and London, England, 1982) has valuable narrative on the European origins of von Karman's career. A number of the Headquarters Air Force Systems Command annual histories written during the early and mid-1960s shed light on the formation of the command, as well as on Project Forecast. The periodical literature on Project Forecast and Project Forecast II is significant, and for the most part found in such defense-oriented publications as Aviation Week and Space Technology and Armed Forces Management. But most of the articles concentrate on the spectacular new technologies promised by the reports, rather than the prosaic processes used to define and assemble science forecasts. Finally, the Air University Review published several articles in the 1960s and 1970s about the Air Force and scientific progress, a good example of which is "Research Horizons: Where the Air Force Ought to be Going," by Col. James Strub in the November-December 1976 issue.

Clearly, the lack of secondary literature on this subject and the availability of primary sources suggests new horizons for historians of science to explore.

GLOSSARY

AAF	Army Air Forces
AEDC	Arnold Engineering Development Center
AFHRC	Air Force Historical Research Center
AFIT	Air Force Institute of Technology
AFLC	Air Force Logistics Command
AFOAR	Air Force Office of Aerospace Research
AFOSR	Air Force Office of Scientific Research
AFRD/OI	Air Force (Deputy Chief of Staff for) Research and Development/ Office Instruction
AFSC	Air Force Systems Command
AFSTC	Air Force Space Technology Center
AFWAL	Air Force Wright Aeronautical Laboratories
AFWL	Air Force Weapons Laboratory
AGARD	(NATO) Advisory Group for Aeronautical Research and Development
AGM-X	Air-to-Ground Missile-Experimental
AI	Artificial Intelligence
AIAA	Aerospace Industries Association of America
AMC	Air Materiel Command
AMPSS	Advanced Manned Precision Strike System
AMST	Advanced Medium Range Short Take-off-and-Landing (Aircraft)
ANSER, Inc.	Analytic Services, Inc.
ARDC	Air Research and Development Command
ASAT	Anti-Satellite
ASD	Aeronautical Systems Division
AWACS	Airborne Warning and Control System
A-X	Attack (Aircraft)--Experimental
BIT	Built-In Test

191

BMEWS	Ballistic Missile Early Warning System
CAD	Computer-Aided Design
Cal Tech	California Institute of Technology
CAM	Computer-Aided Manufacturing
CAS	Computer-Aided Support
	Close Air Support
CEP	Circular Error of Probability
C-X	Cargo (Aircraft)--Experimental
DAG	Division Advisory Group
DCS/RD	Deputy Chief of Staff for Research and Development
DDR&E	Defense Director of Research and Engineering
DOD	Department of Defense
DOE	Department of Energy
DTIC	Defense Technical Information Center
ETO	European Theater of Operations
FII	Project Forecast II
F/B	Fighter/Bomber
FY	Fiscal Year
GALCIT	Guggenheim Aeronautical Laboratory, California Institute of Technology
GPS	Global Positioning System
HQ	Headquarters
ICBM	Intercontinental Ballistic Missile
IDA	Institute for Defense Analyses
IOC	Initial Operational Capability
JPL	Jet Propulsion Laboratory
MAG	Military Advisory Group
MIT	Massachusetts Institute of Technology
MITRE Corp	Massachusetts Institute of Technology Research and Engineering Corp.
MOA	Memorandum of Agreement
MOL	Manned Orbiting Laboratory
MTO	Mediterranean Theater of Operations
NACA	National Advisory Committee on Aeronautics
NAS	National Academy of Sciences

NASA	National Aeronautics and Space Administration
NATO	North Atlantic Treaty Organization
NRC	National Research Council
NTIS	National Technical Information Service
OSD	Office of the Secretary of Defense
POM	Program Objective Memorandum
R&D	Research and Development
RAF	Royal Air Force (U.K.)
RAND Corp.	Research and Development Corp.
RDC	Research and Development Command
RDT&E	Research, Development, Test, and Evaluation
RPV	Remotely Piloted Vehicle
SAB	Scientific Advisory Board
SAC	Strategic Air Command
SAG	Scientific Advisory Group
SOA	Separate Operating Agency
SP	Schriever Papers, Office of Air Force History
SRAM	Short-Range Attack Missile
SRG	Senior Review Group
STOL	Short Take-Off-and-Landing
STOVL	Short Take-Off-and-Vertical Landing
TAC	Tactical Air Command
TDY	Temporary Duty
TVK	Theodore von Karman Collection, California Institute of Technology Archives
U.C.L.A.	University of California, Los Angeles
USAAF	United States Army Air Forces
USAF	United States Air Force
USAFE	United States Air Force—Europe
USDR&E	Under Secretary of Defense for Research and Engineering
USSTAF	United States Strategic Air Forces in Europe
VHSIC	Very High Speed Integrated Circuit
VLSI	Very Large-Scale Integrated (Computer Chips)

INDEX

Aachen Aeronautics Institute: 15, 25
AAF (Army Air Forces): 10
    Consulting Board for Future Research: 18
    Long Range Development Program: 18
Ackeret, Jacob: 33
Advanced Manned Precision Strike System (AMPSS): 109
Advisory Group for Aeronautical Research and
    Development (NATO): 59, 60, 61, 64, 77
Aerial warfare: 20
Aerojet Engineering Corp.: 16
Aerojet General: 18, 103
Aeronautical Research Laboratory: 94
Aeronautical Systems Division (ASD): 112
Aerospace Corp.: 47, 103
AFLC. See Air Force Logistics Command
AFOAR. See Air Force Office of Aerospace Research
AFOSR. See Air Force Office of Scientific Research
AFWAL. See Air Force Wright Aeronautical Laboratories
AGARD. See Advisory Group for Aeronautical Research and
    Development (NATO)
Aircraft types
    A-10: 183
    AMST: 115-116
    B-1: 183
    B-70: 73, 104
    C-5: 115, 183
    C-5A: 113
    C-142B: 113
    CV-X: 113
    C-X: 106
    CX-X: 110, 112, 113
    F-108: 104
    F-111: 113
    high velocity: 17, 20, 38
    hypersonic ramjets: 74
    pilotless: 17, 36, 38, 42
    in Project Forecast II: 163
    scramjet, 114
    short take-off and landing (STOL): 74, 78, 110, 112
    subsonic: 108
    supersonic: 13, 31, 36, 38, 108
    tailless: 30, 31

vertical/short take-off and landing (VSTOL): 113, 119
vertical take-off and landing (VTOL): 73, 104, 107, 108
XP-56: 30
XS-1 (Bell): 13
Air Defense Command: 102
Air Force: 5 See also Air Defense Command; Air Force
   Logistics Command; Air Force Materiel Command; Air
   Force Systems Command; U.S. Army Air Forces
 reform requested for: 49
 research: 123
 science in: 1, 3, 123, 171, 184, 186
Air Force Avionics Laboratory: 115
Air Force Logistics Command: 96, 118
Air Force Office of Aerospace Research: 94
Air Force Office of Scientific Research (AFOSR): 94, 133
Air Force Research Division. See Air Force Office of
   Aerospace Research
Air Force Systems Command (AFSC): 5, 8, 9, 96, 88, 90, 96,
   102, 105, 111, 114-115, 118, 123, 133, 135, 140,
   142-143, 145, 149, 157, 185. See also Division
   Advisory Groups
"Air Force Utilization of Scientific Resources,": 93
Air Force Wright Aeronautical Laboratories (AFWAL): 150
Air Materiel Command (AMC): 95, 96
Air Research and Development Command (ARDC): 4, 5, 48, 63,
   65. See also Air Force Systems Command; Western
   Development Division.
 collaboration with NAS: 66, 67-73, 89-90, 92-96, 123
Allen, Gen. Lew, Jr.: 150
Alperin, Morton: 19
Alsos Mission: 24, 25n
Alvares, Dr. Louis: 19
AMC. See Air Materiel Command; Air Force Logistics
   Command
Analytic Services, Inc. (ANSER): 146-149, 156-160
Anderson, Gen. Samuel E.: 65, 67, 68, 72, 96
Andrews Air Force Base, Md.: 104
Angell, Joseph W.: 100
ANSER. See Analytic Services, Inc.
ARDC. See Air Research and Development Command
Arnold Engineering Development Center: 46
Arnold, Gen. Henry H.: 4, 9, 10, 12
 dream of progress: 13-14, 17-21, 23-24, 26-27, 31-32

ill health of: 33, 34n, 36, 41-44, 45, 60, 77-78, 183, 186
Ashkenas, Irving L.: 20n
Atlantic Alliance: 60
Atlas missile: 73. See also intercontinental ballistic missile
Atomic bomb: 34
Atomic Energy Commission: 118
Atomic energy
    through explosives: 37
    power of: 30
    propulsion by: 30
    weapons: 48
Austrian Air Service: 15

Babcock, Maj. Gen. C. S.: 100
Bacteriological warfare: 20
Baker, George P.: 49
Ballistic Missile Early Warning System (BMEWS): 74
Baumker, Adolph: 24
Belgium: 21
Berger, Col. Robert C.: 132
Bisplinghoff, Dr. Raymond L.: 141
Bombs
    buzz: 20, 25
    robot: 21
    "smart,": 116, 166
Braunschweig: 24
Bray, Charles W.: 19
Britain: 21, 32
Bronk, Dr. Detler V.: 62, 71
Brown, B. P.: 100
Brown, Harold: 105, 120, 121-122
Bryan, Maj. Gen. Thomas L.: 61
Budapest Royal Polytechnic Institute: 15
Burchinal, Lt. Gen. David: 100
Bush, Vannevar: 41

Cabell, Gen. C.: 100

California Institute of Technology: 3, 13, 16, 48, 60, 64
Cambridge Research Laboratories: 94
Cannon, Gen. John K.: 43
Carp, Dr. A.: 100
Carroll, Brig. Gen. Frank: 17
Central Aero-Hydrodynamic Institute, Moscow: 21
Charyk, Joseph V.: 69, 93
China: 32
Churchill, Winston: 27
Close air support: 112, 113, 116
Cobb, Col. J. O.: 100
Cohen, Samuel T.: 91
Commerce Business Daily: 154
Communications: 38, 75, 168
Computers: 8, 112, 166
    data processing: 7
    and information sciences: 167, 168
Consolidated Vultee Aircraft Company: 42
Cooper, Dr. Thomas E.: 145
Corona: 160
Covert, Dr. Eugene: 134, 169
Craigie, Laurence: 47
Crosby, Lt. Col. J. W.: 100

DAGS. See Division Advisory Groups
Davis, Maj. Gen. Leighton I.: 71
Deane, Brig. Gen. John R.: 22, 23
Defense Science Board: 2n
Defense Technical Information Center: 25n
Demler, Brig. Gen. Marvin C.: 61
Department of Defense (DOD): 92, 93, 106, 113-114,
        140-141
Department of Energy (DOE): 141
Dineen, Dr. Gerald: 134
Division Advisory Groups: 93-94, 141
DOD. See Department of Defense
DOE. See Department of Energy
Donovan, A. F.: 100
Doolittle, Gen. James H. (Jimmy): 41, 49, 60-63, 89, 103
Dornberger, Gen. Walter: 25
Douglas, James H.: 66-67

Draper, Dr. Charles: 63
Dryden, Dr. Hugh L.: 16, 19, 22, 25, 32, 34-35, 63-64, 68
DuBridge, Dr. Lee A.: 16, 19, 22, 35
Duffy, Col. R. A.: 100
Durkin, Brig. Gen. Robert F.: 146, 149, 151-152, 160
Duwez, Pol: 19, 68-69
Dyna-Soar: 73-74

Eaglet, Brig. Gen. Robert D.: 141
Eaker, Lt. Gen. Ira C.: 33, 43
Echols, Maj. Gen. Oliver: 17
Eglin Field, Fla.: 16
Eisenhower, Gen. Dwight D.: 22, 23, 45
Electromagnetic radiation techniques: 38
Electronics: 75, 112, 164
Engine designs: 108-109
Estes, Maj. Gen. Howell M.: 67
European Theater of Operations: 22-23, 32, 135

Fairchild, Gen. Muir S.: 43, 48-49
Federal Register: 154
Ferguson, Lt. Gen. James: 92, 100, 121
Finland: 21
Fisk, James B.: 49
Fletcher, Dr. James C.: 100, 103
Foote, Paul D.: 71
Ford, Col. Vincent T.: 91
Forecast East: 104-106, 111
Foster, Dr. John S.: 103
France: 21, 32
Frick, Dr. F. C.: 100
Friel, Col. John: 142, 146, 149, 152-153

Gabriel, Gen. Charles: 143, 145
GALCIT. See Guggenheim Aeronautical Laboratory at the
         California Institute of Technology
Gamow, George A.: 20n

Gasser, Col. Clyde: 91-92
Geisler, Dr. Murray: 118
General Electric Corp.: 18
Germany: 21-24, 26
Getting, Dr. Ivan A.: 16, 20n, 47, 63-64, 103
Giles, Lt. Gen. Barney M.: 18, 22-23
Gilpatrick, Roswell L.: 92, 96, 105
Glantzberg, Col. Frederic E.: 17, 19, 22, 32-33, 34n, 35
Glasgow, Maj. David: 146, 159-160
Global Positioning System (GPS): 139, 140, 166
Goldstayn, Alan: 142, 146, 156
Göttingen University: 15, 25
Graham, W. B.: 100
Gray, Lt. Col. Billy C.: 91
Gropman, Col. Alan: 142
Guggenheim Aeronautical Laboratory at the California
    Institute of Technology (GALCIT): 15, 18
Guggenheim Foundation: 15
Guidance technology: 109

Hammett, Louis P.: 20n
Harriman, Averill: 23, 26
Hasert, Chester: 91
Healy, James F.: 118
Herwald, Dr. Seymour W.: 119
Hetherington, Dr. A.: 100
Hodnette, Brig. Gen. Lovic P.: 135
Holland: 21, 32
Hollomon, John H.: 69
Holzapple, Lt. Joseph R.: 131-132
Holzman, Brig. Gen. Benjamin G.: 94
Horner, Richard E.: 71, 93, 119
Hughes, Lt. Gen. Harley A.: 146
Hunter, Walter S.: 20n

ICBM. See intercontinental ballistic missiles
IDA. See Institute for Defense Analyses
Institute for Defense Analyses: 118
Intercontinental ballistic missiles (ICBM): 31, 41-42,

67-68, 95, 109-110, 114, 116, 183

Jet propulsion: 25, 29
Jet Propulsion Laboratory: 16
Joint Logistics Conference: 142
Jones, Gen. David C.: 7, 134-135, 138, 140
"Junior Indians,": 48, 50, 89

Kaplan, Dr. Joseph: 63, 100, 103
Keegan, Maj. Gen. George J., Jr.: 135
Kellogg, Dr. William: 119
Kelly, Dr. Mervin J.: 61
Kennedy, President John F.: 96: 105
Kenney, Gen. George C.: 33
Kistiakowsky, George: 64
Krick, Irving P.: 20n
Kulp, Dr. Bernard: 146, 159, 161

Lasers: 7, 135, 139-140
Latter, Dr. Albert: 119
Lauritsen, Dr. Charles C.: 103
Lawrence, H. R.: 100
Lawrence Livermore Laboratory: 103
Lawson, Maj. Gen. Richard L.: 135
LeMay, Gen. Curtis E.: 43-45, 48, 65, 71, 92-93, 95, 97,
    105-106, 117-118, 120, 123
Lien, J. R.: 100
Lincoln Laboratory: 118
Loewy, Dr. Robert G.: 134
London: 23, 25
Lovelace, Dr. W. Randolph II: 20n, 35n, 68
Loving, Gen. George P.: 135
Lukeman, Maj. Gen. Robert P.: 135
Lucky, Dr. Robert W.: 169

McConnell, Gen. John P.: 120, 121, 132
McDaniel, Col. Norman A.: 146
MacDougall, Duncan P.: 20n
McHugh, Lt. Col. Godfrey T.: 22, 32, 33, 34n, 35
McKee, Gen. William F. ("Bozo"): 48, 97
McNamara, Robert S.: 92, 93, 96, 97, 105, 115, 131
Manned Orbiting Laboratory (MOL): 110, 112, 142
Markham, John R.: 69
Marsh, Gen. Robert T.: 141-142
Marshall, Gen. George C.: 21-22, 45
Massachusetts Institute of Technology: 3-4, 64
Mathison, Col. Charles: 100
Maxwell, Brig. Gen. J. C.: 100
Meckling, Maj. Gen. Edward P.: 61
Mediterranean Theater of Operations: 22-23
Miller, Maj. Gen. Troup: 61
Millikan, Clark B.: 63, 69
Millikan, Robert A.: 13, 15-16
Minuteman: 73. See also intercontinental ballistic
        missiles
Missiles: 25, 91, 68. See also intercontinental ballistic
        missiles
    hitting missile: 109-110, 112, 115
    short-range attack missile (SRAM): 112
MITRE: 118. See also Massachusetts Institute of
        Technology
Momyer, Gen. William W.: 150
Moore, Maj. Gen. Otis C.: 135
Morgan, Clifford T.: 69, 70
Morton, George A.: 20n
Munich: 113
Murray, Peter R.: 115

NACA. See National Advisory Committee for Aeronautics
NAS. See National Academy of Sciences
NASA. See National Aeronautics and Space Administration
National Academy of Sciences: 4, 16, 62-64, 141, 185
        collaboration with ARDC: 66, 67, 69, 72, 87, 103
National Advisory Committee for Aeronautics: 17, 63
National Aeronautical Laboratories: 21
National Aeronautics and Space Administration: 141

National Contract Management Association: 147
National Technical Information Service (NTIS): 156
NATO. See North Atlantic Treaty Organization
Neireiter, Lt. Col. Donald: 142, 146, 154
Nelson, Brig. Gen. Eric: 142-145, 146, 148-151, 153, 155,
        158-160, 170
New Horizons II: 17, 35
    purpose of: 136-138
    organization chart: 137, 139, 140, 141, 150, 171, 184-186
Newmark, Nathan M.: 20n
Night and all-weather fighter capability: 136
Norstad, Gen. Lauris: 43
North American Aviation Corp.: 42
North Atlantic Treaty Organization (NATO): 59-60, 77
Northrup Aircraft Corp.: 18
Novick, D.: 100
Nuclear power: 38
Nuclear warfare
    controlled response in: 36, 107
    weapons for: 109, 116

Office of Scientific Research: 61, 118, 170
Orly Field: 26
Orr, Verne: 145
OSR. See Office of Scientific Research
Operation Lusty: 24
Overhage, Carl: 49

Page, Maj. Gen. J. D.: 100
Paris: 23-25, 27, 60, 64
Patrick Air Force Base, Fla.: 142
Peenemunde rocket facility: 25
Perkins, Prof. Courtland D.: 68, 93, 118
Phillips Corp.: 21
Pickering, William H.: 20n, 69
Potsdam Conference: 27
Power, Gen. Thomas S.: 4, 61-63, 65, 77
Pradtl, Prof. Ludwig: 15, 25
Project Forecast: 1, 5, 6-9, 88

contributors to: 102
essential features of: 98
flow chart for: 101
organization chart for: 100
recommendations of: 106-107, 110-120, 123-124, 131,
    134-135, 142-144, 155, 159, 172, 185, 186
Project Forecast II: 19, 144, 145
    master technology matrix: 152-153, 154-162, 165-166,
        168-172, 183-186
    occupational affiliation of members: 8
    systems and technologies: 8
Project MX-774: 42
Puckett, Dr. Allen: 69, 100
Purcell, Dr. Edward M.: 16, 20n
Putt, Brig. Gen. Donald L.: 48-50, 60-62, 67, 89, 91-93,
    123

Radar: 9, 20-21, 30-31, 75   See also Project Forecast II;
        Where We Stand
    in navigation: 38
    in communications: 38
Radford, Dr. William H.: 118
RAF. See Royal Air Force
Ralph, Brig. Gen. John E.: 136, 138
Ramo, Dr. Simon: 103
Ramsey, Dr. Norman: 17
RAND. See Research and Development Corp.
Randolph, Gen. Bernard P.: 146
Raytheon: 47
Reed, Dr. John C.: 119
Remote control mechanisms: 38
Research and development
    funding: 20, 21, 28, 36, 42, 113-114, 169
    materials for: 75
    personnel in: 88
Research and Development Corp. (RAND): 94, 103, 118, 136
Ridenour, Louis N.: 49
Ridenour Report: 49, 59
Ritland, Maj. Gen. O. J.: 100
Robotics: 167
Rockets: 72-74

Air Corps research in: 16
nuclear: 74-75
engines for: 108
fuels for: 30
propulsion for: 42, 70
Royal Air Force: 25
Ruina, Dr. Jack: 118
Russia. See Union of Soviet Socialist Republics

SAB. See Scientific Advisory Board
SAC. See Strategic Air Command
SAG. See Scientific Advisory Group
St. Germaine, France: 27
Satellites: 7, 68, 70, 72-73, 77, 139. See also Global
        Positioning System
Saville, Lt. Gen. Gordon P.: 50n, 100
Sawyer, Ralph: 49
Schairer, George: 17, 19, 22
Schlatter, Lt. Gen. David M.: 49-50n
Schriever, Gen. Bernard A.: 5, 6, 7, 48, 62, 67, 88,
        91, 93-97, 98, 102-107, 111-113, 115-118, 123-124,
        131, 140, 142, 147, 150, 172, 183
    background of: 89-90
    retirement of: 114-116
Schubauer, Galen B.: 20n
Schuyler, Col. D. H.: 100
Science
    Air Force in: 186
    materials in: 108
    preeminence of: 38-39
"Science, the Key to Air Supremacy,": 35-36, 38, 40-41,
        42
Scientific Advisory Board: 2, 4-6, 8-9, 41, 45-47,
    102-103, 117-119, 121-124, 131. See also Project
        Forecast II
    decline of: 59, 60, 62-64, 68, 73, 78, 89, 91-95, 100
    1948 revitalization of: 48
    reorganization of: 132, 133-134, 136, 138, 140-141,
        149, 169
    structure of: 59
Scientific Advisory Group: 4, 19, 64, 185

new means of aerial warfare: 20
    mission of: 43-44
    research scope of: 20-21
    travel for information by: 22-24, 26, 31-32, 34, 39,
       40-42
Scowcroft, Gen. Brent: 150
Sears, William R.: 20n, 68, 70
"Seven Man Group,": 141
Sheingold, Dr. Leonard S.: 118-119
Shockley, William: 69
Sherman, G. W.: 100
Skantze, Gen. Lawrence A.: 8, 142-151, 155, 158, 160-161,
      168-169, 183
Slay, Gen. Alton P.: 135, 141
Smith, Maj. Gen. Foster Lee: 134, 136
Soper, Col. Ray E.: 97, 100
Southeast Asia: 113-114, 122, 135
Spaatz, Gen. Carl: 23, 43, 45-47
Space research: 70, 72. See also Sputnik
    Air Force in: 135, 184
    defense systems in: 140
    launch vehicles in: 108, 110
    military use of: 68-69, 73-74n   91
    technical advances in: 136,
    weapons in: 139
Sputnik: 5, 68, 71, 77, 184
Stalin, Josef: 26-27
Standifer, Col. L.: 100
Stebbins, Brig. Gen. Charles F.: 142-143, 146, 148-149,
      151-153, 158-161, 169-170
Stever, Dr. H. Guyford: 63-65, 68, 93, 95, 103, 122, 132,
      184
Stosick, Arthur J.: 20n
Strategic Air Command: 50, 65, 77, 102, 150
Strategic Defense Initiative (SDI): 144
Sweden: 21-22, 32
Sweeney, Gen. Walter: 118-119
Sweeney, William J.: 20n
Switzerland: 21-22, 25, 32
Symington, Stuart: 46

TAC. See Tactical Air Command
Tactical Air Capabilities Task Force: 118, 122
    report of: 7, 120, 124, 131-132
Tactical Air Command: 102, 118
Television: 20
Teller, Dr. Edward: 64
Terhune, Lt. Gen. Charles H., Jr.: 6, 98, 99, 100,
        102-104, 124
Thompson, Louis T. E.: 70
Thompson, Ramo, Wooldridge, Inc.: 103
Thurman, Lt. Gen. William E.: 146
Titan: 73. See also intercontinental ballistic missiles
Toward New Horizons: 1, 3, 4, 6-9,
    content: 35-37
    declassification of: 41
    response to: 40
    results of: 42, 43-46, 50, 59, 61-62, 64, 66-67,
        70-73, 76-78, 118, 135, 138, 151, 172, 183-186
Tsien, Dr. Hsue-shen: 16, 19, 22, 25, 32, 34n
Twining, Gen. Nathan: 41, 60

Union of Soviet Socialist Republics (USSR): 21, 68, 70,
        73, 96, 107, 136
    Academy of Sciences: 26
    laboratory system: 26
    Leningrad: 23
    resistance to granting visa: 22
    science in: 26
    threat posed by: 149
United Kingdom. See Britain
United States Army Air Forces/United States Air Force:
    1, 3, 10, 46-47, 62, 89, 92, 124, 131, 169
United Technology Corp.: 92
USAF. See United States Army Air Forces/United States Air
    Force
USSR. See Union of Soviet Socialist Republics

V-1: 25
V-2: 17, 25

Valley, Dr. George E. Jr.: 16, 20n
Vandenburg, Gen. Hoyt S.: 43, 47-49, 59, 60
Vietnam: 88, 122-123, 135, 140, 171
Von Braun, Dr. Wernher: 25
Von Karman, Maurice: 14-15
Von Karman, Dr. Theodore: 3, 4-5, 7-9, 11-13
    background, 14-15
    chairman, SAB, 60, 61-73, 77-78, 117, 123-124, 131,
        135, 139-140, 147, 151, 172, 183-186
    education, 15, 16-18, 20-27, 30-33, 35-38, 41
    impact on research in the U.S. by, 16, 42, 43-50, 59

Walkowicz, Teddy: 35n, 47-48, 64
Walton, Col. James M.: 142, 146
War Department Documentation Center: 25
Warden, Col. H. E.: 100
Wassell, Brig. Gen. Ralph.: 61
Wattendorf, Dr. Frank C.: 16, 19, 21-22, 25, 32 34n, 35,
        49, 60, 64, 68-69
WDD. See Western Development Division
Weapon systems: 20, 76, 95, 113, 139, 183, 166. See also
        lasers
Welch, Gen. Larry D.: 148
Western Development Division: 62, 90, 93, 103
Where We Stand: 27, 30-31, 34-35, 59
Whisenand, Maj. Gen. J.F.: 100
White, Gen. Thomas D.: 62, 65, 89
White House Science Office: 2n
Wild, John M.: 49
Williams, Lt. Col. Frank W.: 32, 35n, 43
Williams, Lt. Col. John C.: 146
Wilson, Lt. Gen. Roscoe C.: 92
"The Wind and Beyond,": 186
Wind tunnels: 13, 26, 40, 46, 61
Woodrow, Raymond: 49
Woods Hole Summer Study: 1, 5, 63-65, 68, 70, 73, 76-78,
        87, 89, 123-124, 131, 184-185
Woods Hole Summer Study II: 69, 70-72
Wright Field, Ohio: 12, 13, 26, 46, 48, 50, 90

Yarymovych, Dr. Michael I.: 135, 136, 138
York, Dr. Herbert: 103

Zand, Dr. S. J.: 19
Zuckert, Eugene M.: 5, 93, 96-97, 105-106, 116-118, 120,
      123, 183
Zwicky, Fritz: 20n, 35n
Zworykin, Dr. Vladymir K.: 16, 19, 22